TOPIK in 30 days - Intermediate Vocabulary

초판 인쇄	2012년 06월 15일
7쇄 발행	2020년 02월 20일
지은이	김주연, 문선미, 유재선, 이지욱, 최유하
펴낸이	박찬익
펴낸곳	(주)박이정
주소	서울시 동대문구 천호대로 16가길 4
전화	02)922-1192~3
전송	02)928-4683
홈페이지	www.pjbook.com
이메일	pijbook@naver.com
등록	1991년 3월 12일 제1-1182호

ISBN 978-89-6292-293-6(13710)
*책 값은 뒤표지에 있습니다.

Contains more than 2200 words that are highly possible to appear in the upcoming TOPIK after analyzing the past tests.

Intermediate Vocabulary

TOPIK in 30 days

김주연 · 문선미 · 유재선 · 이지욱 · 최유하

self-vocabulary booklet and mp3 files included

교재 집필자 약력

김주연
연세대학교 외국어로서의 한국어교육 석사,
건국대학교 국어국문학과 박사
현 | 건국대학교 국어국문학과 강사,
　　건국대학교 언어교육원 한국어과정 강사
저서 | 『한국어 1』건국대학교 출판부,
　　　『한국어 3』건국대학교 출판부,
　　　『함께 배우는 건국 한국어 1』건국대학교 출판부,
　　　『토픽Ⅱ 필수 문법 150 중급』한글파크,
　　　『토픽Ⅰ 필수 문법 101 초급』한글파크

문선미
연세대학교 외국어로서의 한국어교육 석사
현 | 일본 후쿠오카 진달래 한국어학교 강사
저서 | 『한국어 5』건국대학교 출판부,
　　　『토픽Ⅱ 필수 문법 150 중급』한글파크,
　　　『토픽Ⅰ 필수 문법 101 초급』한글파크

유재선
연세대학교 외국어로서의 한국어교육 석사
현 | 서울대학교 언어교육원 한국어과정 강사
저서 | 『토픽Ⅱ 필수 문법 150 중급』한글파크,
　　　『토픽Ⅰ 필수 문법 101 초급』한글파크,
　　　『서울대 한국어 4급』투판즈 출판사

이지욱
이화여자대학교 국어국문학과 석사,
이화여자대학교 국어국문학과 박사 수료
전 | 건국대학교 언어교육원 한국어과정 강사,
　　한성대학교 언어교육원 한국어과정 강사
저서 | 『한국어 수업을 위한 문법활동집 초급』한글파크,
　　　『토픽Ⅱ 필수 문법 150 중급』한글파크,
　　　『토픽Ⅰ 필수 문법 101 초급』한글파크

최유하
연세대학교 외국어로서의 한국어교육 석사
현 | 건국대학교 언어교육원 한국어과정 강사
저서 | 『한국어 5』건국대학교 출판부,
　　　『토픽Ⅱ 필수 문법 150 중급』한글파크,
　　　『토픽Ⅰ 필수 문법 101 초급』한글파크

Preface

<TOPIK in 30 days> is a textbook for foreigners who are preparing for the TOPIK- intermediate level. It is suitably organized for learners to easily acquire new words that frequently appear on TOPIK and make them able to check their improved capability by solving the review questions.

Many students have trouble preparing for the TOPIK. It is because of the following reasons. First, a textbook that contains a list of required words to prepare for the TOPIK- intermediate level does not exist. Also, there is no textbook that helps students study effectively by themselves. In order to solve these problems, this book has selected the words that must be acquired before taking test, and made a list to help students to easily proceed on their learning.

After closely analyzing questions from the past TOPIK exam, we have selected the words that have most frequently appeared on the test. Then, we have organized these words into a 30 day curriculum and made it possible for the students to go over these words in 30 days. Moreover, the related word for every word is also attached together so that it can help students to better prepare for the test. Also, we provide a section where students can review the words that they know and can check their comprehension.

We wish foreign students positive results by preparing for the test effectively in this 30 day short period by using this book.

Thanks to numerous foreign students who gave precious advice and translators who translated the textbook into the students' mother tongue and also to the people who gave a final review. Also, we appreciate the staffs in 박이정 publisher who put their efforts to complete this TOPIK textbook.

2012. 2. authors

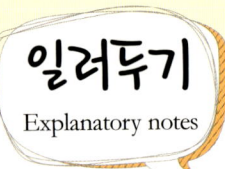

일러두기
Explanatory notes

정확한 발음 확인
Check the accurate pronunciation

제시어와 예문의 발음을 확인하고 익힐 수 있도록 한국인의 발음을 수록하였습니다. MP3형태로 www.pjbook.com 에서 직접 다운로드 받을 수 있습니다.

Includes Korean's voice of pronunciation of given words and example sentences in order to check and master them. Files are available to download from the www.pjbook.com site.

출제 빈도별 우선 순위 어휘
Words organized based on high frequency

토픽에 출제된 어휘들을 빈도 순으로 엄선하고, 30일치 학습 분량으로 나눠 제시하였습니다. 빈도가 가장 높은 중요 단어부터 제시함으로써 학습의 효율성을 높였습니다.

Thoroughly selected the words from past exams based on the frequency, and provided 30 days of curriculum. Increased the efficiency of learning by putting more frequently appeared words in the earlier part of the book.

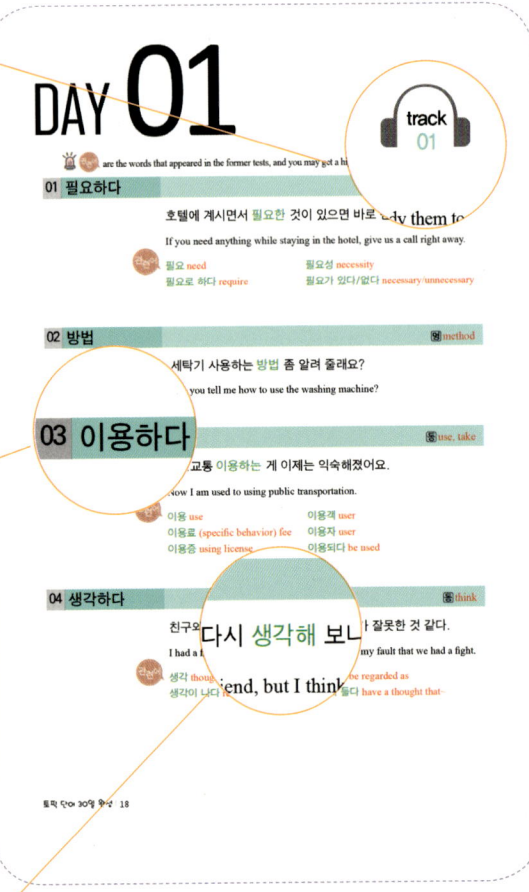

암기력을 높이는 예문
Sample sentences section

제시어의 뜻을 가장 잘 드러낼 수 있는 예문을 해석과 함께 제시하였습니다. 제시어와 함께 예문을 외우면 실제 생활에서도 유용하게 쓸 수 있을 것입니다.

Provides the best sample sentences that clearly shows the suggested meaning together with Korean translation. By memorizing the given word and the sample sentence together, you can also use this in your daily life.

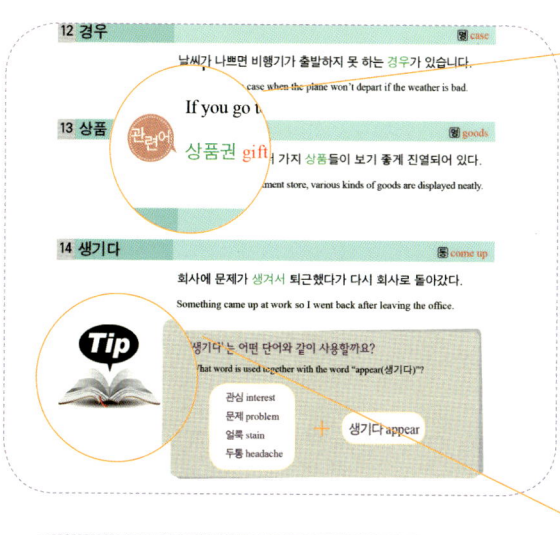

출제된 관련 어휘
Related words from past tests

제시어와 의미상 관련이 있거나 형태상 관련이 있는 어휘들입니다. 이 관련어 역시 토픽에 출제된 어휘들이므로 함께 꼭 외우면 토픽에서 고득점을 받을 수 있을 것입니다.

Words that are related with the given words by meaning or forms. These related words also have appeared in the past TOPIK tests, therefore, it will help you get a high score in the test if you memorize them together.

어휘 정보
Words information

제시어와 혼동하기 쉬운 어휘와의 비교, 제시어와 함께 쓰이는 어휘 제시, 제시어에 대한 더 자세한 정보 등을 실었습니다.

These will have more detailed information about the given words.

출제 경향
Explanation of the latest question trends

제시어가 토픽에서는 어떤 방식으로 출제되었는지 혹은 출제될 가능성이 있는지를 설명했습니다. 그리고 제시어가 토픽 지문에서 주제로 활용되었을 때 자주 사용되는 표현이나 문법을 제시했습니다.

Explains how the given words appear in the actual TOPIK test or how probable the words will appear in the future test. Also, added the frequently used expressions or applied grammar when the given words are used as a topic in the test.

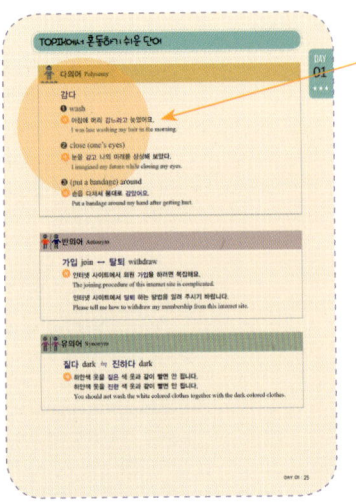

TOPIK에서 혼동하기 쉬운 어휘
Easily confused TOPIK words

토픽에 출제된 유의어, 반의어, 다의어를 예문과 함께 제시해 설명했습니다.

This part explain synonyms, antonyms, and polysemy appeared in the past TOPIK tests along with the sample sentences.

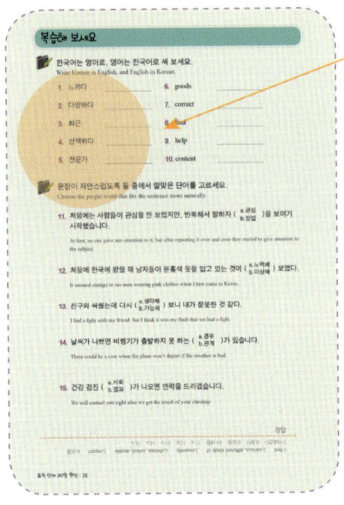

일일 복습
Daily review

그 날 그 날 학습한 어휘를 학습자 스스로 확인할 수 있도록 구성된 복습입니다.

Review that can let the learners check their comprehension of the words on a daily basis.

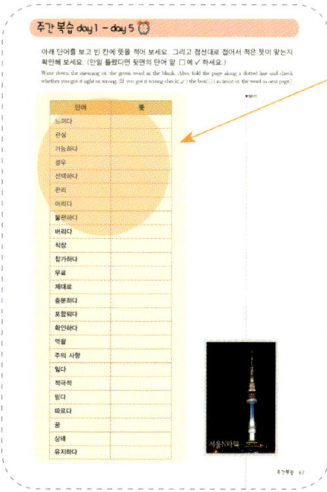

주간 복습
Weekly review

5일마다 제시되는 복습으로 그동안 학습한 어휘를 어느 정도 기억하는지 확인할 수 있도록 구성했습니다.

Review that is provided every 5 days, and is organized to let the learners check how much they remember the words they have learned.

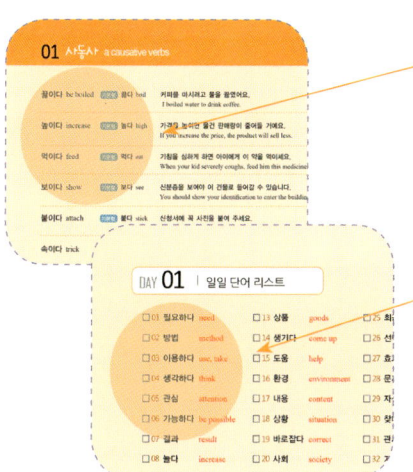

부록
Appendix

토픽에 자주 기출된 핵심 사동사, 피동사, 속담 및 관용표현으로 구성되었습니다.

Part that includes key causative verbs, passive verbs, and proverbs that frequently appeared in the past tests.

단어장
Self-vocabulary booklet

간단하게 잘라서 만들 수 있는 단어장입니다. 시험 전 간편하게 들고 다닐 수 있도록 만들어 보세요!

Provides a booklet that can simply be made only by cutting few pages from the book. Highly required to make one and easily repeat it in your daily life.

차례
Table of Contents

- 머리말 Preface
- 일러두기 Explanatory notes
- 차례 Contents
- 토픽 시험 안내 Guidance for TOPIK
- 학습 스케줄표 Study plan

DAY 01	•017
DAY 02	•027
DAY 03	•037
DAY 04	•047
DAY 05	•057
주간복습 Weekly review	•067

DAY 06	•069
DAY 07	•079
DAY 08	•089
DAY 09	•099
DAY 10	•109
주간복습 Weekly review	•119

DAY 11	•121
DAY 12	•131
DAY 13	•141
DAY 14	•151
DAY 15	•161
주간복습 Weekly review	•171

DAY 16	•173
DAY 17	•183
DAY 18	•193
DAY 19	•203
DAY 20	•213
주간복습 Weekly review	•223

DAY 21	•225
DAY 22	•235
DAY 23	•245
DAY 24	•255
DAY 25	•265
주간복습 Weekly review	•275

DAY 26	•277
DAY 27	•287
DAY 28	•297
DAY 29	•307
DAY 30	•317
주간복습 Weekly review	•327

사동사 causative verbs	•330
피동사 passive verbs	•333
속담 및 관용표현 proverbs, idomatic expressions	•335
단어장 Self-vocabulary booklet	•339
INDEX	•355

TOPIK 시험 안내

1. 시행시기

- 연간 총 4회 실시

시기		시행 지역	미주·유럽·아프리카	아시아·오세아니아	한국
상반기	1월경	국내	-	-	일요일
	4월경	국내 외	토요일	일요일	일요일
하반기	7월경	국내	-	-	일요일
	9월경	국내 외	토요일	일요일	일요일

2. 시험의 등급

- 시험 수준 : 초급, 중급, 고급
- 시험 등급 : 6개 등급(1급~6급)

시험 수준	초급		중급		고급	
시험 등급	1급	2급	3급	4급	5급	6급
등급 결정	시험 성적에 따라 응시한 시험 내에서 평가 등급 결정					

3. 문항 구성

- 영역별 구성

교시	제 1교시			제 2교시		계
영역	어휘·문법	쓰기		듣기	읽기	4영역
유형	선택형	서답형	선택형	선택형	선택형	선택형 / 서답형
문항수	30	4~6	10	30	30	104~106
배점	100	60	40	100	100	400

- 연간 총 4회 실시
  - 선택형 문항(4지 택 1형)
  - 서답형 문항(쓰기 영역)
  - 문장/문단 완성하기, 문장/문단 쓰기
  - 작문(초급 150~300자, 중급 400~600자, 고급 700~800자) : 1문항

4. 합격 판정

- 전 영역(어휘·문법, 쓰기, 듣기, 읽기) 평균 점수가 급별 합격 점수에 도달하고, 평가 영역별 과락 점수가 없어야 함

급수	시험 등급	합격 점수	과락 점수
초급	1급	50점 이상	40점 미만
	2급	70점 초과	50점 미만
중급	3급	50점 이상	40점 미만
	4급	70점 초과	50점 미만
고급	5급	50점 이상	40점 미만
	6급	70점 초과	50점 미만

5. 결과 발표

- 발표 시기 : 응시원서 접수 시 안내, TOPIK 홈페이지 공지
- 발표 방법 : 토픽 홈페이지(www.topik.go.kr) 게재 및 개인별 성적통지표 발송
- 홈페이지에 접속하여 자기 성적을 확인할 경우 회차, 수험번호, 생년월일이 필요함

• 성적 통지표 발급

성적통지표는 합격·불합격 여부에 관계없이 응시자 전원에게 발급
- 응시수준, 평가영역별 점수, 총점, 평균점수 및 합격 여부 표기

• 연간 총 4회 실시

발송 대상		시험 응시자 전원
발송 지역	한국	개인별 우편 발송
	해외	해외 시행기관에 일괄 송부 후 시행기관별 배부

! 국외 응시자도 인터넷(www.topik.go.kr)을 통해 자기 성적 확인 가능

• 성적증명서 출력
- 대학, 기업 등 외부 기관에 제출하기 위한 성적증명서를 홈페이지 성적증명서 발급란을 통해 직접 출력 가능

! 한국과 인터넷 환경이 호환 가능하고, 온라인 결제가 가능하여야 함

Guidance for TOPIK

1. Exam Dates

- Tests held 4 times a year
  - The above test dates are subject to change according to the area or affiliate institution's circumstances.

Dates		Area	The Americas/Europe / Africa	Asia/Australia	Korea
First Half Year	January		-	-	Sunday
	April	Korea/Overseas	Saturday	Sunday	Sunday
Second Half Year	July	Korea	-	-	Sunday
	September	Korea/Overseas	Saturday	Sunday	Sunday

2. Exam Levels and Difficulties

- Exam Difficulties: Elementary, Intermediate, Advanced
- Exam Levels: 6 Levels (Level 1~6)

Difficulty	Elementary		Intermediate		Advanced	
Level	1	2	3	4	5	6
Determination of Level	Level is determined according to test result within given difficulty					

3. Question Composition

- Composition by Area

Section	1st section			2nd section		Total
Area	Vocabulary/Grammar	Writing		Listening	Reading	4 Areas
Type of questions	Multiple Choice	Written Answers	Multiple Choice	Multiple Choice	Multiple Choice	Multiple Choice / Written Answers
Number of Questions	30	4-6	10	30	30	105-107
Score	100	60	40	100	100	400

- Types of Problems
  - Multiple Choice (4 Choices)
  - Written Answers (Writing)
  - Complete Sentence/Paragraph, Writing Sentences/Paragraphs
  - Short Essay Writing (Elementary: 150~300 letters, Intermediate: 400~600 letters, Advanced: 700~800 letters): 1 question Composition.

4. Pass and Fail Scores

Difficulty	Levels	Pass Score	Fail Score
Beginner	Level1	50 or above	Lower than 40
	Level2	Over 70	Lower than 50
Intermediate	Level3	50 or above	Lower than 40
	Level4	Over 70	Lower than 50
Advanced	Level5	50 or above	Lower than 40
	Level6	Over 70	Lower than 50

5. Test Result

- Test scores will be announced when application is received, and on the TOPIK website.
- Test results will be announced at the TOPIK website(www.topik.go.kr) and individual score reports.
- When checking through the website, you must know the test number, application number and birth date.

- **Score Report Issuance**
  Score reports will be sent to all testees regardless of pass or fail.
  - Level applied, area-specific score, total score, average score, and pass or fail will be declared on scroe report.

Who		All testees
Location	Korea	Individual mail sent out
	Overseas	All score reports sent to the affiliated institution of that nation, who will be responsible for distributing to each testee.

! Those who took the test overseas can confirm their score on the website (www.topik.go.kr).

- **Printing the Score Report**
  - For the purpose of submitting score reports to institutions such as colleges or companies, score reports can be printed out on the website print page.
  ! The internet must be adaptable with Korea, and online payment must be possibleScore Report Shipping.

Hey, everyone! There is a Korean saying, "A journey of 1000 miles begins with a single step." It means that no matter how hard the task is, at some point you will reach your goal when you accomplish your task one by one every day.
How about well planning your schedule and settling down to your studies?
Now, let's write down the days that you can study in the graph below.
Do not plan overwhelming tasks since you may give up while you are doing it.

Now, cheer up until you reach the mid-level of TOPIK!

월 일 DAY 01	월 일 DAY 02	월 일 DAY 03	월 일 DAY 04	월 일 DAY 05
월 일 DAY 06	월 일 DAY 07	월 일 DAY 08	월 일 DAY 09	월 일 DAY 10
월 일 DAY 11	월 일 DAY 12	월 일 DAY 13	월 일 DAY 14	월 일 DAY 15
월 일 DAY 16	월 일 DAY 17	월 일 DAY 18	월 일 DAY 19	월 일 DAY 20
월 일 DAY 21	월 일 DAY 22	월 일 DAY 23	월 일 DAY 24	월 일 DAY 25
월 일 DAY 26	월 일 DAY 27	월 일 DAY 28	월 일 DAY 29	월 일 DAY 30

DAY 01

확인해 보세요

빨간 시트지로 가리고 단어의 뜻을 알면, □에 ✓ 해 보세요.
After covering up the words with red cover, please check(✓) the box (□) when you know the meaning of the word.

- ☑ 01 필요하다 need
- □ 02 방법 method
- □ 03 이용하다 use, take
- ☑ 04 생각하다 think
- □ 05 관심 attention
- □ 06 가능하다 be possible
- □ 07 결과 result
- □ 08 늘다 increase
- □ 09 바꾸다 exchange
- ☑ 10 노력하다 make an effort
- ☑ 11 느끼다 feel
- □ 12 경우 case
- □ 13 상품 goods
- □ 14 생기다 come up
- ☑ 15 도움 help
- □ 16 환경 environment
- □ 17 내용 content
- □ 18 상황 situation
- □ 19 바로잡다 correct
- □ 20 사회 society
- □ 21 생활 living
- ☑ 22 이상하다 strange
- □ 23 경험 experience
- □ 24 다양하다 various, different kinds of
- ☑ 25 최근 recently
- □ 26 선택하다 choose, select, decide
- □ 27 효과 effect
- ☑ 28 문제 problem
- □ 29 자신 oneself
- ☑ 30 찾다 find
- □ 31 관계 relationship
- □ 32 기간 period
- □ 33 전문가 expert

DAY 01

 track 01

 관련어 are the words that appeared in the former tests, and you may get a higher grade if you study them together.

01 필요하다   형 need

호텔에 계시면서 **필요한** 것이 있으면 바로 전화 주세요.

If you need anything while staying in the hotel, give us a call right away.

 필요 need   필요성 necessity
필요로 하다 require   필요가 있다/없다 necessary/unnecessary

02 방법   명 method

세탁기 사용하는 **방법** 좀 알려 줄래요?

Can you tell me how to use the washing machine?

03 이용하다   동 use, take

대중교통 **이용하는** 게 이제는 익숙해졌어요.

Now I am used to using public transportation.

 이용 use   이용객 user
이용료 (specific behavior) fee   이용자 user
이용증 using license   이용되다 be used

04 생각하다   동 think

친구와 싸웠는데 다시 **생각해** 보니 내가 잘못한 것 같다.

I had a fight with my friend, but I think it was my fault that we had a fight.

 생각 thought   생각되다 be regarded as
생각이 나다 remember   생각이 들다 have a thought that~

05 관심 　　　　　　　　　　　　　　　　　　　명 attention

처음에는 사람들이 관심을 안 보였지만, 반복해서 말하자 관심을 보이기 시작했습니다.

At first, no one gave any attention to it, but after repeating it over and over they started to give attention to the subject.

관심을 갖다(가지다) give attention to　　관심이 있다 be interested in
관심을 끌다 draw attention

06 가능하다 　　　　　　　　　　　　　　　　형 be possible

가능하면 그렇게 처리해 주십시오.

If it is possible, please process it as such.

가능 possible　　　　　　가능성 possibility

07 결과 　　　　　　　　　　　　　　　　　　　명 result

건강 검진 결과가 나오면 연락을 드리겠습니다.

We will contact you right after we get the result of your checkup.

08 늘다 　　　　　　　　　　　　　　　　　　동 increase

백화점 세일 덕분에 판매량이 30%정도 늘었다고 합니다.

It is known that the sales have increased approximately 30% because of the sales.

> **출제 경향** how this word appears in the test
>
> 그래프 문제를 풀 때는 항상 나오는 단어입니다. 이 단어의 반대어인 '줄다'의 의미도 확인하세요.
>
> This word always appears in the question that includes graphs. Be sure to check the meaning of "줄다(decrease)" along with this word.

09 바꾸다 　　　　　　　　　　　　　　　　　동 exchange

여기서 한국 돈을 일본 돈으로 바꿀 수 있어요?

May I exchange Korean won to Japanese yen here?

10 노력하다　　　　　　　　　　　　　동 make an effort

노력하면 안 되는 일이 어디 있겠어요?
There is no such thing that you cannot do if you make an effort.

 노력 effort

11 느끼다　　　　　　　　　　　　　동 feel

그 영화를 보고 느낀 점을 말해 봅시다.
Tell us what you felt after watching the movie.

 느낌 feeling

 12 경우　　　　　　　　　　　　　명 case

날씨가 나쁘면 비행기가 출발하지 못 하는 경우가 있습니다.
There could be a case when the plane won't depart if the weather is bad.

13 상품　　　　　　　　　　　　　명 goods

백화점에 가면 여러 가지 상품들이 보기 좋게 진열되어 있다.
If you go to the department store, various kinds of goods are displayed neatly.

 상품권 gift card

14 생기다　　　　　　　　　　　　　동 come up

회사에 문제가 생겨서 퇴근했다가 다시 회사로 돌아갔다.
Something came up at work so I went back after leaving the office.

'생기다'는 어떤 단어와 같이 사용할까요?
What word is used together with the word "appear(생기다)"?

| 관심 interest |
| 문제 problem | +   생기다 appear
| 얼룩 stain |
| 두통 headache |

15 도움   명 help

처음 미국에 갔을 때 그 친구에게 많은 도움을 받았습니다.

When I first went to the states, that buddy helped me out a lot.

 돕다 help   도우미 helper

16 환경   명 environment

우리의 환경을 지키기 위한 노력이 필요합니다.

We need to make an effort to protect our environment.

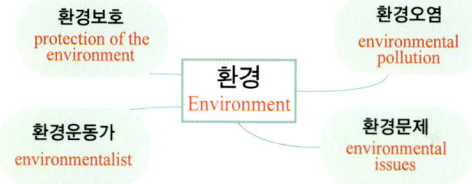

환경보호 protection of the environment

환경오염 environmental pollution

환경 Environment

환경운동가 environmentalist

환경문제 environmental issues

17 내용   명 content

이 책은 내용이 어려워서 이해하기 어렵다.

The content of this book is too hard to understand.

18 상황   명 situation

지진 피해 상황에 대한 뉴스가 계속 보도되고 있다.

The news that shows the situation of the earthquake's aftermath is constantly being reported.

19 바로잡다   동 correct

아이가 잘못을 하면 부모가 당연히 바로잡아야 한다.

When the child does something wrong, the parents must correct them.

20 사회　　　　　　　　　　　　　　　　　　　　　　명 society

우리 사회에는 좋은 일과 나쁜 일이 모두 존재한다.

Both good and bad things coexist in our society.

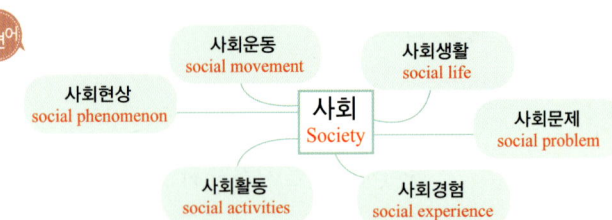

21 생활　　　　　　　　　　　　　　　　　　　　　　명 living

유학 생활은 힘들지만 좋은 추억을 많이 만들 수 있다.

Studying abroad is hard, but it will let you have many good memories.

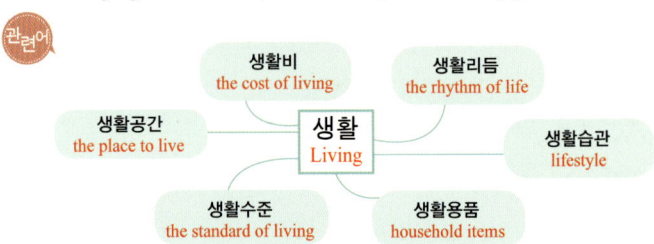

22 이상하다　　　　　　　　　　　　　　　　　　　　형 strange

처음에 한국에 왔을 때 남자들이 분홍색 옷을 입고 있는 것이 이상해 보였다.

It seemed strange to see men wearing pink clothes when I first came to Korea.

23 경험　　　　　　　　　　　　　　　　　　　　　　명 experience

학력보다는 그 사람이 어떠한 경험을 했는가가 중요합니다.

The kind of experience a person did is more important than what kind of academic background he has.

 경험하다 experience　　　　사회경험 social experience

24 다양하다 · 형 various, different kinds of

요즘 서점에서는 **다양한** 잡지를 접할 수 있습니다.

Nowadays, you can read many different kinds of magazines in the book store.

 다양성 diversity

25 최근 · 명 recently

이 지역은 **최근** 3년 동안 많은 변화가 나타났습니다.

This area has gone through a big change in the recent 3 years.

26 선택하다 · 동 choose, select, decide

전공은 오랫동안 고민한 후에 **선택해야** 후회가 없다.

When choosing your major, you will not regret your decision only if you make up your mind after thinking it over a lot.

 선택 decision   선택되다 be selected

27 효과 · 명 effect

꾸준히 운동했더니 마침내 **효과**가 나타났어요.

After constantly exercising, the result finally appeared.

 효과적 effective

28 문제 · 명 problem

문제가 좀 생겼는데 와서 도와줄래요?

I have a problem, can you help me with it?

문제점 problem   문젯거리 problem
문제가 되다 become a problem

29 자신   명 oneself

자기 자신에 대한 사랑 없이 남을 사랑할 수 없다.

You can never love other people if you do not love yourself.

30 찾다   동 find

외출해야 하는데 열쇠를 찾을 수가 없어요.

I should go out, but I cannot find my keys.

찾아 오다 visit   찾아 가다 pay a visit
찾아 내다 find out   찾아 보다 look for
찾아 뵙다 pay a visit   찾아 다니다 look around for

31 관계   명 relationship

성공한 사람들은 대부분 인간 관계가 좋았다고 합니다.

Most of the successful men have good personal relationships.

관계자 the persons concerned   관계당국 the authorities concerned
관계 없다 have no relation to

32 기간   명 period

A/S 기간은 구입 후 1년입니다.

The limited warranty is one for a period of year.

33 전문가   명 expert

이 분야의 전문가가 되고 싶습니다.

I want to be an expert in this area.

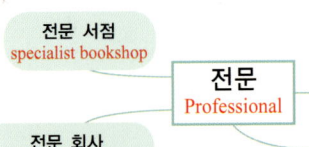

전문 서점 specialist bookshop
전문 지식 expertise
전문 Professional
전문 회사 specialized company
전문 요리사 professed cook

TOPIK에서 혼동하기 쉬운 단어

다의어 Polysemy

감다

❶ wash
예 아침에 머리 감느라고 늦었어요.
I was late washing my hair in the morning.

❷ close (one's eyes)
예 눈을 감고 나의 미래를 상상해 보았다.
I imagined my future while closing my eyes.

❸ (put a bandage) around
예 손을 다쳐서 붕대로 감았어요.
Put a bandage around my hand after getting hurt.

반의어 Antonym

가입 join ↔ 탈퇴 withdraw

예 인터넷 사이트에서 회원 가입을 하려면 복잡해요.
The joining procedure of this internet site is complicated.

인터넷 사이트에서 탈퇴 하는 방법을 알려 주시기 바랍니다.
Please tell me how to withdraw my membership from this internet site.

유의어 Synonym

짙다 dark ≒ 진하다 dark

예 하얀색 옷을 짙은 색 옷과 같이 빨면 안 됩니다.
하얀색 옷을 진한 색 옷과 같이 빨면 안 됩니다.
You should not wash the white colored clothes together with the dark colored clothes.

DAY 01

복습해 보세요

 한국어는 영어로, 영어는 한국어로 써 보세요.
Write Korean in English, and English in Korean.

1. 느끼다   To feel
2. 다양하다 various
3. 최근   recently
4. 선택하다 to select / choose
5. 전문가   expert
6. goods   상품
7. correct 바로잡다
8. find   찾다
9. help   도움
10. content 내용

 문장이 자연스럽도록 둘 중에서 알맞은 단어를 고르세요.
Choose the proper word that fits the sentence more naturally.

11. 처음에는 사람들이 관심을 안 보였지만, 반복해서 말하자 (a.관심 / b.방법)을 보이기 시작했습니다.

    At first, no one gave any attention to it, but after repeating it over and over they started to give attention to the subject.

12. 처음에 한국에 왔을 때 남자들이 분홍색 옷을 입고 있는 것이 (a.노력해 / b.이상해) 보였다.

    It seemed strange to see men wearing pink clothes when I first came to Korea.

13. 친구와 싸웠는데 다시 (a.생각해 / b.가능해) 보니 내가 잘못한 것 같다.

    I had a fight with my friend, but I think it was my fault that we had a fight.

14. 날씨가 나쁘면 비행기가 출발하지 못 하는 (a.경우 / b.관계)가 있습니다.

    There could be a case when the plane won't depart if the weather is bad.

15. 건강 검진 (a.사회 / b.결과)가 나오면 연락을 드리겠습니다.

    We will contact you right after we get the result of your checkup.

정답

1.feel 2.various, different kinds of 3.recently 4.choose, select, decide 5.expert 6.상품 7.바로잡다 8.찾다 9.도움 10.내용 11.a 12.b 13.a 14.a 15.b

DAY 02

확인해 보세요

빨간 시트지로 가리고 단어의 뜻을 알면, □ 에 ✓ 해 보세요.
After covering up the words with red cover, please check(✓) the box (□) when you know the meaning of the word.

- ☒ 01 행사 — event
- ☐ 02 대상 — target
- ☐ 03 설명하다 — explain
- ☐ 04 연구 — research
- ☐ 05 직접 — in person, directly
- ☐ 06 대부분 — most (of)
- ☐ 07 물건 — thing, object
- ☐ 08 안내하다 — show
- ☐ 09 직장 — job
- ☐ 10 참여하다 — participate
- ☒ 11 시작하다 — start
- ☐ 12 변화 — change
- ☒ 13 편하다 — comfortable
- ☒ 14 성공하다 — succeed
- ☐ 15 영향 — influence
- ☒ 16 걱정하다 — worry about
- ☐ 17 교통 — traffic
- ☐ 18 모으다 — save
- ☐ 19 세계 — world
- ☐ 20 신청 — apply
- ☐ 21 오히려 — rather
- ☐ 22 지역 — area
- ☐ 23 판매하다 — sell
- ☒ 24 계속 — continue
- ☒ 25 버리다 — throw away
- ☐ 26 경력 — experience
- ☒ 27 계획 — plan
- ☒ 28 끝나다 — finish
- ☒ 29 어리다 — young
- ☐ 30 직원 — employee
- ☐ 31 관리 — management
- ☒ 32 사실 — truth
- ☒ 33 불편하다 — inconvenient

DAY 02

 are the words that appeared in the former tests, and you may get a higher grade if you study them together.

01 행사   명 event

비가 와서 **행사**가 취소되었습니다.

The event was canceled because of the rain.

 행사장 event hall

02 대상   명 target

대학생들을 **대상**으로 취직에 관한 설문조사를 실시했습니다.

The survey of employment was carried out targeting the university students.

03 설명하다   동 explain

이 문제가 이해가 잘 안 되는데 다시 한번 **설명해** 주세요.

It is hard to understand this question, so can you explain it one more time?

 설명 explanation   설명서 manual
설명회 presentation

04 연구   명 research

암에 대한 **연구**가 활발히 진행되고 있습니다.

The cancer research is being carried out actively.

 연구원 researcher   연구소 research laboratory
연구 결과 the result of research   연구하다 research

05 직접

명 in person, directly

그런 일은 네가 직접 말하는 것이 좋겠어.

It would be better for you to tell that in person.

 직접적 directly

06 대부분

명 most (of)

책의 내용이 너무 어려워서 대부분 이해가 안 돼요.

The content of the book is so challenging that I can't understand most of it.

07 물건

명 thing, object

이 물건은 어디에 사용하는 거예요?

What is this thing for?

08 안내하다

동 show

외국에서 온 손님들에게 우리 학교를 안내할 거예요.

We will show our school around to the visitors from other countries.

 안내 show   안내문 notice
안내소 information desk

 출제 경향 how this word appears in the test

읽기와 듣기 영역에 '안내문' 문제가 항상 출제됩니다. 안내문과 관련된 단어는 다음과 같습니다.

The questions that consist of "안내문(notification)" always appear in the reading and listening sections. The words that are related to the topic are as the following.

일시(Time), 장소(place), 모집(recruit), 대상(targeting group), 기간(deadline), 자격(qualification), 참가(participate), 접수(apply), 응모(entry), 문의(inquiry), 결과 발표(announcement of the result)

위의 단어들은 반드시 알아 두세요.
Don't forget to remember these words.

09 직장 명 job

지영 씨가 드디어 좋은 직장을 구했대요.

Ji-young finally got a good job.

직장인 office worker   직장 생활 work life
직장 상사 boss   일자리 (job)occupation

10 참여하다 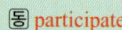 동 participate

모든 일에 적극적으로 참여하는 태도가 필요합니다.

You need to participate more actively in every work you do.

참여 participation

11 시작하다 동 start

수업을 시작하기 전에 출석을 먼저 부르겠어요.

I will call role before I start the class.

시작 start   시작되다 being started

12 변화 명 change

나이가 많은 사람들은 젊은 사람들보다 변화에 적응하기 어렵다.

The old has more trouble adapting to the change.

변화하다 change   변화시키다 make one change

13 편하다 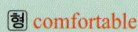 형 comfortable

이 신발은 정말 편하네요.

These shoes are really comfortable.

> '편하다'와 '편리하다'는 어떤 차이가 있을까요?
> What is the difference between "편하다(comfortable)" and "편리하다(convenient)"?
> '편하다'는 주로 몸과 마음이 안정된 상태에 많이 사용하고 '편리하다'는 기술의 발달로 생활이 좋아졌을 때 사용합니다.
> "편하다(comfortable)" is mostly used in the case that the subject is going through a physical and psychological stability, and "편리하다(convenient)" is used when daily life has changed positively because of the technical development.

14 성공하다 동 succeed

여러 번의 실패를 거듭한 후 드디어 그 실험에 성공했다.
After failing many times, the experiment finally succeeded.

성공 success   성공적 successful

15 영향 명 influence

화가이신 어머니의 영향으로 일찍부터 그림을 배우기 시작했어요.
My mother, being the artist, influenced me to learn to draw very early.

영향을 받다 get influenced by   영향을 주다 give influence to
영향을 미치다 influence

16 걱정하다 동 worry about

그 문제는 잘 해결될 테니까 너무 걱정하지 마세요.
The problem will turn out fine, so do not worry about it.

걱정 worry   걱정거리 anxiety
걱정스럽다 be anxious about

17 교통 명 traffic

우리 학교는 다 좋지만 교통이 불편해요.
The only problem that my school has is the inconvenient transportation.

교통비 transportation fee   교통문제 transportation problem
교통질서 traffic order   교통수단 means of transportation

18 모으다 동 save

세계 여행을 하기 위해서 돈을 모으고 있어요.
I am saving money to travel around the world.

모임 gathering   모이다 gather

19 세계 — 명 world

세계 여러 나라 선수들이 한자리에 모였다.

Athletes from all around the world gathered in one place.

 세계화 globalization   세계적 global

20 신청 — 명 apply

다음 학기 신청은 이번주까지예요.

The due date to apply for the next semester is by this week.

 신청서 application   신청 기간 a period for application
신청 방법 how to apply   신청하다 apply

21 오히려 — 부 rather

약속 시간에 늦은 친구가 오히려 나에게 화를 냈다.

My friend was late for the appointment but she was mad rather than me.

22 지역 — 명 Area

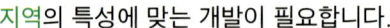

지역의 특성에 맞는 개발이 필요합니다.

The development that suits the aspect of the area under concern is needed.

 지역성 regionality   지역문제 regional problem

23 판매하다 — 동 sell

현재 약국에서 판매하는 약을 앞으로 편의점에서 판매할 거라고 해요.

It has been said that the drugs that are now sold in the pharmacy will be sold in the convenience store.

 판매 sell   판매량 sales volume
판매원 salesperson

24 계속　　　　　　　　　　　　　　　　　　　　　명 continue

계속 한국에서 살기로 결정했습니다.

I have decided to keep on living in Korea.

계속적 continuously　　　　　계속되다 be continued
계속하다 do continuously

25 버리다　　　　　　　　　　　　　　　　　　　동 throw away

이 가방은 아직 쓸 만하니까 버리지 마세요.

This bag is still usable so do not throw it away.

26 경력　　　　　　　　　　　　　　　　　　　명 experience

교육 경력이 5년 이상 되시는 분들만 지원할 수 있습니다.

Only the ones who have more than 5 years of teaching experience can apply for the position.

27 계획　　　　　　　　　　　　　　　　　　　　명 plan

아무리 계획을 세워도 지키지 않으면 소용이 없겠지요.

It is no use if you plan things over and over and not do it.

계획적 premeditated　　　　　계획하다 plan

28 끝나다　　　　　　　　　　　　　　　　　　　동 finish

수리가 끝났으니까 찾아가시기 바랍니다.

The repair is done so you should come and pick it up.

끝 end　　　　　　　　　　끝내 finally
끝내다 finish　　　　　　　　끝맺다 end
끝없이 endlessly　　　　　　끝으로 at last

29 어리다 [형] young

그 사람은 어린 나이에 이 분야에서 성공했다.

He became successful in this area at a young age.

 어린이 a child   어린시절 youth
어린아이 a child

30 직원 [명] employee

다음 달에 직원을 새로 뽑으려고 합니다.

We are planning to hire a new employee next month.

 직원 교육 membership training   직원 채용 hire people

31 관리 [명] management

가죽 옷은 멋있기는 하지만 관리가 힘들어요.

Leather clothes are fashionable but hard to manage.

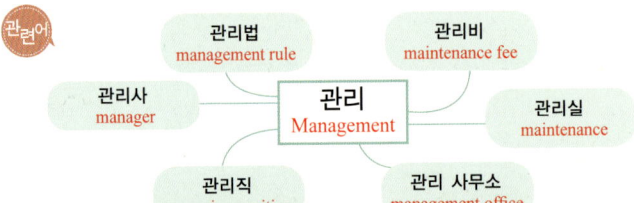

- 관리법 management rule
- 관리비 maintenance fee
- 관리사 manager
- 관리 Management
- 관리실 maintenance
- 관리직 managing position
- 관리 사무소 management office

32 사실 [명] truth

더 이상 숨기지 말고 사실을 말해 주세요.

Do not disguise anymore and just tell me the truth.

 사실적 realistic

33 불편하다 [형] inconvenient

엘리베이터가 고장나서 불편했다.

The elevator was out of order and it was inconvenient.

 불편 inconvenience   불편을 겪다 go through inconvenience
불편을 느끼다 feel inconvenience

TOPIK에서 혼동하기 쉬운 단어

다의어 Polysemy

걸다

❶ hang
> 예) 겉옷은 옷걸이에 걸어서 장롱 안에 넣으시면 됩니다.
> You should hang your outerwear inside the closet.

❷ make
> 예) 안 그래도 전화를 걸려던 참이었어.
> I was just about to make a phone call.

❸ hit on
> 예) 저 여자에게 말을 걸어 보고 싶은데 용기가 안 나.
> I want to hit on that girl, but I don't have the courage.

반의어 Antonym

감소하다 decrease ↔ 증가하다 increase

> 예) 매년 출산율이 감소하는데 원인이 무엇일까요?
> The annual birth rate is constantly decreasing and what do you consider as the reason?
>
> 싱글족이 증가함에 따라서 1인용 물건이 잘 팔린다고 합니다.
> They say the single items sell well as the single person household increases.

유의어 Synonym

게다가 all the more ≒ 더구나 moreover

> 예) 안 그래도 길이 복잡한데 교통사고가 났다. 게다가 공사까지 해서 하루종일 차가 막혔다.
> 안 그래도 길이 복잡한데 교통사고가 났다. 더구나 공사까지 해서 하루종일 차가 막혔다.
> The road was already crowded but there was an accident. Moreover, on-going construction has jammed the traffic all day.

복습해 보세요

 한국어와 영어를 알맞게 연결해 보세요.
Connect the Korean words with the English words of same meaning.

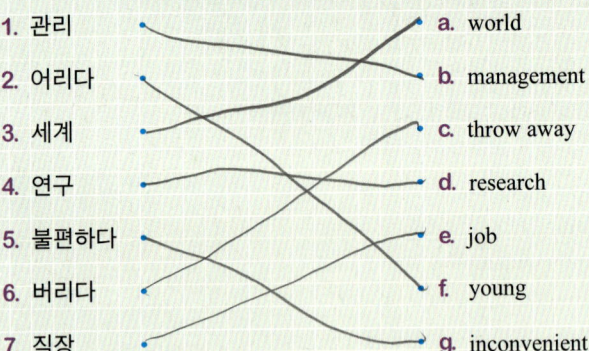

1. 관리   a. world
2. 어리다   b. management
3. 세계   c. throw away
4. 연구   d. research
5. 불편하다   e. job
6. 버리다   f. young
7. 직장   g. inconvenient

 다음 빈 칸에 알맞은 단어를 〈보기〉에서 골라 쓰세요.
Pick and write the suitable word among <the options> in the blank space.

〈보기〉
  a. 대부분   b. 행사가   c. 모으고   d. 오히려

8. 비가 와서 (B) 취소되었습니다.
   The event was canceled because of the rain.

9. 책의 내용이 너무 어려워서 (A) 이해가 안 돼요.
   The content of the book is so challenging that I can't understand most of it.

10. 세계 여행을 하기 위해서 돈을 (C) 있어요.
    I am saving money to travel around the world.

11. 약속 시간에 늦은 친구가 (D) 나에게 화를 냈다.
    My friend was late for the appointment but she was mad rather than me.

정답

1.b 2.f 3.a 4.d 5.g 6.c 7.e 8.b 9.a 10.c 11.d

DAY 03

확인해 보세요

빨간 시트지로 가리고 단어의 뜻을 알면, □ 에 ✓ 해 보세요.
After covering up the words with red cover, please check(✓) the box (□) when you know the meaning of the word.

□ 01 소비	consumption	□ 13 통하다	through	☒ 25 기회	chance
□ 02 실제로	actually	□ 14 참가하다	participate in	□ 26 무료	free of charge
□ 03 충분하다	plenty of, be enough	□ 15 문화	culture	□ 27 상대방	counterpart
□ 04 표현하다	express	☒ 16 받다	receive	☒ 28 색	color
□ 05 해결하다	solve	□ 17 발생	occurrence	□ 29 알려주다	notice
□ 06 개인	individual, personal	□ 18 심하다	severe	□ 30 포함되다	be included
□ 07 경제	economy	□ 19 장소	place	☒ 31 힘	power
☒ 08 늦다	be late	□ 20 제대로	properly	□ 32 대회	competition
□ 09 따라하다	follow	□ 21 개발하다	develop	□ 33 발표	presentation
☒ 10 인기	popularity	□ 22 구입하다	purchase		
□ 11 장단점	strong and weak points	☒ 23 기분	mood		
□ 12 지키다	keep	□ 24 기억	memory		

DAY 03

  are the words that appeared in the former tests, and you may get a higher grade if you study them together.

01 소비 　　　　　　　　　　　　　　　　　　　　　　　명 consumption

날씨가 더워지면서 아이스크림의 소비가 증가했다.

As the weather became hotter, the consumption of ice cream increased.

관련어 　소비량 consumption　　　소비자 consumer
　　　　소비하다 consume

*Commercial consumption

02 실제로 　　　　　　　　　　　　　　　　　　　　　　　부 actually

그 법을 실제로 지키는 사람은 거의 없다.

No one actually observes that law.

관련어 　실제 actual　　　　　　　실제적 practical

03 충분하다 　　　　　　　　　　　　　　　　　　형 plenty of, be enough

이 정도면 5명이 먹기에 충분합니다.

This will be enough food for 5 people to eat.

관련어 　충분히 plentiful

04 표현하다 　　　　　　　　　　　　　　　　　　　　　동 express

그 사람은 자기의 감정을 잘 표현하는 편이에요.

That person is good at expressing his feelings.

관련어 　표현 expression

05 해결하다   동 solve

그건 내가 해결할 수 있는 문제가 아니네요.

That is not a problem that I can solve.

해결 solve   해결되다 be solved

06 개인   명 individual, personal

개인 정보가 유출되지 않도록 주의해 주십시오.

Be cautious not to leak personal information.

개개인 every individual   개인적 personally
개인 공간 personal space

07 경제   명 economy

세계 경제 위기가 심각한 수준에 이르렀습니다.

The crisis of the global economy has reached a severe level.

경제계 economic world   경제력 economic power
경제적 economical   경제학 economics
경제 회복 economic renewal

08 늦다   동 be late

아무리 늦어도 12시까지는 보내 드리겠습니다.

I will send it no later than 12 o'clock.

늦추다 postpone   늦어지다 be delayed

09 따라하다   동 follow

그 가수의 춤은 보기에는 쉬운데 따라하면 어려워요.

That singer's dance looks easy but hard to follow.

따라오다 follow   따라가다 follow

10 인기　　　　　　　　　　　　　　　　명 popularity

요즘 인기 있는 노래가 뭐예요?

What is the latest popular song recently?

 인기요인 popular factor　　　인기를 끌다 gain popularity

11 장단점　　　　　　　　　　　　　　명 strong and weak points

자기 자신의 장단점에 대해 말해 줄 수 있어요?

Can you tell me about your strong and weak point?

 장점 strength　　　　　단점 weakness

12 지키다　　　　　　　　　　　　　　　　　동 keep

사업을 할 때 약속을 지키는 것이 가장 중요하다.

When you are doing business, the most important thing for you is to always keep the promised time.

13 통하다　　　　　　　　　　　　　　　　동 through

유학원을 통해서 이 학교에 오게 되었습니다.

I came to this school through the academy that helped me go abroad for study.

14 참가하다　　　　　　　　　　　　　　　동 participate in

참가하는 인원을 정확하게 알려 주세요.

Tell me the exact people who are participating.

 참가 participate　　　　　　참가비 participation fee
　　　　참가자 participant　　　　　참가 신청 applying for the participation

 how this word appears in the test

'참가하다, 참여하다, 참석하다'는 토픽에 자주 나오는 단어들이니까 꼭 기억하세요! "참가하다(Participate)", "참여하다(take part in)", "참석하다(attend)" are the words that frequently appear in the TOPIK test, therefore you should remember them.

15 문화 　　　　　　　　　　　　　　　　　　　　　　　　명 culture

각 나라마다 독특한 문화가 있다.

Every country has its own special culture.

 문화재 cultural assets

16 받다 　　　　　　　　　　　　　　　　　　　　　　　　동 receive

이번에 개봉한 전쟁 영화는 많은 사람들의 주목을 받고 있다.

The war movie that was released recently is receiving great attention from many people.

 받아들이다 admit

17 발생 　　　　　　　　　　　　　　　　　　　　　　　　명 occurrence

휴가철이 되면서 교통 사고 발생 건수가 증가하고 있다.

As the vacation season begins, the traffic accidents are occurring more frequently.

 발생률 the incidence 　　　　　 발생하다 occur

18 심하다 　　　　　　　　　　　　　　　　　　　　　　　　형 severe

감기가 심해서 집에서 쉬어야겠어요.

Because of my severe cold, I should stay home and rest.

19 장소 　　　　　　　　　　　　　　　　　　　　　　　　명 place

이번 모임 장소는 한국 호텔입니다.

The place of our meeting is Hankuk hotel.

20 제대로 　　　　　　　　　　　　　　　　　　　　　　　　부 properly

이번 일을 제대로 처리하지 못해 죄송합니다.

I apologize for not doing the work properly.

21 개발하다 　 동 develop

새로운 기술을 개발하기 위하여 노력하고 있습니다.

We are trying hard to develop a new technology.

 개발 develop　　　개발자 developer
개발되다 be developed

22 구입하다 　 동 purchase

며칠 전에 스마트폰을 구입했습니다.

I purchased a new smart phone.

 구입 purchase

23 기분 　 명 mood

그 노래를 들으면 기분이 좋아집니다.

I feel better after hearing this music.

 기분전환 refresh oneself

24 기억 　 명 memory

어릴 때 같이 놀던 기억이 납니다.

I remember playing together when I was young.

 기억력 memory　　　기억나다 be remembered of
기억하다 remember

25 기회 　 명 chance

이번 기회를 놓치지 마십시오.

Do not lose this chance.

26 무료 — 몡 free of charge

만 4세 이하는 무료 입장입니다.

Children below 4 can enter free of charge.

27 상대방 — 몡 counterpart

대화를 잘 하려면 상대방의 말을 잘 들어줘야 한다.

You should listen carefully to what your counterpart says if you want to be good at conversing with others.

 상대 counterpart

28 색 — 몡 color

나에게는 이 색이 잘 어울린다.

This color suits me well.

 색깔 color   색상 color
색다르다 be out of ordinary

29 알려주다 — 동 notice

약속 시간이 정해지면 저에게도 알려주세요.

If you set the time of appointment, please let me know.

 알림 notice   알리다 inform
알려지다 be well known   알려드리다 let one know

30 포함되다 — 동 be included

기숙사비에 전기세가 포함되나요?

Is the electricity fee included in the whole dormitory fee?

 포함 include   포함하다 include

31 힘 power

목소리에 힘이 없는 걸 보니 불합격했나 봐요.

Based on his weak voice tone, I think he failed to pass the test.

 힘쓰다 put one's effort   힘이 되다 become a power to someone

32 대회 명 competition

이번 수영 대회는 부산에서 열릴 예정입니다.

This upcoming swimming competition will be held in Busan.

33 발표 명 presentation

다음 주에 발표가 있어서 좀 바빠요.

I am busy because I have a presentation next week.

 발표자 presenter   발표되다 be presented
발표하다 give a presentation

TOPIK에서 혼동하기 쉬운 단어

다의어 Polysemy

구하다

❶ get
> 오후 내내 방을 **구하러** 다녔지만 마음에 드는 방이 없었다.
> I have looked all around to get a new room, but there was no room that I liked.

❷ save
> 친구의 도움으로 목숨을 **구할** 수 있었다.
> I was able to save my life because of my friend's help.

❸ get
> 대학 생활에 대해 선배에게 조언을 **구해야겠다**.
> I should get some advice from my elders.

반의어 Antonym

감추다 hide ↔ 드러내다 reveal

> 본심을 **감추고** 상대방을 대하면 친구가 될 수 없다.
> If you hide your true feelings when you communicate with others, you will never find a friend.

> 그 사람은 속마음을 좀처럼 **드러내지** 않는 편이에요.
> He tends not to reveal his true feelings.

유의어 Synonym

마련하다 prepare ≒ 준비하다 prepare

> 더 추워지기 전에 겨울옷을 빨리 **마련해야겠다**.
> 더 추워지기 전에 겨울옷을 빨리 **준비해야겠다**.
> We should quickly prepare our winter clothes before it gets colder.

복습해 보세요

 한국어는 영어로, 영어는 한국어로 써 보세요.
Write Korean in English, and English in Korean.

1. 참가하다   Participate   6. purchase   구입하다
2. 따라하다   to follow   7. power   힘
3. 무료   free charge   8. properly   제대로
4. 실제로   actually   9. occurrence 발생
5. 충분하다   Plenty enough   10. severe   심하다

문장이 자연스럽도록 둘 중에서 알맞은 단어를 고르세요.
Choose the proper word that fits the sentence more naturally.

11. 그 사람은 자기의 감정을 잘 (**a.표현하는** / b.해결하는) 편이에요.
    That person is good at expressing his feelings.

12. 사업을 할 때 약속을 (**a.지키는** / b.통하는) 것이 가장 중요하다.
    When you are doing business, the most important thing for you is to keep the promised time.

13. 어릴 때 같이 놀던 (a.기분 / **b.기억**)이 납니다.
    I remember playing together when I was young.

14. 이번 수영 (a.문화 / **b.대회**)는 부산에서 열릴 예정입니다.
    This upcoming swimming competition will be held in Busan.

15. 기숙사비에 전기세가 (a.알려주나요 / **b.포함되나요**)?
    Is the electricity fee included in the whole dormitory fee?

정답
1.participate in 2.follow 3.free of charge 4.actually 5.plenty of, be enough 6.구입하다 7.힘 8.제대로 9.발생 10.심하다 11.a 12.a 13.b 14.b 15.b

DAY 04

확인해 보세요

빨간 시트지로 가리고 단어의 뜻을 알면, □에 ✓해 보세요.
After covering up the words with red coyer, please check(✓) the box (□) when you know the meaning of the word.

☒ 01 소개하다 introduce	☒ 13 들어오다 come	□ 25 차이 difference
□ 02 역할 role, part	☒ 14 사고 accident	□ 26 책임 responsibility
□ 03 일반적 in general	☒ 15 소리 sound	□ 27 행동하다 act
□ 04 입장 entrance	☒ 16 연락하다 contact	□ 28 확인하다 check
□ 05 자료 data	□ 17 모습 appearance	□ 29 광고 advertisement
□ 06 제품 product	□ 18 오래되다 old	□ 30 급하다 urgent
□ 07 주변 surroundings	□ 19 원인 reason	□ 31 실시하다 practice
□ 08 주의 사항 matters that require attention	☒ 20 인간 man, human	□ 32 작품 work
□ 09 피해 be harmed	□ 21 잃다 lose	□ 33 적극적 active
□ 10 부탁 request	□ 22 자리 seat	
☒ 11 고르다 pick	□ 23 조사하다 investigate	
☒ 12 돌아가다 go back (to)	□ 24 주민 (local) resident	

DAY 04

 are the words that appeared in the former tests, and you may get a higher grade if you study them together.

01 소개하다 　　　　　　　　　　　　　　　　　　　　　　　　　동 introduce

여러분께 이번에 새로 나온 상품을 소개하도록 하겠습니다.
I will now introduce the newly produced product.

 소개 introduce　　　　　소개되다 be introduced
소개받다 be introduced to

02 역할 　　　　　　　　　　　　　　　　　　　　　　　　　　　명 role, part

어떤 역할을 맡고 있든지 최선을 다해야 한다고 생각합니다.
Whatever role you take, you should do your best.

03 일반적 　　　　　　　　　　　　　　　　　　　　　　　　　　명 in general

일반적으로 남성보다 여성의 수명이 길다고 한다.
Women live longer than men in general.

일반인 ordinary people　　　　일반화 generalization

04 입장 　　　　　　　　　　　　　　　　　　　　　　　　　　　명 entrance

콘서트장 입장 시간이 거의 다 되었네요.
It is almost time to enter.

 입장권 entrance ticket　　　입장료 entrance fee
입장하다 enter

05 자료 　　　　　　　　　　　　　　　　　　　　　　　　　　　명 data

리포트 자료를 찾기 위해 도서관에 가요.
Let's go to the library to find some data for the report.

06 제품　　　　　　　　　　　　　　　　　　　　　명 product

제품의 홍보는 인터넷을 활용하는 것이 좋겠습니다.

It should be better to use the internet to publicize the product.

07 주변　　　　　　　　　　　　　　　　　　　　　명 surroundings

학교 주변에 있는 맛있는 식당을 소개해 주세요.

Tell me a good place to eat around the school.

 주변 환경 surroundings

08 주의 사항　　　　　　　　　　　　　　　명 matters that require attention

이번 대회 참가자들은 주의 사항을 잘 확인해 주세요.

The participants in this competition should carefully check the matters that require attention.

주의 be cautious　　　　　　　　주의력 attention
주의하다 be cautious　　　　　　주의할 점 the things that you should be aware of
주의를 주다 warn　　　　　　　　주의를 기울이다 pay attention (to)

09 피해　　　　　　　　　　　　　　　　　　　　　명 be harmed

다른 사람에게 피해를 주지 않기 위해 노력해야 합니다.

You should try not to harm other people.

 피해자 victim

 how this word appears in the test

토픽에는 재난에 관한 기사가 자주 출제됩니다. 다음 표현들을 '피해'와 함께 공부해 보세요.
Many articles that deal with disaster frequently appear in TOPIK test. Study the following words together with the word "피해(be harmed)".

사고(accident), ＿ 모 씨(an unnamed person), 시경(around o'clock), 목격자(witness), 부상(report an accident, be injured), 치료(cure), 발생하다(occur), 구조하다(save), 밝혀지다(reveal), 정도가 심하다(in severe degree), 'N에 따르면(according to N)

10 부탁   명 request

아이의 부탁대로 맛있는 케이크를 사서 집에 돌아왔다.
I bought a cake on my way home as the kid requested.

 부탁하다 request

11 고르다   동 pick

친구 선물을 고르느라고 하루종일 명동을 돌아다녔습니다.
I looked around Myeongdong the whole day to find a present for my friend.

12 돌아가다   동 go back (to)

다음 달 말에 고향에 돌아갈 예정이에요.
I am planning to go back to my hometown late next month.

 돌아오다 come back

13 들어오다   동 come

오늘 집에 들어올 때 사과 좀 사 와.
Get some apples when you come home today.

 들어가다 go in   들어서다 go in

14 사고   명 accident

집에 오는 길에 교통 사고가 나서 병원에 갔다.
I had an accident when I was coming home so I went to the hospital.

 사고 경위 details of the accident 사고가 나다 accident occurred

15 소리 sound

밤에 밖에서 갑자기 이상한 소리가 들려서 깜짝 놀랐다.
I was surprised to hear a strange sound from outside last night.

소리치다 yell out loud   소리가 나다 sound
소리를 지르다 scream

16 연락하다 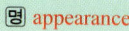 contact

고향에 계신 부모님께 자주 연락해요?
Do you often call your parents in your hometown?

연락 contact   연락처 contact number
연락(이) 오다 hear from (someone)
연락(을) 주다 contact someone

17 모습 ⑬ appearance

아이가 자는 모습을 보면 그렇게 예쁠 수가 없어요.
If you watch how babies sleep, they are adorable.

Tip

'모습'과 '모양'은 어떤 차이가 있을까요?
What is the difference between "모습(appearance)" and "모양(shape)"?

'모습'은 사람이나 자연에 대해서 주로 사용해요.
"모습(appearance)" is the term that is used when you explain about a person or nature.

예) 아버지의 뒷 모습 (the appearance of my father's back)
    어린 아이의 우는 모습 (the appearance of the crying baby)

반면에, '모양'은 주로 비교적 작은 사물에 대해서 사용해요.
However, "모양(shape)" is used for the relatively smaller objects.

예) 강아지 모양 필통 (puppy shaped pencil case)
    세모 모양 지우개 (triangle shaped eraser)

18 오래되다　　　　　　　　　　　　　　　　　　　　형 old

오래된 물건을 버리지말고 재활용합시다.
Please recycle old stuff instead of throwing them out.

오래 old　　　　　　　　　　　오래가다 last long
오랫동안 for a long time

19 원인　　　　　　　　　　　　　　　　　　　　　　명 reason

요즘 이혼율이 높아지는 원인이 무엇입니까?
What do you think is the reason for the increasing divorce rate nowadays?

20 인간　　　　　　　　　　　　　　　　　　　명 man, human

인간은 사회적 동물이다.
Men are social animals.

인간적 humane　　　　　　　　인간관계 human relationship

21 잃다　　　　　　　　　　　　　　　　　　　　　　동 lose

건강을 잃지 않으려면 꾸준한 운동을 해야 한다.
You should constantly exercise in order to not lose your health.

22 자리　　　　　　　　　　　　　　　　　　　　　　명 seat

실례지만, 자리 좀 바꿔 주실 수 있나요?
Excuse me, would you mind changing your seat?

자리가 있다/없다 have a seat/does not have a seat
자리를 바꾸다 change the seat

23 조사하다

 investigate

경찰은 이번 사건을 오늘에서야 **조사하기** 시작했다.

The police only started to investigate the case today.

조사 investigate   조사되다 be investigated
조사 결과 the result of the investigation

24 주민

명 (local) resident

우리 아파트는 **주민**들의 편의를 위해 노력하고 있습니다.

Our apartment is trying its best to make the residents more comfortable.

주민등록증 identification card

25 차이

명 difference

쌍둥이도 많은 면에서 **차이**가 있는 것으로 나타났다.

It is known that even twins have differences in many ways.

차이점 difference

26 책임

명 responsibility

이 일의 **책임**을 맡은 사람이 누구지요?

Who is responsible for this?

책임감 responsibility   책임지다 be responsible for
책임을 묻다 ask for the responsibility
책임을 다하다 discharge responsibility

27 행동하다

 act

생각한 것을 **행동할** 수 있는 용기가 필요해요.

You need the courage to act on what you think.

행동 action

28 확인하다　　　　　　　　　　　　　　　　　　동 check

공지 사항은 미리 확인해 주십시오.
Please check the announcement beforehand.

29 광고　　　　　　　　　　　　　　　　　　명 advertisement

텔레비전 광고를 보고 찾아오는 손님들이 늘었습니다.
The number of costumers who paid a visit after watching the advertisement has increased.

30 급하다　　　　　　　　　　　　　　　　　　형 urgent

급하게 해결해야 할 일이 있어요.
There is an urgent problem that you should solve.

 급히 in a hurry　　　　　성격이 급하다 be impetuous

31 실시하다　　　　　　　　　　　　　　　　　　동 practice

몇 년 전부터 초등학교에서 무료 급식을 실시하고 있어요.
The elementary schools have offered the free lunch for the past several years.

 실시되다 be practiced

32 작품　　　　　　　　　　　　　　　　　　명 work

이 작품은 최고의 걸작으로 평가 받는다.
This work is being assessed as a masterpiece.

33 적극적　　　　　　　　　　　　　　　　　　명 active

그 문제를 해결하기 위해 적극적인 태도를 취하고 있다.
He is showing an active attitude to solve the problem.

 소극적 passive

TOPIK에서 혼동하기 쉬운 단어

다의어 Polysemy

나가다

❶ participate in
예) 이번 올림픽에 나가게 되었습니다.
Become a participant in the following Olympics.

❷ go out
예) 우리 아이는 밖에 나가서 노는 걸 좋아하는 편이에요.
I'll be participating in the upcoming Olympics.

❸ go out
예) 여러 사이트에서 물건이 나가다보니 확인이 어렵습니다.
This goes out to many different sites, so it is hard to confirm.

❹ quit
예) 그런 일로 회사를 나간다니요!
You should not quit your job because of that!

반의어 Antonym

거절하다 reject ↔ 승낙하다 accept

예) 다른 사람의 부탁을 잘 거절하지 못하는 성격이다.
He is not a person that can reject other people's request.

그 사람과의 결혼을 승낙해 주십시오.
Please accept my marriage proposal with that person.

유의어 Synonym

사용하다 use ≒ 이용하다 use

예) 사람처럼 도구를 사용하는 동물도 있습니다.
사람처럼 도구를 이용하는 동물도 있습니다.
There are animals that use tools like people do.

복습해 보세요

 한국어와 영어를 알맞게 연결해 보세요.
Connect the Korean words with the English words of same meaning.

1. 확인하다 •　　　　　　　　• a. man, human
2. 자료 •　　　　　　　　　• b. practice, implement
3. 실시하다 •　　　　　　　　• c. check
4. 작품 •　　　　　　　　　• d. data
5. 인간 •　　　　　　　　　• e. active
6. 적극적 •　　　　　　　　　• f. work
7. 잃다 •　　　　　　　　　• g. lose

 다음 빈 칸에 알맞은 단어를 〈보기〉에서 골라 쓰세요.
Pick and write the suitable word among <the options> in the blank space.

〈보기〉
a. 소리가　　b. 급하게　　c. 역할을　　d. 주의 사항을

8. 이번 대회 참가자들은 (　　　　) 잘 확인해 주세요.
The participants in this competition should carefully check the matters that require attention.

9. 밤에 밖에서 갑자기 이상한 (　　　　) 들려서 깜짝 놀랐다.
I was surprised to hear a strange sound from outside last night.

10. (　　　　) 해결해야 할 일이 있어요.
There is an urgent problem that you should solve.

11. 어떤 (　　　　) 맡고 있든지 최선을 다해야 한다고 생각합니다.
Whatever role you take, you should do your best.

정답

1.c　2.d　3.b　4.f　5.a　6.e　7.g　8.d　9.a　10.b　11.c

DAY 05

확인해 보세요

빨간 시트지로 가리고 단어의 뜻을 알면, ☐ 에 ✓ 해 보세요.
After covering up the words with red cover, please check(✓) the box (☐) when you know the meaning of the word.

☐ 01	정보	information	☐ 13	따르다	follow	✓ 25	이해하다	understand
☐ 02	할인되다	discount	☐ 14	모집	recruitment	☐ 26	정리하다	organize
☐ 03	활용하다	apply, use	✓ 15	믿다	trust	☐ 27	방식	method
✓ 04	꿈	dream	☐ 16	부족하다	be short of	☐ 28	감정	emotion
☐ 05	노인	older people	☐ 17	상태	status, condition	☐ 29	과학	science
☐ 06	반면	on the other hand	☐ 18	시민	citizen	☐ 30	나타나다	appear
✓ 07	자기	self	☐ 19	공연	performance	☐ 31	따로	apart
☐ 08	키우다	raise	☐ 20	여성	female	☐ 32	밝히다	disclose
☐ 09	해외	abroad	☐ 21	역사	history	✓ 33	벌써	already
☐ 10	각종	of every kind	☐ 22	예전	back in the days			
☐ 11	고민	worry	✓ 23	원하다	desire			
☐ 12	글	(a piece of) writing	☐ 24	유지하다	maintain			

DAY 05

 are the words that appeared in the former tests, and you may get a higher grade if you study them together.

01 정보   명 information

많은 **정보**보다 올바른 정보를 갖는 것이 중요하다.

It is important to have right information rather than having much information.

 정보실 information office   정보화 사회 informational society

02 할인되다   동 discount

혹시 이 식당에서 **할인되는** 카드를 가지고 있어?

Do you have a card that can get us a discount in this restaurant?

 할인 discount   할인율 discount rate
할인받다 get a discount   할인제도 discount policy
할인하다 discount

03 활용하다   동 apply, use

인터넷을 **활용한** 수업을 진행 중입니다.

We are taking a class using the internet.

 활용도 applying degree

04 꿈   명 dream

꿈이 없는 사람은 불행한 사람이다.

The person who does not have a dream is an unhappy person.

 꿈을 꾸다 have a dream   꿈을 버리다 give up one's dream
꿈을 이루다 realize one's dream

05 노인 　명 senior citizen

노인들을 위한 시설을 더 늘려야겠습니다.

We should increase the number of the facilities for the senior citizen.

 노인 회관 hall for the elderly

06 반면 　명 on the other hand

어디나 좋은 사람도 있는 반면에 나쁜 사람도 있다.

Good people exist wherever you go, on the other hand, bad people also exist wherever you go.

07 자기 　명 oneself

그 사람은 자기 스스로에 대한 자부심이 강한 사람이다.

He is a person who has a strong self-esteem.

 자기 개발 self-development   자기 소개서 a letter of self-introduction

08 키우다 　동 raise

라디오 소리가 너무 작아요. 좀 키워 주세요.

The sound of the radio is too small. Can you please raise the volume?

09 해외 　명 abroad

이번 연휴에 해외로 출국하는 사람들이 작년보다 늘어났대요.

Over the last holiday, the number of people going abroad increased compared to last year.

10 각종　　　　　　　　　　　　　　　　　　　　　　명 of every kind

각종 여행 상품을 한 자리에 모았습니다.

We have gathered every kind of travel package here.

관련어
각각 each　　　　　　　각자 each one
각국 each country　　　 각기 each
각지 every place

11 고민　　　　　　　　　　　　　　　　　　　　　　　　명 worry

밤에 잠을 못 자는 걸 보니 고민이 생겼나 봐요.

He must have some worries, since he cannot get any sleep at nights.

관련어
고민하다 worry about

12 글　　　　　　　　　　　　　　　　　　　　　명 (a piece of) writing

잘 쓰여진 글은 사람들에게 감동을 줍니다.

A well- written piece of writing moves many people.

13 따르다　　　　　　　　　　　　　　　　　　　　　　　　동 follow

수영 실력으로는 우리 학교에서 내 동생을 따를 사람이 없어요.

There is no one who can beat my brother in swimming.

14 모집　　　　　　　　　　　　　　　　　　　　　　　명 recruitment

우리 회사는 능력 있는 직원을 모집 중입니다.

Our company is recruiting a worker with high ability.

관련어
모집하다 recruit

15 믿다
동 trust

그 친구는 정말 믿을 만한 사람이에요.
He is a trustworthy friend.

 믿음 trust

16 부족하다
형 be short of

시험 볼 때 시간이 너무 부족했어요.
I was short of time while I was taking the test.

 부족 shortage

17 상태
명 status, condition

수술 후 그 사람의 상태는 더 안 좋아졌다.
His condition got worse after the surgery.

18 시민
명 citizen

서울시에서는 정책에 시민들의 의견을 반영하고 있다.
The city of Seoul is reflecting on the opinion of the citizens regarding the policy that they execute.

19 공연
명 performance

예술의 전당에서는 다양한 공연을 개최하고 있습니다.
Many kinds of performances are being held in the arts center.

 공연장 theatre   공연되다 be performed
공연하다 perform

 how this word appears in the test

읽기 영역에서 뮤지컬, 콘서트, 연극, 오페라 등의 포스터를 자주 볼 수 있어요. 포스터의 내용을 확인하는 문제로 많이 출제됩니다.

In the reading comprehension test, you can easily see many posters of musicals, concerts, plays, operas etc. They ask the specific information that you can check based on the information that is written on the poster.

20 여성　　　　　　　　　　　　　　　　　　　　명 female

많은 백화점에서는 여성 고객을 잡기 위해 여러가지 이벤트를 한다.

Many department stores are having various kinds of events to attract female customers.

 여성운동가 female activist　　　남성 male

21 역사　　　　　　　　　　　　　　　　　　　　명 history

한국의 역사를 알고 싶은데 어떤 책이 좋을까요?

What kind of books do you recommend in order to know the history of the Republic of Korea?

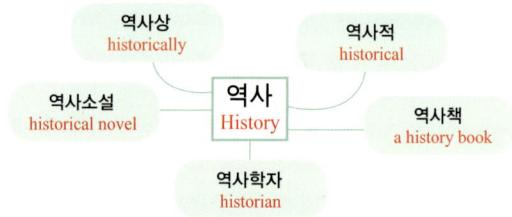

22 예전　　　　　　　　　　　　　　　　　　　　명 back in the days

예전에는 지구가 평평하다고 생각했다.

People believed that the earth is flat back in the days.

23 원하다　　　　　　　　　　　　　　　　　　　동 desire

원하는 일을 하고 있다는 것만으로 행복합니다.

It is happy just to be able to do what I desire.

24 유지하다　　　　　　　　　　　　　　　　　　동 maintain

다이어트 후에도 요요현상을 막기 위해 운동량을 유지하고 있다.

I am keeping the same hours of work out in order to not regain the weight.

 유지 maintain　　　　　　유지되다 be maintained
유지시키다 have something maintained

25 이해하다 동 understand

입장을 바꿔 생각해 보면 상대방을 더 잘 이해할 수 있을 거예요.
You will understand better if you consider from the other's point of view.

이해 understanding   이해력 understanding ability
이해심 understanding   이해되다 be understood
이해시키다 make one understand

26 정리하다 동 organize

고향으로 가기 위해 짐을 정리하고 있어요.
I am packing to visit my hometown.

정리 organize   정리되다 be organized

27 방식 명 method

김 대리와 저는 일하는 방식이 서로 달라서 가끔 마찰이 있어요.
Sometimes I have a trouble with Mr. Kim since the way that we work is totally different from each other.

28 감정 명 emotion

평소에 자신의 생각이나 감정을 잘 표현하는 연습이 필요합니다.
It is necessary to practice expressing your thoughts and emotions eloquently.

감정 조절 emotion control   감정적 emotional

29 과학 명 science

과학의 발달로 생활이 편리해졌다.
Life has become more convenient because of the scientific development.

과학자 scientist   과학적 scientific

30 나타나다　　　⑧ appear

최근 서울시 산 근처 도로에 맷돼지가 나타났다고 합니다.

It is said that the boars recently appeared in the roads near the mountain.

 나타내다 appear

31 따로　　　㉿ apart

저는 부모님과 따로 살고 있어요.

I live apart from my parents.

32 밝히다　　　⑧ disclose

강이 오염된 원인이 밝혀졌다고 합니다.

The reason that polluted the river was disclosed.

33 벌써　　　㉿ already

벌써 10시네요. 이제 그만 집에 가야겠어요.

It is already 10 o'clock. I should go home.

TOPIK에서 혼동하기 쉬운 단어

다의어 Polysemy

나다

❶ start
예) 본인도 모르게 소문이 **났던** 것 같아요. The rumors got started even before I noticed it.

❷ start
예) 아침부터 기침도 **나고** 콧물도 났어요. I started to cough and have a runny nose from this morning.

❸ get
예) 아무리 화가 **나도** 참아야지요. You should control your emotion even when you get angry.

❹ happen
예) 핸드폰이 고장 **나서** 서비스센터에 다녀왔어요.
My cell phone was broken and I went to the service center to get it fixed.

❺ appear
예) 저쪽에서 무슨 소리가 **나는** 것 같지 않아요? Don't you hear something?

❻ occur
예) 어제 옆동에서 불이 **나서** 사람이 죽었대요.
There was a fire in the next building yesterday and people died.

❼ arise
예) 아까부터 이상한 냄새가 **나는걸**. A weird smell is coming from somewhere.

반의어 Antonym

게으르다 lazy ↔ 부지런하다 diligent

예) 게으른 사람은 성공할 수 없다.
A lazy person cannot succeed.

부지런하게 일하다 보면 너에게도 기회가 생길 것이다.
If you work diligently, you will have your chance.

유의어 Synonym

상의하다 consult ≒ 의논하다 discuss

예) 유학을 갈지 안 갈지 부모님과 **상의한** 후에 결정할 거예요.
유학을 갈지 안 갈지 부모님과 **의논한** 후에 결정할 거예요.
I will decide whether to go abroad and study after discussing with my parents.

DAY 05

복습해 보세요

 한국어는 영어로, 영어는 한국어로 써 보세요.
Write Korean in English, and English in Korean.

1. 과학 _____
2. 믿다 _____
3. 따르다 _____
4. 이해하다 _____
5. 부족하다 _____

6. dream _____
7. apply, use _____
8. method _____
9. back in the days _____
10. already _____

 문장이 자연스럽도록 둘 중에서 알맞은 단어를 고르세요.
Choose the proper word that fits the sentence more naturally.

11. 다이어트 후에도 요요현상을 막기 위해 운동량을 (a.정리하고 / b.유지하고) 있다.
    I am keeping the same hours of work out in order to not regain the weight.

12. 수술 후 그 사람의 (a.정보 / b.상태)는 더 안 좋아졌다.
    His condition got worse after the surgery.

13. 강이 오염된 원인이 (a.밝혀졌다고 / b.키워졌다고) 합니다.
    The reason that polluted the river was disclosed.

14. (a.원하는 / b.나타나는) 일을 하고 있다는 것만으로 행복합니다.
    It is happy only to be able to do what I desire.

15. 밤에 잠을 못 자는 걸 보니 (a.감정 / b.고민)이 생겼나 봐요.
    He must have some worries, since he cannot get any sleep at nights.

정답

1.science 2.trust 3.follow 4.understand 5.be short of 6.꿈 7.활용하다 8.방식 9.예전 10.벌써 11.b 12.b 13.a 14.a 15.b

주간 복습 day 1 – day 5

아래 단어를 보고 빈 칸에 뜻을 적어 보세요. 그리고 점선대로 접어서 적은 뜻이 맞는지 확인해 보세요. (만일 틀렸다면 뒷면의 단어 앞 □ 에 ✓ 하세요.)

Write down the meaning of the given word in the blank. Also, fold the page along a dotted line and check whether you got it right or wrong. (If you got it wrong check(✓) the box(□) in front of the word in next page.)

▼접는선

단어	뜻
느끼다	
관심	
가능하다	
경우	
선택하다	
관리	
어리다	
불편하다	
버리다	
직장	
참가하다	
무료	
제대로	
충분하다	
포함되다	
확인하다	
역할	
주의 사항	
잃다	
적극적	
믿다	
따르다	
꿈	
상태	
유지하다	

서울N타워

주간복습 | 67

주간 복습 day 1 - day 5

빈 칸에 한국어 단어를 3번 적고 다시 외워 봅시다.
Write down the Korean word 3 times in the blank and try to memorize it again.

뜻	단어		
☐ feel	느끼다		
☐ attention	관심		
☐ be possible	가능하다		
☐ case	경우		
☐ choose, select, decide	선택하다		
☐ management	관리		
☐ young	어리다		
☐ inconvenient	불편하다		
☐ throw away	버리다		
☐ job	직장		
☐ participate in	참가하다		
☐ free of charge	무료		
☐ properly	제대로		
☐ plenty of, be enough	충분하다		
☐ be included	포함되다		
☐ check	확인하다		
☐ role, part	역할		
☐ matters that require attention	주의 사항		
☐ lose	잃다		
☐ active	적극적		
☐ trust	믿다		
☐ follow	따르다		
☐ dream	꿈		
☐ status, condition	상태		
☐ maintain	유지하다		

DAY 06

확인해 보세요

빨간 시트지로 가리고 단어의 뜻을 알면, □에 ✓ 해 보세요.
After covering up the words with red cover, please check(✓) the box (□) when you know the meaning of the word.

□ 01 삶	life	□ 13 기능	function	□ 25 동료	coworker
□ 02 성격	characteristic	□ 14 꾸준히	constantly	□ 26 떠나다	leave
□ 03 습관	habit	☒ 15 맛	taste	□ 27 그만두다	quit
□ 04 업무	work	□ 16 신경	nerve	□ 28 무조건	unconditionally
☒ 05 위험하다	dangerous	□ 17 심각하다	serious	□ 29 물론	as well as
□ 06 자녀	children	□ 18 인정하다	appreciate (one's ability)	□ 30 바라다	wish
□ 07 자연스럽다	it is natural to	□ 19 진행되다	in progress	□ 31 발명되다	be invented
□ 08 치료하다	cure	☒ 20 하루	a day	□ 32 방문	visit
☒ 09 함께	together	☒ 21 행복하다	be happy	□ 33 방송	broadcasting
☒ 10 혼자	alone	□ 22 적당하다	proper		
□ 11 등등	etc. (et cetera), ~and so on	□ 23 정부	administration, government		
□ 12 국내	domestic	□ 24 내리다	decrease		

DAY 06

 관련어 are the words that appeared in the former tests, and you may get a higher grade if you study them together.

01 삶   명 life

우리 삶에서 제일 중요한 것이 무엇인지 잘 생각해 봐야 한다.
You should deeply think about what is the most important thing in our life.

 살다 live

02 성격   명 characteristic

그 사람은 성격이 좋아서 친구가 많은 편이다.
He has a good characteristic and has many friends.

성격에 맞다 fit one's characteristic

03 습관   명 habit

어릴 때부터 좋은 습관을 키우는 것은 매우 중요하다.
It is important to develop a good habit when you are young.

04 업무   명 work

요즘 그 사람은 회사 업무 때문에 정신없이 바쁘다.
Recently, he is overly busy with his work.

 업무내용 job description   업무시간 office time

05 위험하다   형 dangerous

이 곳은 깊어서 어린 아이가 수영하기에 위험합니다.
It is dangerous for children to swim in this area since it is too deep.

 위험 danger   위험성 dangerousness

06 자녀
명 children

자녀에 대한 부모의 큰 기대가 오히려 자녀를 망칠 수 있다.
Too much expectation of the parents to their children rather harms their children.

 출제 경향 how this word appears in the test

교육과 관련된 주제의 문제가 자주 나옵니다. 예를 들면, 자녀의 교육 문제, 입시 문제, 청소년 비행 문제 등이 나오고 주로 중심생각을 묻거나 글쓴이의 태도를 묻는 질문이 많은 편입니다.
Many questions that are related to education often appear in the test. For instance, there are many questions that give some contents related to child's educational problem, admission test problem, and teenager misdeed etc. Then, asks about the main idea or the writer's attitude.

07 자연스럽다
형 it is natural to

외국어를 배울 때는 자연스럽게 말하는 연습이 필요합니다.
Practicing to speak naturally is essential when you learn a foreign language.

 자연적 natural   자연현상 natural phenomenon

08 치료하다
동 cure

이는 조금 썩었을 때 빨리 치료해야 합니다.
You should go for treatment when your teeth are a little bit rotten.

 치료 treatment

09 함께
부 together

친구들과 함께 극장에 갔습니다.
I went to the theater with my friends.

10 혼자
명 alone

혼자 밥을 먹으면 맛이 없어요.
It does not taste good when you eat alone.

 혼자서 alone   둘이서 two people together
셋이서 three people together

11 등등   명 etc. (et cetera), ~and so on

한국의 환경, 경제, 산업 기타 등등에 대해 정리한 자료를 보내 드리겠습니다.

I will send you documents that include the contents about South Korea's environment, economy and industry etc.

12 국내   명 domestic

추천할 만한 국내 여행지는 어디일까요?

Is there any domestic destination that you recommend?

 국내외 the inside and outside of the country

13 기능   명 function

이 컴퓨터에는 새로운 기능이 추가되었다고 합니다.

They say there is a new function added to this computer.

14 꾸준히   부 constantly

꾸준히 노력하면 언젠가는 합격할 거예요.

If you constantly try hard, you will pass the test some time or other.

 꾸준하다 constant

15 맛   명 taste

국이 다 됐는데, 맛 좀 볼래?

The soup is ready, want to taste it?

Tip
맛에는 또 뭐가 있을까요?
What kind of taste do we have?
단맛(sweet), 매운 맛(hot), 신맛(sour), 쓴맛(bitter), 짠맛(salty) etc.

16 신경   명 nerve

요즘 너무 바빠서 가족들을 신경 쓸 정신이 없어요.
I am too busy these days, and do not have any time to pay attention to my family.

관련어 신경을 쓰다 pay attention to

17 심각하다   형 serious

환경 오염이 점점 심각해지고 있다.
The environmental pollution is becoming more serious than before.

18 인정하다   동 appreciate (one's ability)

그 사람의 그림을 직접 본다면 실력을 인정할 수밖에 없다.
If you see his painting in person, you have no choice but to appreciate his ability.

관련어 인정받다 be recognized

19 진행되다   동 in progress

아침 9시부터 오후 6시까지 진행된 행사에 많은 사람들이 참여했습니다.
Many people joined the event that was in progress from 9am to 6pm.

관련어 진행 progress   진행자 presenter
진행하다 present

20 하루   명 a day

하루에 물을 7잔 마시면 좋대요.
It is good for you to drink 7 cups of water a day.

관련어 하루종일 all day

DAY 06
★★★

21 행복하다   혱 be happy

사람들은 모두 행복한 삶을 살고 싶어합니다.

Everyone wants to live happy.

행복 happiness   불행 unhappiness
행복감 euphoria   불행하다 unhappy

22 적당하다   혱 proper

적당한 실내 온도는 20도라고 한다.

The proper temperature indoors is 20 degree Celsius.

적당히 properly

23 정부   명 administration, government

이번 정부는 국민들로부터 많은 지지를 받고 있다.

This administration is getting a great deal of support from the citizens.

24 내리다   동 decrease

주사를 맞자 열이 내렸어요.

After getting a shot, the temperature decreased.

25 동료   명 coworker

직장 동료들과 좋은 관계를 유지하고 있다.

I am maintaining a good relationship with the coworkers.

26 떠나다   동 leave

최근 고향을 떠나는 사람들이 많아지고 있다.

There are many people leaving their hometowns.

27 그만두다   동 quit

다음 달부터 아르바이트를 그만두려고요.
I am planning to quit the part time job from next month on.

Tip '그만두다'는 어떤 단어와 같이 사용할까요?
What kind of word is used together with the word "그만두다(quit)"?

회사 job
일 work
학교 school
+ 그만두다 quit

28 무조건   부 unconditionally

무조건 아이를 야단치지 말고 왜 그런 행동을 했는지 물어 보세요.
Don't just scold your child, ask why he behaved like he did.

29 물론   부 as well as

그 사람은 영어는 물론 한국어도 잘해요.
He speaks fluent Korean as well as English.

30 바라다   동 wish

건강하고 행복하게 지내기를 바랍니다.
I wish you live happy and healthily.

 바람 wish

31 발명되다   동 be invented

최근에 전기로 가는 자동차가 발명되었다.
Recently, the automobile that operates by electricity was invented.

 발명 invention   발명가 an inventor
발명품 invention

32 방문   명 visit

오늘 오후 3시에 **방문**이 가능할까요?

May I visit you at 3 o'clock this afternoon?

 방문객 visitor   방문하다 pay a visit

33 방송   명 broadcasting

어제 라디오 **방송**에 제 사연이 소개됐어요.

My story was introduced in the radio broadcasting yesterday.

방송국 broadcasting station   방송사 broadcasting company
방송인 broadcaster   방송되다 be broadcasted

TOPIK에서 혼동하기 쉬운 단어

다의어 Polysemy

나오다

❶ be introduced
예) 새 모델이 곧 **나온다고** 하니까 조금 더 기다렸다가 사요.
The new model will be introduced soon, so wait a while then buy it.

❷ appear
예) 영화가 시작되기 전에는 항상 광고가 **나옵니다**.
The commercials always appear before the movie starts.

❸ attend
예) 동창회에 빠지지 않고 **나오는** 사람은 10명도 안 돼요.
It is less than 10 people who constantly attend the reunion.

❹ come out
예) 요즘 무리를 했더니 어제부터 목소리가 **나오지** 않아요.
After working hard for the past several days, I lost my voice.

❺ emit
예) 전자파가 **나오니까** 전자레인지 앞에 서 있지 마세요.
The electromagnetic waves emit from the microwaves, so don't stand before it.

반의어 Antonym

귀하다 precious ↔ **흔하다** common

예) 내 자식이 **귀하면** 남의 자식도 귀한 법이다.
If my kid is precious, then other people's kid is also precious.

1975년에 가장 **흔한** 여자 이름은 '미영' 이었다.
The mostly common name in the 1975 was Mi Young.

유의어 Synonym

마침내 finally(at last) ≒ **드디어** finally(at last)

예) **마침내** 기다리고 기다리던 대학교 시험 결과가 발표되었다.
드디어 기다리고 기다리던 대학교 시험 결과가 발표되었다.
The result of the university test has finally been announced.

DAY 06

복습해 보세요

 한국어와 영어를 알맞게 연결해 보세요.
Connect the Korean words with the English words of same meaning.

1. 자녀 • • a. characteristic
2. 내리다 • • b. taste
3. 맛 • • c. children
4. 적당하다 • • d. nerve
5. 자연스럽다 • • e. decrease
6. 신경 • • f. naturally
7. 성격 • • g. proper

 다음 빈 칸에 알맞은 단어를 〈보기〉에서 골라 쓰세요.
Pick and write the suitable word among <the options> in the blank space.

〈보기〉
   a. 치료해야   b. 꾸준히   c. 행복한   d. 정부는

8. (   ) 노력하면 언젠가는 합격할 거예요.
   If you constantly try hard, you will pass the test some time or other.

9. 이는 조금 썩었을 때 빨리 (   ) 합니다.
   You should go for treatment when your teeth are a little bit rotten.

10. 사람들은 모두 (   ) 삶을 살고 싶어합니다.
    Everyone wants to live happy.

11. 이번 (   ) 국민들로부터 많은 지지를 받고 있다.
    This administration is getting a great deal of support from the citizens.

정답
1.c 2.e 3.b 4.g 5.f 6.d 7.a 8.b 9.a 10.c 11.d

DAY 07

확인해 보세요

빨간 시트지로 가리고 단어의 뜻을 알면, ☐ 에 ✓ 해 보세요.
After covering up the words with red cover, please check(✓) the box (☐) when you know the meaning of the word.

☐ 01	붙다	stick	☐ 13	조건	condition	☒ 25	거의	almost
☒ 02	비슷하다	be similar to	☒ 14	조심하다	be careful	☐ 26	결국	finally
☐ 03	상담하다	consult	☐ 15	즐기다	enjoy	☐ 27	공공장소	public place
☐ 04	시설	facility	☐ 16	증가하다	increase	☐ 28	관광객	tourist
☒ 05	실수	mistake	☐ 17	취업하다	get a job	☒ 29	기대하다	expect
☐ 06	안전하다	be safe	☒ 18	팔다	sell	☒ 30	대신하다	replace, instead (of)
☐ 07	없애다	get rid of	☒ 19	프로그램	program	☐ 31	대중교통	public transportation
☐ 08	자격	qualification	☐ 20	피하다	avoid	☐ 32	미리	in advance
☐ 09	작가	writer	☐ 21	넘다	after	☐ 33	반응	reaction
☐ 10	전하다	send	☐ 22	발길	coming and going			
☐ 11	제공하다	provide	☐ 23	가득하다	be filled with			
☐ 12	제시하다	suggest	☐ 24	가지다(=갖다)	have			

DAY 07

  are the words that appeared in the former tests, and you may get higher grade if you study them together.

01 붙다 　　　　　　　　　　　　　　　　　　　　　　⟨동⟩ stick

옷에 껌이 **붙었는데** 어떻게 해야 할지 모르겠다.

I have gum stuck on my clothes, and I don't know what to do.

02 비슷하다 　　　　　　　　　　　　　　　　　　　⟨형⟩ be similar to

나와 우리 언니는 성격이 **비슷하다**.

My sister and I have very similar personalities.

03 상담하다 　　　　　　　　　　　　　　　　　　　⟨동⟩ consult

공부 방법에 대해서 선생님께 **상담하러** 갈 것이다.

I am planning to consult with my teacher about my studying habits.

　상담 consultation　　　　　상담 전문가 consulting expert
　　상담 창구 consulting window　　상담소 counseling center
　　상담원 consultant

04 시설 　　　　　　　　　　　　　　　　　　　　　　⟨명⟩ facility

우리 병원은 국내 최고의 **시설**을 자랑합니다.

Our hospital has the best facilities in the whole country.

　시설물 facility

05 실수 　　　　　　　　　　　　　　　　　　　　　　⟨명⟩ mistake

실수를 무서워하면 큰 일을 할 수 없어요.

You can never accomplish a big thing if you are afraid of making mistakes.

　실수하다 make a mistake

06 안전하다 　　　　　　　　　　　　　　　[형] be safe

운전할 때는 휴대전화를 사용하지 않는 것이 안전하다.

It is safe not to use your cell phone while you are driving.

 관련어

07 없애다 　　　　　　　　　　　　　　　[동] get rid of

남녀 차별을 없애기 위해 많은 사람들이 노력해야 한다.

Many people should try their best effort to get rid of the discrimination between men and women.

08 자격 　　　　　　　　　　　　　　　　[명] qualification

입사 지원 자격이 어떻게 되나요?

What is the qualification required to apply for the company?

 관련어

자격증 certificate(license)

> **출제 경향** how this word appears in the test
>
> '자격'은 공고문에 항상 나오는 단어입니다. 다음 단어의 의미를 꼭 확인하세요.
> The word "자격(qualification)" always appears in the notification. Always remember the following words.
>
> 참가자격(qualification to participate), 응모자격(qualification to enter),
> 출전자격(qualification to compete), 자격요건(requirements).

09 작가 　　　　　　　　　　　　　　　　[명] writer

해리포터를 쓴 작가가 한국을 방문할 것이라고 한다.

They say the writer who wrote Harry Potter is planning to visit Korea.

 관련어

글쓴이 writer

10 전하다 　　　　　　　　　　　　　　　　　　　동 send

지현 씨에게 안부 좀 전해 주세요.

Please send regards to Ji-hyun.

11 제공하다 　　　　　　　　　　　　　　　　　동 provide

대회 참가자에게는 도시락과 물을 제공해 드립니다.

A packed lunch and bottle of water will be given to every participant of this competition.

제공 provide　　　　　　제공되다 be provided

12 제시하다 　　　　　　　　　　　　　　　　동 suggest

이 문제는 해결책을 제시하기가 힘들다.

It is hard to suggest a solution to this problem.

제시되다 be suggested

13 조건 　　　　　　　　　　　　　　　　　　명 condition

이 회사에 지원하려면 어떤 조건을 갖춰야 합니까?

What is the condition required to apply for this company?

14 조심하다 　　　　　　　　　　　　　　　　동 be careful

길이 미끄러우니 조심해서 걸어야 합니다.

You should be careful while you walk since the road is slippery.

15 즐기다 　　　　　　　　　　　　　　　　　동 enjoy

이 운동은 남녀노소 누구나 즐길 수 있어요.

This sport can be enjoyed by men and women of all ages.

16 증가하다

최근 이혼율이 증가하는 원인이 무엇입니까?

What is the cause that made the divorce rate increase?

 증가 increase   증가폭 increase

> **출제 경향** how this word appears in the test
>
> 읽기와 쓰기에서는 그래프 문제가 자주 출제됩니다. 그래프 문제를 풀기 위해서는
> The question that uses the graphs often appears in the reading and writing sections.
> In order to solve those questions, you should be aware of the words such as
> 이상(over), 이하(under), 경향(tendency), 비중(weight), 비율(ratio), 수치(figure),
> 대상(object), N 별(지역별, 성별)(by N groups) (by regional groups, by gender groups),
> 증가하다(increase), 감소하다(decrease)
> 등의 단어를 공부해야 합니다.
> and so on.

17 취업하다   동 get a job

요즘 대학을 졸업해도 취업하기가 쉽지 않습니다.

Lately, it is hard to get a job even after you graduate from university.

취업 getting a job
취업생 job applicant
취업률 employment rate
여성취업 a female employment

실업 unemployment
실업자 the unemployed
실업률 unemployment rate
청년실업 youth unemployment

18 팔다   동 sell

컴퓨터 부품을 파는 데가 어디에 있어요?

Where do they sell computer parts?

19 프로그램   명 program

이번 주말에 볼 수 있는 TV 프로그램을 확인해 보세요.

Check the television program for the weekend.

20 피하다 　　　　　　　　　　　　　　　　　[동] avoid

자전거를 피하려다가 넘어졌어요.

I fell down trying to avoid the bicycle.

21 넘다 　　　　　　　　　　　　　　　　　　[동] after

6시가 넘으면 우체국은 문을 닫아요.

The post office closes after six.

22 발길 　　　　　　　　　　　　　　　[명] coming and going

제주도를 찾는 사람들의 발길이 이어지고 있습니다.

The trend of people visiting Jeju will likely continue.

 발걸음 visit

23 가득하다 　　　　　　　　　　　　　　[형] be filled with

웃음이 가득한 집에는 행복이 찾아온다.

The happiness will visit the house filled with laughter.

 가득 full　　　　　　가득히 full

24 가지다(=갖다) 　　　　　　　　　　　　　　[동] have

꿈을 가지고 도전해 보세요.

Have a dream and challenge.

Tip '가지다'는 어떤 단어와 같이 사용할까요?
What word is used together with the word "가지다(have)"?

가지다 have ＋ 꿈 a dream
희망 a hope
관심 an interest
자신감 a self esteem

25 거의　　　　　　　　　　　　　　　　　　　　　　　　图 almost

거의 한 달 내내 비가 오는 것 같다.

I think it is has been raining almost all month long.

26 결국　　　　　　　　　　　　　　　　　　　　　　　　图 finally

무리하게 일을 하다가 결국 병에 걸렸습니다.

I finally got sick after working too hard.

27 공공장소　　　　　　　　　　　　　　　　　　　　　图 public place

공공장소에서는 담배를 피울 수 없습니다.

You cannot smoke in the public place.

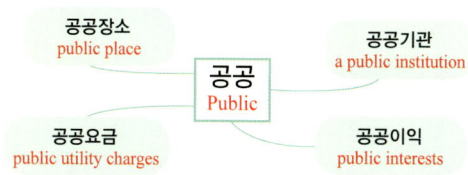

28 관광객　　　　　　　　　　　　　　　　　　　　　　　图 tourist

한국을 찾는 외국인 관광객이 늘었다고 합니다.

They say the number of foreign tourists has increased.

관광지 tourist site　　　　　　관광 명소 tourist site

29 기대하다　　　　　　　　　　　　　　　　　　　　　　图 expect

이번 시험에 합격하기를 기대하겠습니다.

I expect you to pass the test.

기대 expectation　　　　　　기대치 expected value

30 대신하다　　　　　　　　　통 replace, instead (of)

누구도 다른 사람의 인생을 대신해서 살아 줄 수는 없어요.

No one can live other people's life instead.

 대신 instead of

31 대중교통　　　　　　　　　명 public transportation

더욱 편리하게 대중교통을 이용할 수 있도록 정부에서 노력을 기울이고 있다.

The government is putting its effort to make it easier for people to use public transportation.

 대중 the public　　　　　대중적 popular
대중매체 mass media

32 미리　　　　　　　　　　　부 in advance

시험까지 아직 시간이 많이 남았지만 미리 준비해 놓으세요.

There is plenty of time until the test, but you should prepare in advance.

33 반응　　　　　　　　　　　명 reaction

이번 사건에 대한 사람들의 반응은 다 다르다.

The reaction to this case differs from people to people.

 반응하다 react

TOPIK에서 혼동하기 쉬운 단어

다의어 Polysemy

낫다

❶ be cured
예 할머니의 병이 나아서 다행이에요.
It is nice to see my grandmother getting cured.

❷ better than
예 부모님에게 하는 것을 보면 동생이 나보다 나을 때가 있어요.
Based on what my brother does to our parents, he can sometimes be better than me.

반의어 Antonym

긍정적 positive ↔ 부정적 negative

예 이번 일에 대해서는 긍정적으로 검토해 보겠습니다.
I will positively review this occasion.

부정적인 사고 방식으로는 성공할 수 없습니다.
You will never be successful with a negative attitude.

유의어 Synonym

결심하다 make up one's mind ≒ 마음먹다 decide

예 이제부터 열심히 공부하기로 결심했습니다.
이제부터 열심히 공부하기로 마음먹었습니다.
I have made up my mind to study hard from now on.

복습해 보세요

한국어는 영어로, 영어는 한국어로 써 보세요.
Write Korean in English, and English in Korean.

1. 비슷하다 _____
2. 상담하다 _____
3. 증가하다 _____
4. 공공장소 _____
5. 대중교통 _____

6. mistake _____
7. writer _____
8. get a job _____
9. reaction _____
10. provide _____

문장이 자연스럽도록 둘 중에서 알맞은 단어를 고르세요.
Choose the proper word that fits the sentence more naturally.

11. 우리 병원은 국내 최고의 (a.시설을 / b.발길을) 자랑합니다.

    Our hospital has the best facilities in the whole country.

12. 이 회사에 지원하려면 어떤 (a.관계를 / b.조건을) 갖춰야 합니까?

    What is the condition required to apply for this company?

13. 운전할 때는 휴대전화를 사용하지 않는 것이 (a.안전하다 / b.불편하다).

    It is safe not to use your cell phone while you are driving.

14. 자전거를 (a.피하려다가 / b.제시하려다가) 넘어졌어요.

    I fell down trying to avoid the bicycle.

15. 이번 시험에 합격하기를 (a.대신하겠습니다 / b.기대하겠습니다).

    I expect you to pass the test.

정답: 1.be similar to 2.consult 3.increase 4.public place 5.public transportation 6.실수 7.작가 8.취직하다 9.반응 10.제공하다 11.a 12.b 13.a 14.a 15.b

DAY 08

확인해 보세요

빨간 시트지로 가리고 단어의 뜻을 알면, ☐ 에 ✓ 해 보세요.
After covering up the words with red cover, please check(✓) the box (☐) when you know the meaning of the word.

- ☐ 01 봉사하다 — volunteer
- ☒ 02 서비스 — service
- ☒ 03 스트레스 — stress
- ☐ 04 시청 — watch
- ☐ 05 신문 — newspaper
- ☐ 06 움직이다 — move
- ☐ 07 가격 — price
- ☐ 08 전통 — tradition
- ☐ 09 젊다 — young
- ☐ 10 점 — point
- ☐ 11 정확하다 — precise
- ☒ 12 주문하다 — order
- ☐ 13 지나치다 — excessively
- ☐ 14 지원하다 — apply for
- ☐ 15 청소년 — teenager
- ☐ 16 추억 — memory
- ☒ 17 현재 — present, now
- ☐ 18 활동하다 — be active
- ☐ 19 희망하다 — look forward to
- ☐ 20 관람하다 — watch
- ☐ 21 기준 — standard
- ☐ 22 감상하다 — appreciate
- ☐ 23 경쟁 — competition
- ☐ 24 공기 — air
- ☐ 25 담다 — contain
- ☒ 26 도시 — city
- ☒ 27 뛰다 — run
- ☒ 28 분위기 — atmosphere
- ☒ 29 빛 — light
- ☐ 30 생명 — life
- ☐ 31 세탁하다 — wash
- ☐ 32 안정 — stability
- ☐ 33 어울리다 — go with

DAY 08

 are the words that appeared in the former tests, and you may get a higher grade if you study them together.

01 봉사하다
⑧ volunteer

이번 방학 때는 농촌에 가서 봉사하려고 해요.

I am planning to provide a voluntary service in the rural area during this vacation.

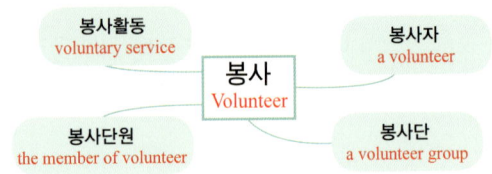

02 서비스
⑲ service

백화점은 시장보다 물건값이 비싸기는 하지만 더 좋은 서비스를 받을 수 있다.

Even though the price of the goods in the department store is more expensive than that of other markets, you can get better services as well.

03 스트레스
⑲ stress

요즘에 스트레스를 너무 많이 받아서 밤에 잠이 잘 안 온다.

I have trouble sleeping because of too much stress.

04 시청
⑲ watch

하루에 한 시간 이상의 TV 시청은 시력에 좋지 않다고 한다.

They say it is bad for your eyes to watch television more than one hour a day.

시청률 (viewer) ratings   시청자 viewer

05 신문　　　　　　　　　　　　　　　　　　　　　명 newspaper

매일 신문을 읽으면 요즘 어떤 일이 있는지 잘 알 수 있어요.

If you read the newspaper every day, you will be aware of what is happening these days.

 신문지 newspaper　　　　　신문기사 news article

06 움직이다　　　　　　　　　　　　　　　　　　　동 move

다리를 다쳐서 움직이는 것이 힘들어요.

It is hard for me to move since I have hurt my leg.

 움직임 movement

07 가격　　　　　　　　　　　　　　　　　　　　　명 price

최근 서울의 아파트 가격이 떨어졌습니다.

The price of Seoul's apartment has fallen recently.

'가격'과 비슷한 뜻을 가진 단어는 뭐가 있을까요?
What are the words that have the similar meaning as the word "가격(price)"?

단어	예
금액 The amount of money	계약 금액, 보험 금액 the deposit for the contract, the amount of money for the insurance
비용 Expense	수술 비용 export expense, 이사 비용 moving expense
N 값 The cost of N	기름값 the coffee cost, 커피값 the oil cost
요금 Charge	핸드폰 요금 the cell phone charge, 전기 요금 electricity cost, 수도 요금 the charge of water
N 료 bill	전기료 electricity bill, 수도료 water bill, 도시가스료 gas bill
N 비 Fare	버스비 the bus fare, 목욕비 fare to bathe

08 전통　　　　　　　　　　　　　　　　　명 tradition

나라마다 전통을 지키고자 많은 노력을 하고 있다.

Each country is doing their best to protect their tradition.

 전통적 traditional　　　　　　전통 악기 traditional musical instrument
전통 문화 traditional culture　　전통 연구소 traditional research office

09 젊다　　　　　　　　　　　　　　　　　형 young

나이보다 정말 젊어 보이시네요.

You look younger than you really are.

젊음 youth　　　　　　　　　젊은이 young person
젊은 사람 young people　　　젊은 시절 in one's youth

10 점　　　　　　　　　　　　　　　　　명 point

궁금한 점이 있으면 언제든지 연락해 주시기 바랍니다.

If you have anything to ask, please contact me.

11 정확하다　　　　　　　　　　　　　　　동 precise

정확하고 자세한 설명 부탁드립니다.

Please give a precise and specific explanation.

 정확 precision　　　　　　정확히 precisely

12 주문하다　　　　　　　　　　　　　　동 order

손님, 주문하신 음료 나왔습니다.

Sir, here is your drink that you ordered.

주문 order

13 지나치다　　　　　　　　　　　　　　동 excessively

이 물건이 좋기는 하지만 지나치게 비싸지 않아요?

This is really good, but isn't it excessively expensive?

14 지원하다 　　　　　　　　　　　　　　　　　　　　　통 apply for

그 대학교에 지원하려면 뭐가 필요합니까?

What do I need to apply for that university?

관련어　지원 apply　　　　　　지원서 application
　　　　지원자 applicant

15 청소년 　　　　　　　　　　　　　　　　　　　　　명 teenager

청소년들을 대상으로 하는 음악회가 열립니다.

A concert for teenagers will be held.

출제 경향　how this word appears in the test

청소년 관련 문제는 최근에 한국에서 일어나는 여러 문제들에 대한 내용이 많습니다.
Many questions consist of the problem of the teenagers occurred recently in the South Korea.
Also, many topics related to 폭력(violence), 흡연(smoking), and 교사의 체벌 논란(bullying)
appears often in the tests).

16 추억 　　　　　　　　　　　　　　　　　　　　　명 memory

사진을 보니 학교 다닐 때 추억이 떠오른다.

When I look at the picture, it reminds me of the time when I was in school.

17 현재 　　　　　　　　　　　　　　　　　　　　　명 present, now

현재 상영되는 영화 중에 뭐가 제일 인기 있어요?

What is the most popular movie playing now?

18 활동하다 　　　　　　　　　　　　　　　　　　　　　통 be active

고양이는 주로 밤에 활동하는 동물입니다.

The cat is an animal that is mostly active at night.

관련어　활동 act　　　　　　활동량 active mass
　　　　활동내용 contents of acctivities

19 희망하다 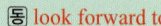 look forward to

이 회사에 입사하기를 희망하고 있습니다.
I am looking forward to getting a job in your company.

 희망 hope   희망자 person who has a hope

20 관람하다   watch

공연을 관람하려는 사람들이 길게 늘어서 있다.
The audiences are standing in line to watch the show.

관람객 audience   관람권 an admission ticket

21 기준 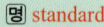 standard

신입 사원을 뽑는 기준을 알려 주세요.
Please tell me the standard that is applied in the recruitment.

22 감상하다 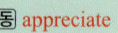 appreciate

이 수업은 한국의 현대시를 이해하고 감상하는 수업입니다.
This class is to understand and appreciate the Korean modern poetry.

 감상 appreciate   감상문 report
감상평 reviewa

23 경쟁  competition

매년 입시 경쟁이 심해지고 있습니다.
The competition of the admission is getting more intensified each year.

경쟁력 competitiveness

24 공기   air

실내의 공기를 바꾸었더니 머리가 아프지 않습니다.
After changing the indoor air, I no longer have headache.

25 담다 　　　　　　　　　　　　　　　　　　　　　　⑧ contain

이 소설은 젊은 세대의 여러 가지 고민을 담고 있습니다.

This novel contains many concerns of the young generation.

26 도시 　　　　　　　　　　　　　　　　　　　　　　⑲ city

도시 생활에 지쳐서 시골로 내려가는 사람들이 증가하는 추세다.

The number of people who move to rural areas after being exhausted by the city life is increasing.

 도심 the central city 　　　　시골 rural area

27 뛰다 　　　　　　　　　　　　　　　　　　　　　　⑧ run

학교에 늦을 것 같은데 우리 뛸까?

I think we will be late for school, want to run?

뛰어가다 run to 　　　　　　　뛰어오다 run back
뛰어내리다 run off 　　　　　　뛰어다니다 run around
뛰어나가다 run out

28 분위기 　　　　　　　　　　　　　　　　　　　　　⑲ atmosphere

이 식당의 분위기가 마음에 들어서 자주 온다.

I often come to this restaurant because of the good atmosphere.

29 빛 　　　　　　　　　　　　　　　　　　　　　　　⑲ light

길을 잃었지만 멀리 보이는 빛을 보고 다시 길을 찾을 수 있었다.

I was lost, but I could find my way after seeing the light from far away.

빛나다 light

30 생명 　　　　　　　　　　　　　　　　　　　　　　⑲ life

그 의사는 환자의 생명을 살리기 위해 노력했다.

The doctor tried hard to save the life of the patient.

 생명력 vitality

31 세탁하다 wash

옷에 김치가 묻었을 때 빨리 세탁하면 없앨 수 있어요.

When you get stains from Kimchi on your clothes, you can get rid of it if you wash them quickly.

32 안정 명 stability

정부는 물가 안정을 위해서 노력하고 있다.

The government is trying to stabilize the prices.

안정성 stability   안정적 stable
안정되다 be stabled   안정시키다 set at ease

33 어울리다 동 go with

이 옷은 이 신발과 전혀 어울리지 않아요.

The clothes do not even slightly match with the shoes.

TOPIK에서 혼동하기 쉬운 단어

다의어 Polysemy

두다

❶ have
- 예) 요즘은 아이를 셋 둔 집이 많이 는 것 같아요.
  It seems that the number of families with 3 kids has increased recently.

❷ give weight to
- 예) 이번 신입사원 면접에서는 인성에 비중을 두었습니다.
  In this recruiting interview, we gave weight to the importance of the personality.

❸ have
- 예) 유명한 연예인들은 모두 보디가드를 두고 있어요.
  All of the famous celebrities have bodyguards.

반의어 Antonym

낯설다 unfamiliar with ~ ↔ 익숙하다 get used to

- 예) 처음에는 낯선 곳에 와서 많이 힘들었습니다.
  At first, I was unfamiliar with the surroundings because I was a new comer.

  한국에서의 생활도 점점 익숙해지고 있습니다.
  I am getting used to living in Korea.

유의어 Synonym

모자라다 be short of ≒ 부족하다 be insufficient

- 예) 음식이 모자라면 곤란하니까 넉넉하게 준비하세요.
  음식이 부족하면 곤란하니까 넉넉하게 준비하세요.
  It would be embarrassing for us to be short of food, therefore prepare plenty of food.

복습해 보세요

 한국어와 영어를 알맞게 연결해 보세요.
Connect the Korean words with the English words of same meaning.

1. 봉사하다 •   • a. excessively
2. 시청 •   • b. volunteer
3. 지나치다 •   • c. appreciate
4. 추억 •   • d. watch
5. 경쟁 •   • e. life
6. 생명 •   • f. memory
7. 감상하다 •   • g. competition

 다음 빈 칸에 알맞은 단어를 〈보기〉에서 골라 쓰세요.
Pick and write the suitable word among <the options> in the blank space.

〈보기〉
a. 활동하는   b. 전통을   c. 지원하려면   d. 안정을

8. 나라마다 (   ) 지키고자 많은 노력을 하고 있다.
   Each country is doing their best to protect their tradition.

9. 그 대학교에 (   ) 뭐가 필요합니까?
   What do I need to apply for that university?

10. 고양이는 밤에 주로 (   ) 동물입니다.
    The cat is an animal that is mostly active at night.

11. 정부는 물가 (   ) 위해서 노력하고 있다.
    The government is trying to stabilize the prices.

정답

1.b 2.d 3.a 4.f 5.g 6.e 7.c 8.b 9.c 10.a 11.d

DAY 09

확인해 보세요

빨간 시트지로 가리고 단어의 뜻을 알면, ☐ 에 ✓ 해 보세요.
After covering up the words with red cover, please check(✓) the box (☐) when you know the meaning of the word.

☐ 01	연장하다	extend	☐ 13	다치다	injured	✓ 25	음식	food
☐ 02	옮기다	move	☐ 14	마침	just (about to)	✓ 26	의미	(the) meaning
☐ 03	유행하다	be in fashion	☐ 15	물질	material	☐ 27	일시적	temporary
☐ 04	일부	part, portion, section	✓ 16	미래	future	☐ 28	일으키다	raise
☐ 05	전시회	exhibition	☐ 17	미술	art	☐ 29	자신감	self-esteem
☐ 06	처리하다	handle	✓ 18	별로	particularly	☐ 30	재산	asset, property
✓ 07	처음	for the first time	☐ 19	분석하다	analyze	☐ 31	정신	mind
✓ 08	선배	senior alumnus	☐ 20	비교하다	compare	☐ 32	얻다	get, gain
✓ 09	고생	(have) a hard time + ~ing	✓ 21	사무실	office	☐ 33	제도	policy
☐ 10	구매하다	purchase	☐ 22	살펴보다	look around			
☐ 11	기업	firm	☐ 23	어른	an adult			
☐ 12	남	other people	☐ 24	예방하다	prevent			

DAY 09

  are the words that appeared in the former tests, and you may get a higher grade if you study them together.

01 연장하다 — 동 extend

비자를 연장하기 위해서는 어떤 서류가 필요합니까?
What kind of documents do I need to extend my visa?

연장 extension   연장되다 be extended
연장 신청 apply for extension

02 옮기다 — 동 move

한국에서 직장을 자주 옮기는 것은 사회성에 문제가 있어 보일 수 있다.
Changing jobs frequently in Korea may be considered as a problem in sociality.

03 유행하다 — 동 be in fashion

요즘은 짧은 머리에 짧은 치마가 유행한대요.
They say wearing short skirts with short hair is in fashion these days.

유행 fashion   유행을 따르다 follow the fashion

04 일부 — 명 part, portion, section

생존자들 가운데 일부는 사고의 충격으로 정신과 치료가 필요하다.
Some people among the survivors got a shock from the accident and should receive psychotherapy.

05 전시회 — 명 exhibition

시간 있으면 주말에 전시회에 같이 갈래?
Do you want to go to an exhibition in the weekend if you have time?

전시장 exhibition hall   전시되다 be exhibited
전시하다 exhibit

06 처리하다　　　　　　　　　　　　　　　　동 handle

밀린 일을 다 처리하느라고 퇴근이 늦었어요.

I left the office late after handling some things.

 처리 handle

07 처음　　　　　　　　　　　　　　　　명 for the first time

처음 듣는 노래인데 왠지 익숙하네요.

I am hearing this song for the first time, but it sounds familiar.

08 선배　　　　　　　　　　　　　　　　명 senior alumnus

퇴근 후에 대학교 선배를 만나서 같이 식사하기로 했다.

I am having dinner with one of my seniors from university after work.

 선배님 senior　　　　　　후배 junior

09 고생　　　　　　　　　　　　　　　　명 (have) a hard time + ~ing

부모님께서는 저희들 때문에 고생을 많이 하셨습니다.

Parents had a hard time raising us.

10 구매하다　　　　　　　　　　　　　　　　동 purchase

사치품을 구매하려는 사람들이 점점 늘어나고 있다.

People who are trying to buy luxurious goods are increasing.

 구매 purchase

11 기업　　　　　　　　　　　　　　　　명 firm

삼성은 한국을 대표하는 기업입니다.

Samsung is one of the firms that represents the Republic of Korea.

 기업인 business man

12 남 명 other people

남들 앞에만 서면 얼굴이 빨개져서 큰일이에요.
Every time I am in front of other people, I can't help myself blushing.

13 다치다 동 injured

다리를 다쳐서 걸을 수가 없어요.
I injured my leg and cannot walk.

14 마침 부 just (about to)

친구에게 전화하려고 했는데 마침 전화가 왔어요.
My friend called me when I was just about to call him.

15 물질 명 material

인스턴트 음식에는 몸에 좋지 않은 물질이 들어 있으니까 먹지 마세요.
Do not eat instant foods since they are filled with bad materials for your health.

16 미래 명 future

아이의 미래를 생각해서 유학을 보내기로 했어요.
I have decided to let my son study abroad since it is good for his future.

관련어 미래가 없다 there is no future

17 미술 명 art

미술을 공부하기 위해서 프랑스로 유학가게 되었습니다.
I decided to go to France to study art.

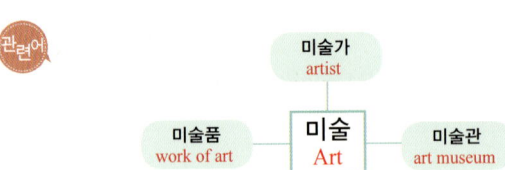

18 별로
particularly (부)

고기는 별로 좋아하지 않는 편이에요.
I do not particularly like meat.

19 분석하다
analyze (동)

그 연구원은 설문 조사를 분석해서 그 결과를 발표했다.
The researcher analyzed the result of the survey and announced it.

분석되다 be analyzed

20 비교하다
compare (동)

좋은 물건을 사려면 여러 물건을 비교한 후에 사야 한다.
You should compare many products before you purchase in order to get a good one.

비교 comparison   비교적 comparatively

21 사무실
office (명)

어려운 문제가 생기면 사무실에 와서 이야기하세요.
If you have something bothering you, please come to the office and tell me.

22 살펴보다
look around (동)

중고 물건을 살 때는 문제가 없는지 잘 살펴보고 사야 한다.
When you are buying the used product, you should look carefully whether the product has any problems.

23 어른
an adult (명)

어린 아이들은 어른들의 행동을 쉽게 따라한다.
Children behave like the adults do.

24 예방하다 — 동 prevent

손을 자주 씻는 것만으로도 많은 질병을 예방할 수 있다.
You can prevent yourself from getting a disease only by washing your hands often.

관련어 예방 prevention

25 음식 — 명 food

한국 음식 중에서 불고기는 외국인들에게 인기가 많아요.
The Bulgogi is one of the most popular food that is loved by foreigners.

관련어 음식점 restaurant   음식물 food
음식물 쓰레기 food garbage

26 의미 — 명 (the) meaning

비싸지 않아도 의미가 있는 선물을 하고 싶어요.
I want to buy a product that has a special meaning even though it is not expensive.

27 일시적 — 명 temporary

일시적인 문제이니 곧 해결될 것입니다.
It is only a temporary matter, and therefore it will soon be solved.

28 일으키다 — 동 raise

그 사람의 무례한 말이 싸움을 일으켰다.
His insulting words raised an argument.

29 자신감 — 명 self-esteem

무슨 일이든 자신감을 갖고 일하는 것이 중요하다.
It is important for you to always have your self-esteem whatever you do.

30 재산   명 asset, property

그 사업가는 자신의 재산을 모두 사회에 환원했다.

The businessman donated his whole property to the society.

 재산피해 property damage

31 정신   명 mind

너무 정신이 없어서 밥 먹는 것조차 잊었네요.

It drove me out of my mind, and I even forgot to eat.

 정신적 psychological   정신차리다 be awakened

32 얻다   통 get, gain

인터넷을 통해 많은 정보를 얻을 수 있다.

You can get much information from using the internet.

Tip '얻다'는 어떤 단어와 같이 사용할까요?
What kind of word can be used together with the word "얻다(get)"?

인기 popularity
기회 chance
결과 result
공감 sympathy
반응 reaction

+ 얻다 get

33 제도   명 policy

어려운 이웃을 위한 다양한 제도가 필요하다.

You need various kinds of policy to help the neighbors who are going through difficulties.

TOPIK에서 혼동하기 쉬운 단어

다의어 Polysemy

뜨다

❶ rise
예) 새해에는 해가 뜨는 것을 같이 보고 싶습니다.
I want to see the sunrise with you on the New Year's Day.

❷ knit
예) 크리스마스 선물로 장갑이랑 목도리를 떴어요.
I knitted gloves and a muffler for the Christmas gifts.

반의어 Antonym

드물다 rare, unusual ↔ 흔하다 common

예) 그렇게 정직한 사람은 드문 편이에요.
It is hard to find a man who is as honest as he is.

제주도에는 돌이 가장 흔합니다.
Rocks are the most common thing in Jeju.

유의어 Synonym

갑자기 suddenly ≒ 문득 all of a sudden

예) 산책을 하다가 갑자기 고등학교 때 친구가 보고 싶어졌다.
산책을 하다가 문득 고등학교 때 친구가 보고 싶어졌다.
While walking around, I suddenly missed my friend from high school.
While walking around, I missed my friend from high school all of a sudden.

복습해 보세요

 한국어는 영어로, 영어는 한국어로 써 보세요.
Write Korean in English, and English in Korean.

1. 유행하다 _____
2. 전시회 _____
3. 기업 _____
4. 분석하다 _____
5. 비교하다 _____

6. handle _____
7. self-esteem _____
8. purchase _____
9. look around _____
10. asset, property _____

 문장이 자연스럽도록 둘 중에서 알맞은 단어를 고르세요.
Choose the proper word that fits the sentence more naturally.

11. 비자를 (a.살펴보기 / b.연장하기) 위해서는 어떤 서류가 필요합니까?
    What kind of documents do I need to extend my visa?

12. 퇴근 후에 대학교 (a.선배를 / b.건물을) 만나서 같이 식사하기로 했다.
    I am having dinner with one of my seniors from university after work.

13. (a.노력을 / b.미술을) 공부하기 위해서 프랑스로 유학가게 되었습니다.
    I decided to go to France to study art.

14. 손을 자주 씻는 것만으로도 많은 질병을 (a.예방할 / b.활동할) 수 있다.
    You can prevent yourself from getting a disease only by washing your hands often.

15. 인스턴트 음식에는 몸에 좋지 않은 (a.물질이 / b.물건이) 들어 있으니까 먹지 마세요.
    Do not eat instant foods since they are filled with bad materials for your health.

정답

1. be in fashion 2. exhibition 3. firm 4. analyze 5. compare 6. 처리하다 7. 자신감 8. 구매하다 9. 둘러보다 10. 재산 11. b 12. a 13. b 14. a 15. a

한국의 행정구역 Regional Districts of Korea

- 서울
- 인천
- 강원도
- 경기도
- 충청남도
- 대전
- 충청북도
- 경상북도
- 대구
- 전라북도
- 울산
- 광주
- 경상남도
- 부산
- 전라남도
- 제주도

DAY 10

확인해 보세요

빨간 시트지로 가리고 단어의 뜻을 알면, ☐ 에 ✓ 해 보세요.
After covering up the words with red cover, please check(✓) the box (☐) when you know the meaning of the word.

- ☐ 01 제출하다   submit
- ☐ 02 지속되다   continue
- ☐ 03 집중하다   concentrate (on)
- ☐ 04 체험하다   experience
- ☐ 05 최선   do one's best
- ☐ 06 평소   usual
- ☐ 07 학습하다   learn
- ☐ 08 고객   customer
- ☐ 09 고려하다   consider
- ☐ 10 고장나다   break
- ☐ 11 교환   exchange
- ☒ 12 그냥   just
- ☐ 13 기술   technology
- ☒ 14 나중에   afterward
- ☐ 15 드러내다   reveal
- ☒ 16 디자인   design
- ☐ 17 마찬가지   as ~ as
- ☐ 18 초대하다   invite
- ☐ 19 목표   goal
- ☐ 20 방해하다   bother
- ☒ 21 보내다   send
- ☐ 22 빌리다   borrow
- ☐ 23 설문조사   survey
- ☐ 24 사건   incident, case
- ☒ 25 실패하다   fail
- ☐ 26 실험   experiment
- ☐ 27 아무리   no matter
- ☒ 28 아이디어   idea
- ☐ 29 안타깝다   feel sorry for
- ☐ 30 알아보다   recognize
- ☐ 31 연결되다   be connected
- ☐ 32 예   example
- ☐ 33 변하다   change

DAY 10

 are the words that appeared in the former tests, and you may get a higher grade if you study them together.

01 제출하다   통 submit

입학 관련 서류를 내일까지 **제출해** 주세요.

Please submit your admission document by tomorrow.

 제출 submission   제출시기 the deadline for the document

02 지속되다   통 continue

당분간 장마가 **지속될** 것 같네요.

The monsoon will continue for a while.

 지속 continue   지속적 continuous

03 집중하다   통 concentrate (on)

짧은 시간이라도 **집중해서** 공부하는 것이 효과적입니다.

It is effective for you to concentrate on your study even though it is for a short period of time.

 집중력 concentration   집중되다 be concentrated in

04 체험하다   통 experience

한국의 전통 시골집을 **체험하신** 기분이 어떠세요?

What does it feel like to experience Korea's traditional cottage?

 체험 experience   체험비 experience fee
체험학습 learning by experience

05 최선　　　　　　　　　　　　　　　　　　　명 do one's best

우리가 할 수 있는 최선을 다하겠습니다.

We will do the best we can.

06 평소　　　　　　　　　　　　　　　　　　　부 usual

오늘은 차가 많아서 평소보다 시간이 더 걸렸어요.

It took more time today since there were much more cars in the street than usual.

07 학습하다　　　　　　　　　　　　　　　　　동 learn

한국의 문화를 학습하고자 박물관에 갔습니다.

We paid a visit to the museum to learn the Korean culture.

관련어　학습 learn　　　　　　　학습능력 learning ability
　　　　학습자 learner

08 고객　　　　　　　　　　　　　　　　　　　명 customer

고객의 입장에서 다시 한번 생각해 주십시오.

Please rethink the issue from the position of the customer.

관련어　고객센터 customer service center

09 고려하다　　　　　　　　　　　　　　　　　동 consider

여러 가지로 고려했어야 했는데 그렇게 못해서 죄송합니다.

I should have considered the issue from various points of view, I apologize for not doing that.

10 고장나다　　　　　　　　　　　　　　　　　동 break

컴퓨터가 고장나서 자료를 모두 날렸어요.

My computer crashed and all of my files were gone.

11 교환　　　　　　　　　　　　　　　　　　명 exchange

교환 학생들을 위한 다양한 프로그램이 필요합니다.
We need various kinds of programs for the exchange students.

 교환하다 exchange　　　환불 refund

12 그냥　　　　　　　　　　　　　　　　　　부 just

주말에 특별한 일이 없어서 **그냥** 집에 있었어요.
I had no special plans for the weekend so I just stayed home.

13 기술　　　　　　　　　　　　　　　　　　명 technology

한국은 IT **기술**이 발달된 나라입니다.
Korea is a country with high Information Technology (IT).

 기술적 technical

14 나중에　　　　　　　　　　　　　　　　　부 afterward

나중에 자세히 말씀드릴게요.
I will tell you the details afterward.

15 드러내다　　　　　　　　　　　　　　　　동 reveal

민호 씨는 자신의 감정을 **드러내는** 경우가 별로 없는 것 같아요.
It seems that Minho rarely reveals his inner feelings.

 드러나다 be revealed

16 디자인　　　　　　　　　　　　　　　　　명 design

전자제품을 살 때 기능만큼이나 **디자인**도 많이 봐요.
When purchasing an electronic product, I consider the product's design as much as the function.

17 마찬가지
명 as ~ as

어머니와 **마찬가지**로 아버지의 역할도 중요합니다.
The father's role is as important as that of the mother's.

18 초대하다
동 invite

결혼식에 **초대할** 사람들은 결정했어요?
Have you decided who to invite to the wedding?

초대 invitation   초대장 invitation

19 목표
명 goal

저는 금메달을 **목표**로 이 올림픽에 참가했습니다.
I have participated in this Olympics with a goal to win the gold medal.

목표를 세우다 set a goal

20 방해하다
동 bother

공부를 하려고 하는데 동생이 **방해했다**.
I was trying to study, but my brother bothered me.

방해 bother   방해가 되다 get in the way

21 보내다
동 send

제가 부탁한 자료를 내일까지 이메일로 **보내** 주세요.
Please send me the files that I have asked for via e-mail by tomorrow.

22 빌리다
동 borrow

도서관에서 **빌린** 책을 오늘까지 갖다 줘야 한다.
I have to return the book that I have borrowed from the library by today.

빌려 주다 lend

23 설문조사 survey

기업 선호도에 대한 설문조사를 실시하였다.

We carried out a survey to get information about the preference that customers have for the firm.

 설문 survey

 how this word appears in the test

쓰기 영역에서는 '설문조사'의 결과를 서술하는 문제가 항상 출제되고 있습니다. 이때 자주 사용되는 문법 항목은 다음과 같습니다.

The question that asks about the result of the "설문조사(survey)" is frequently appearing in the past test. The word usage that is often used in this section are the following.

N을/를 대상으로(targeting N)
N을/를 조사하다(investigate N)
N(으)로 나타나다(appear as N)
N율(독서율, 저축률, 흡연율 등) (N rate (reading rate, savings rate, smoking rate etc.))

24 사건  incident, case

올해는 나에게 여러 가지 사건이 일어나서 정신이 없다.

Many incidents have happened to me this year and it drove me out of my mind.

25 실패하다 fail

이번 시험에서 또 실패했지만 절대로 포기하지 않을 거예요.

I have failed this test again, but I will never give up.

 실패 failure

26 실험 experiment

이번 실험은 위험해서 안전에 대한 준비를 많이 해야 한다.

This experiment is dangerous. Therefore there should be many preparation on safety.

 실험실 experiment lab   실험하다 perform an experiment

27 아무리   튄 no matter

아무리 힘들어도 나는 끝까지 이 일을 할 것이다.

I will finish this work no matter how hard it is.

28 아이디어   명 idea

새로운 상품 광고에 대한 좋은 **아이디어**가 있으면 말씀해 주세요.

If you have any good idea for the new product commercial, please let me know.

29 안타깝다   형 feel sorry for

그 친구는 열심히 노력하지만 항상 실패해서 참 **안타까워요**.

I feel sorry for him always failing even though he tries his best all the time.

30 알아보다   동 recognize

오랜만에 친구를 만났는데 많이 달라져서 처음에는 못 **알아봤다**.

I met my friend a while ago, and I could not recognize him when I met him since he looked so different.

알아내다 find out   알아듣다 understand
알아차리다 realize

31 연결되다   동 be connected

컴퓨터 선이 잘 **연결되어** 있나요?

Is the computer line well connected?

연결 connection   연결하다 connect
연결시키다 get something connected to

32 예   명 example

잘 이해가 안 되니까 **예**를 들어 설명해 주세요.

Please give an example since I do not understand.

33 변하다

동 change

5년 만에 대학교 때 친구를 만났는데 모습이 많이 변했더라고요.
I met my friend from college in 5 years, and his appearance was changed a lot.

 변함없이 as always   변함이 없다 have no change

 '변함없이'와 '그대로'는 어떤 차이가 있을까요?
What is the difference between "변함없이(as always)" and "그대로(as it is)"?

'변함없이'는 긴 시간 동안에 변화가 없을 때 사용하고 '그대로'는 보다 짧은 시간 동안 변화가 없을 때 사용해요.
"변함없이(as always)" is used when there is no change during the long period of time and "그대로(as it is)" is used when the change did not occur only for the short period of time.

 이런 전통은 300년을 변함없이 이어져 내려오고 있다.
This tradition has been passed on for the past 300 years without change.

이제 사진을 찍을 거니까 그대로 있어요.
I will take a picture, so stay as you are.

TOPIK에서 혼동하기 쉬운 단어

DAY 10 ★★★

다의어 Polysemy

맞다

❶ get soaked (in the rain)
  예 1시간 정도 비를 맞고 감기에 걸렸다.
  I caught a cold after getting soaked in the rain for an hour.

❷ fit one
  예 저는 적성에 맞는 직업을 찾고 싶습니다.
  I want to work in the company that fits me.

❸ agree with
  예 저랑 민호 씨는 서로 의견이 잘 안 맞을 때가 많아요.
  There are a lot of times when Minho and I disagree with each other.

반의어 antonym

마중하다 greet ↔ 배웅하다 see someone off

예 해외 여행을 다녀오시는 부모님을 마중하러 공항에 가는 길이에요.
I am now on my way to the airport to greet my parents coming back from the overseas trip.

집에 놀러 왔다가 돌아가는 친구들을 큰 도로까지 배웅해 주었다.
I saw my friends out to the main street after paying a visit to our place.

유의어 Synonym

기르다 raise ≒ 키우다 raise

예 애완동물을 기르는 것이 치매 예방에 좋습니다.
애완동물을 키우는 것이 치매 예방에 좋습니다.
Raising a pet helps you to prevent from getting Alzheimer's disease.

복습해 보세요

 한국어와 영어를 알맞게 연결해 보세요.
Connect the Korean words with the English words of same meaning.

1. 지속되다 •　　　　　　　　• a. customer
2. 체험하다 •　　　　　　　　• b. exchange
3. 고객 •　　　　　　　　• c. bother
4. 교환 •　　　　　　　　• d. continue
5. 방해하다 •　　　　　　　　• e. experiment
6. 실험 •　　　　　　　　• f. experience
7. 연결되다 •　　　　　　　　• g. be connected

 다음 빈 칸에 알맞은 단어를 〈보기〉에서 골라 쓰세요.
Pick and write the suitable word among <the options> in the blank space.

〈보기〉
　a. 실패했지만　b. 아이디어가　c. 집중해서　d. 목표로

8. 짧은 시간이라도 (　　　) 공부하는 것이 효과적입니다.
It is effective for you to concentrate on your study even though it is a short period of time.

9. 이번 시험에서 또 (　　　) 절대로 포기하지 않을 거예요.
I have failed this test again, but I will never give up.

10. 새로운 상품 광고에 대한 좋은 (　　　) 있으면 말씀해 주세요.
If you have any good idea for the new product commercial, please let me know.

11. 저는 금메달을 (　　　) 이 올림픽에 참가했습니다.
I have participated in this Olympics with a goal to win the gold medal.

정답

1.d 2.f 3.a 4.b 5.c 6.e 7.g 8.c 9.a 10.b 11.d

주간 복습 day 6 - day 10

아래 단어를 보고 빈 칸에 뜻을 적어 보세요. 그리고 점선대로 접어서 적은 뜻이 맞는지 확인해 보세요. (만일 틀렸다면 뒷면의 단어 앞 □ 에 ✓ 하세요.)
Write down the meaning of the given word in the blank. Also, fold the page along a dotted line and check whether you got it right or wrong. (If you got it wrong check(✓) the box(□) in front of the word in next page.)

▼접는선

단어	뜻
신경	
내리다	
자연스럽다	
적당하다	
정부	
증가하다	
제공하다	
시설	
조건	
봉사하다	
연장하다	
생명	
활동하다	
안정	
지나치다	
전시회	
비교하다	
구매하다	
물질	
예방하다	
체험하다	
방해하다	
실패하다	
집중하다	
목표	

북촌한옥마을

주간 복습 day 6 – day 10

빈 칸에 한국어 단어를 3번 적고 다시 외워 봅시다.
Write down the Korean word 3 times in the blank and try to memorize it again.

◀ 접는선

뜻	단어		
☐ nerve	신경		
☐ decrease	내리다		
☐ it is natural to	자연스럽다		
☐ proper	적당하다		
☐ administration, government	정부		
☐ increase	증가하다		
☐ provide	제공하다		
☐ facility	시설		
☐ condition	조건		
☐ volunteer	봉사하다		
☐ extend	연장하다		
☐ life	생명		
☐ be active	활동하다		
☐ stability	안정		
☐ excessively	지나치다		
☐ exhibition	전시회		
☐ compare	비교하다		
☐ purchase	구매하다		
☐ material	물질		
☐ prevent	예방하다		
☐ experience	체험하다		
☐ bother	방해하다		
☐ fail	실패하다		
☐ concentrate (on)	집중하다		
☐ goal	목표		

DAY 11

확인해 보세요

빨간 시트지로 가리고 단어의 뜻을 알면, ☐ 에 ✓ 해 보세요.
After covering up the words with red cover, please check(✓) the box (☐) when you know the meaning of the word.

- ☐ 01 운전 drive
- ☐ 02 이미 already
- ☐ 03 조용하다 be quite
- ☐ 04 주로 mainly
- ☐ 05 주차장 parking lot
- ☐ 06 직업 occupation
- ☐ 07 특징 (special) feature
- ☐ 08 평균 average
- ☐ 09 끌다 draw (attention)
- ☐ 10 포기하다 give up
- ☐ 11 현상 phenomenon
- ☐ 12 현실 reality
- ☐ 13 현장 scene
- ☐ 14 홈페이지 homepage
- ☐ 15 환영하다 welcome
- ☐ 16 양 quantity
- ☐ 17 걸리다 catch
- ☐ 18 경기 game
- ☐ 19 기타 other, further
- ☐ 20 긴장 tension
- ☐ 21 깊다 deep
- ☐ 22 낭비하다 waste
- ☐ 23 낮잠 nap
- ☐ 24 농사 farming
- ☐ 25 능력 ability
- ☐ 26 단 only
- ☐ 27 안심하다 calm down
- ☐ 28 대형 big
- ☐ 29 대화 conversation
- ☐ 30 도로 (take it) back
- ☐ 31 떠오르다 come up
- ☐ 32 만족하다 satisfy
- ☐ 33 멀리하다 keep away from

DAY 11

  are the words that appeared in the former tests, and you may get a higher grade if you study them together.

01 운전   명 drive

그 교통 사고는 운전자의 졸음 운전으로 일어났다.

Drowsy driving was a major cause of that car accident.

운전석 driver's seat   운전자 driver
운전 면허 driver's license   음주운전 drunk driving

02 이미   부 already

내가 역에 도착했을 때 기차는 이미 떠나고 없었다.

The train had already left when I arrived at the station.

벌써 already

03 조용하다   형 be quite

방학이 되면 학교가 조용하다.

The school is quite during the vacation.

조용히 quietly

04 주로   부 mainly

평일에는 주로 이 식당에서 밥을 먹어요.

During the weekdays I mainly eat in this restaurant.

보통 usually

05 주차장   명 parking lot

공연장 근처에 주차장이 있지만 가능하면 대중교통을 이용해 주세요.

Even though there are parking lots around the concert hall, please use the public transportation if possible.

주차 parking   주차난 the parking problems
주차비 parking fee   주차하다 park

06 직업　　　　　　　　　　　　　　　명 occupation

사람마다 **직업**을 선택하는 기준이 다르다.

People has different standards in choosing his or her occupation.

07 특징　　　　　　　　　　　　　　명 (special) feature

이 제품의 **특징**은 무엇입니까?

What is the special feature of this product?

08 평균　　　　　　　　　　　　　　　명 average

이번 중간 시험 **평균**이 높지 않습니다.

The average of this mid-term is not high.

09 끌다　　　　　　　　　　　　　　동 draw (attention)

이번 전시회에서는 아이디어 제품들이 눈길을 **끌었다**.

In this exhibition, so called "The idea product" draw the audiences' attention.

> **Tip**
> '끌다'는 어떤 단어와 같이 사용할까요?
> What are the words that are used together with the word "끌다(draw)"?
>
> | 끌다　draw (attention) |
> | --- |
> | 관심을 끌다 (draw attention) |
> | 시선을 끌다 (catch one's sight) |
> | 인기를 끌다 (catch popularity) |
> | 흥미를 끌다 (attract one's interest) |

10 포기하다　　　　　　　　　　　　동 give up

아무리 힘들어도 **포기하**지 마세요.

Do not give up no matter how hard it is.

11 현상 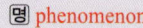 phenomenon

요즘 고령화 **현상**이 큰 문제가 되고 있어요.
The aging phenomenon is becoming a big issue these days.

 how this word appears in the test
시험에 'N 현상' 이 주제가 되는 경우가 많습니다.
There are many cases when "N 현상(N phenomenon)" is the topic of the test question.
예를 들면 온난화 현상, 고령화 현상 등이 있습니다.
For instance, there are the cases of "온난화 현상(global warming)" and "고령화 현상 (aging phenomenon)" etc.
이런 현상의 원인 및 이로 인한 피해 등에 대한 지식이 있다면 문제를 풀기 쉽겠지요?
Therefore, if you have some knowledge about these themes, it would be easier to solve the problem, wouldn't it?

12 현실 reality

드라마와 **현실**은 다릅니다.
Drama is different from the reality.

 현실성 reality 현실적 realistic

13 현장  scene

사고 **현장**에 경찰이 바로 왔어요.
The police came to the crime scene right away.

14 홈페이지  homepage

학교 **홈페이지**에 자세한 정보가 있습니다.
Detailed information is on the school homepage.

15 환영하다  welcome

이 곳에 오신 모든 분들을 **환영**합니다.
We welcome you all who came here.

 환영 welcome 환영식 the welcoming ceremony

16 양   명 quantity

시간이 지날수록 내리는 눈의 양이 점점 많아졌다.

As the time passed the snow fell more and more.

질 quality   질량 mass
수량 quantity

17 걸리다   동 catch

언니가 여름에 독감에 걸려서 고생을 하고 있다.

My sister caught the flu in the summer and she is going through a hard time.

18 경기   명 game

축구 경기 규칙을 알아 둘 걸 그랬어요.

I should have learned the rules for the soccer game.

19 기타   명 other, further

기타 문의사항이 있으신 분들은 아래로 연락해 주시기 바랍니다.

If you have any further questions to ask, feel free to call the number written below.

20 긴장   명 tension

차라도 한 잔 드시면서 긴장을 풀어 보세요.

Drink a cup of tea, and release your tension.

긴장감 tension   긴장하다 be nervous
긴장을 풀다 release the tension   긴장을 줄이다 decrease the tension

21 깊다   형 deep

수심이 깊어서 수영할 수 없습니다.

The water is too deep to swim.

22 낭비하다 waste

시간을 낭비하면 나중에 후회하게 됩니다.
If you waste your time, you will regret it later.

 낭비 waste

 **Tip**
'낭비하다' 는 어떤 단어와 같이 사용할까요?
What word is used together with the word "낭비하다(waste)"?

낭비하다 Waste + 돈 money
시간 time
자원 resource
(전기,물,종이 등
electricity, water,
paper etc.)

23 낮잠 nap

낮잠을 많이 잤더니 밤에 잠이 안 오네요.
I cannot fall asleep because I took a long nap.

 늦잠 oversleep

24 농사 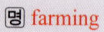 farming

도시 생활을 그만두고 시골로 가서 농사를 짓는 사람들이 늘어나고 있다.
The number of people who quit their city life and go to the rural area farm is increasing.

농촌 rural   농업 agriculture
농사철 farming season   농산물 farm products
농작물 crop   농어촌 farming and fishing village
농수산업 agriculture and fishery

25 능력　　　　　　　　　　　　　　　　　　　명 ability

학력보다 능력을 중요하게 생각하는 분위기가 확산되고 있어요.
The atmosphere of emphasizing one's capability over his or her academic backgrounds are widely spreading.

26 단　　　　　　　　　　　　　　　　　　　　부 only

단 한번 만났을 뿐인데 금방 알아보시네요!
We only met once, but you recognized me right away.

27 안심하다　　　　　　　　　　　　　　　　동 calm down

경찰이 도착했으니까 안심하세요.
The police arrived, so you should calm down.

28 대형　　　　　　　　　　　　　　　　　　　명 big

어제 고속도로에서 대형 교통사고가 나서 많은 사람들이 죽었습니다.
There was a big accident in the highway yesterday and many people died.

관련어
소형 small　　　　　　　　중형 mid-sized
대형 사고 big-sized accident　　대형 마트 large sized market

29 대화　　　　　　　　　　　　　　　　　　명 conversation

마음이 맞는 친구들과의 대화는 언제나 즐겁다.
The conversation with close friends is always fun to have.

관련어
대화하다 converse

30 도로　　　　　　　　　　　　　　　　부 (take it) back

이런 비싼 선물은 받을 수 없으니까 도로 가지고 가세요.
This is too expensive for me to accept it, so please take it back.

DAY 11

31 떠오르다  come up

여행을 하다가 좋은 아이디어가 떠올랐다.

A good idea came up while we were traveling.

 떠올리다 recall

32 만족하다 동 satisfy

이 식당의 서비스에 손님들이 모두 만족해했습니다.

The customers were all satisfied with the service from this restaurant.

 만족감 satisfaction   만족도 level of satisfaction
만족시키다 make one satisfied

33 멀리하다 동 keep away from

나쁜 친구는 멀리하는 것이 좋아요.

You should keep away from the bad friends.

 멀리 far   멀리서 from a distance

TOPIK에서 혼동하기 쉬운 단어

다의어 Polysemy

맞추다

❶ fit
> 나이에 **맞춰서** 옷을 입어야 가장 자연스럽고 아름답다.
> Wearing clothes that fits your age is most natural and beautiful.

❷ correct
> 시험이 끝나고 친구들이랑 정답을 **맞춰** 봤다.
> After the test was over, I checked my answers with my friends.

❸ adjust
> 망원경의 초점을 잘 **맞춰야** 제대로 볼 수 있어요.
> The focus of the telescope should properly be adjusted in order to see the view.

반의어 Antonym

맡기다 take ↔ 찾다 pick up

> 출근하는 길에 세탁소에 옷을 **맡겼다**.
> I took my clothes to the dry cleaners on my way to work.

> 공항에서 짐을 **찾기** 위해 기다리는 중이다.
> I am waiting to pick up my baggage.

유의어 Synonym

반드시 certainly ≒ 틀림없이 surely

> 지금까지 열심히 공부했으니까 **반드시** 대학교에 합격할 거야.
> 지금까지 열심히 공부했으니까 **틀림없이** 대학교에 합격할 거야.
> You will surely get into the university since you have studied hard.

복습해 보세요

 한국어는 영어로, 영어는 한국어로 써 보세요.
Write Korean in English, and English in Korean.

1. 안심하다 _____
2. 평균 _____
3. 현장 _____
4. 포기하다 _____
5. 낮잠 _____

6. parking lot _____
7. tension _____
8. drive _____
9. big _____
10. farming _____

 문장이 자연스럽도록 둘 중에서 알맞은 단어를 고르세요.
Choose the proper word that fits the sentence more naturally.

11. 요즘 고령화 (a.유행이 / b.현상이) 큰 문제가 되고 있어요.
    The aging phenomenon is becoming a big issue these days.

12. 시간을 (a.안전하면 / b.낭비하면) 나중에 후회하게 됩니다.
    If you waste your time, you will regret it later.

13. 이 제품의 (a.특징은 / b.가격은) 무엇입니까?
    What is the special feature of this product?

14. 평일에는 (a.주로 / b.평균) 이 식당에서 밥을 먹어요.
    During the weekdays I mainly eat in this restaurant.

15. 이 식당의 서비스에 손님들이 모두 (a.멀리했습니다 / b.만족해했습니다).
    The customers were all satisfied with the service from this restaurant.

정답
1.calm down 2.average 3.scene 4.give up 5.nap 6.주차장 7.긴장 8.공짜 9.대형 10.농사 11.b 12.b 13.a 14.a 15.b

DAY 12

확인해 보세요

빨간 시트지로 가리고 단어의 뜻을 알면, □에 ✓해 보세요.
After covering up the words with red cover, please check(✓) the box (□) when you know the meaning of the word.

□ 01 목적	goal	□ 13 설득하다	persuade	□ 25 전달하다	give
□ 02 문의	inquire	□ 14 본	this	□ 26 점점	more and more
□ 03 및	and	□ 15 성장하다	grow	□ 27 정기적	regular
□ 04 바라보다	look	□ 16 소중하다	be precious	□ 28 정작	actually
□ 05 발견하다	find out	□ 17 숲	forest	□ 29 정치	politics
□ 06 보고서	report	□ 18 시각	vision	□ 30 즐겁다	enjoy
□ 07 부담	pressure	□ 19 영양	ingredient	□ 31 진정하다	calm down
□ 08 부분	part	□ 20 옛	old	□ 32 집안일	housework
□ 09 분야	area	□ 21 운동	movement, campaign	□ 33 축제	festival
□ 10 상상력	imagination	□ 22 일정하다	steady		
□ 11 서두르다	hurry	□ 23 자원봉사	volunteer		
□ 12 서류	document	□ 24 재료	ingredient		

DAY 12

 are the words that appeared in the former tests, and you may get a higher grade if you study them together.

01 목적 goal

한국어를 공부하는 목적이 뭐예요?
What is your goal to study Korean?

 목적지 destination

02 문의 inquire

드라마 주인공이 입었던 옷에 대한 문의 전화가 많이 왔다.
Phone calls flooded in inquiring about the clothes worn by the main character that starred in the drama.

 문의처 a reference   문의하다 inquire

03 및 and

이 자료에는 각각의 보험에 대한 설명 및 비교 내용이 들어 있습니다.
This data contains the explanation and the comparison of the each insurance.

 how this word appears in the test

이 단어는 모집 공고문이나 안내문 등에 주로 쓰입니다.
This word is mostly used in a notice or an instruction.
단어의 뜻을 정확하게 알아야 정답을 맞출 수 있겠지요?
In order to find the correct answer, wouldn't you need to know the meaning accurately?
'N 및 N'으로 제시되면 두 가지 모두 포함된다는 것을 꼭 기억하세요.
You should always remember that when it is said "N 및 N(N and N)," it means the two are included.

04 바라보다 look

그 사람은 말없이 바다를 바라보고 있었다.
He was looking at the sea in silence.

05 발견하다
동 find out

이번에 병원에서 검사를 받으면서 암을 발견했어요.

I found out that I had cancer from the last test I got from the hospital.

 발견되다 be found

06 보고서
명 report

보고서를 쓰려고 지금 자료를 모으고 있어요.

I am now collecting the data to write a report.

보고 report 　　　　　보고하다 report
논문 thesis 　　　　　리포트 report

07 부담
명 pressure

부모님이 너무 기대하시고 계시니까 정말 부담이 커요.

I feel so much pressure, because my parents have great expectation for me.

 부담감 a great pressure   부담스럽다 feel pressure

08 부분
명 part

소설의 앞 부분은 별로 재미가 없는데 뒤로 가면서 아주 재미있어진다.

The parlier part of the novel is somewhat boring, but it becomes interesting towards the end.

09 분야
명 area

그 사람은 이 분야에서 가장 유명한 전문가다.

He is the most famous expert in this area.

10 상상력
명 imagination

그 사람은 상상력이 풍부해서 재미있는 이야기를 잘 만들어낸다.

He is filled with imagination since he is good at making up interesting stories.

상상 imagine   상상하기 어렵다 it is hard to imagine

11 서두르다   동 hurry

비행기를 놓치지 않으려면 빨리 서두르세요.

You should hurry to not miss your flight.

12 서류   명 document

요즘 대학원 입학에 필요한 서류를 준비하느라 바쁘다.

I am busy preparing the document required for getting admission from graduate school.

 서류 심사 document screening

13 설득하다   동 persuade

반대 의견을 갖고 있던 사람을 설득하는데 성공했다.

I was successful to persuade the person with the opposite opinion.

 설득 persuasion   설득시키다 persuade one to

14 본   관 this

본 제품은 치료를 위한 것이 아니라 영양 보충을 위한 것입니다.

This product is not for the treatment but to supplement the nutrition.

'본 N'의 형태로 쓰이는 것은 또 뭐가 있을까요?
What other words are used in the form of "본 N(this N)"?

본 This + 사업 business
계획 plan
연구 research
발표 presentation

15 성장하다 grow

우리 나라 경제가 빠르게 성장하고 있다.
Our country's economy is growing fast.

 성장 growing   성장률 growth rate

16 소중하다  be precious

나에게는 무엇보다 어머니가 써 주신 편지가 소중하다.
For me, the most precious thing is the letter from my mom.

17 숲 forest

숲 속에서 산책을 하면 마음이 편안해진다.
When I take a walk in the forest, I feel comfortable.

 숲길 forest road

18 시각 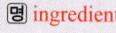 vision

큰 사고로 그 사람은 시각을 잃었다.
That person lost his vision because of a big accident.

Tip 다른 감각에는 또 뭐가 있을까요?
What other senses do human beings have?
미각(sense of taste), 청각(sense of hearing), 촉각(sense of touch), 후각(sense of smell) 등이 있어요.

19 영양 ⑱ ingredient

성장기에 영양을 골고루 섭취하는 것이 중요합니다.
It is important to take a broad variety of nutrients while you're growing up.

 영양소 ingredients

20 옛   🅟 old

남대문의 옛 모습을 복원하기 위해 여러 분야의 전문가들이 노력하고 있다.

Experts are doing their best to restore the original image of Namdaemun.

 옛날 the old days   옛말 old saying

21 운동   🅝 movement, campaign

환경의 날을 맞이하여 환경 보호 운동이 전국에서 일어났다.

To welcome the Environment day the environmental campaign was held across the country.

 캠페인 campaign

22 일정하다   🅥 steady

수입이 일정하지 않아서 살기가 힘들어요.

It is hard to manage living since I don't have a steady income.

23 자원봉사   🅝 volunteer

이번 여름 방학 때에는 자원봉사를 하기로 했다.

I have decided to do volunteer work for this summer vacation.

 자원봉사자 volunteer (worker)

24 재료   🅝 ingredient

이 요리의 재료는 주변에서 쉽게 살 수 없는 것이군요.

The ingredients for this dish are not the ones that you can easily get from the nearest stores.

 재료비 the cost of ingredients

25 전달하다　　　　　　　　　　　　　　　통 give

이 소포를 룸메이트에게 전달해 주세요.

Please give this package to your roommate.

 전달 give　　　　　　전달되다 be given

26 점점　　　　　　　　　　　　　　　　부 more and more

그 사람이 점점 좋아지기 시작했다.

I am starting to like him more and more.

27 정기적　　　　　　　　　　　　　　　명 regular

정기적인 모임을 갖기 위해 노력해 봅시다.

Let us try to have a regular meeting.

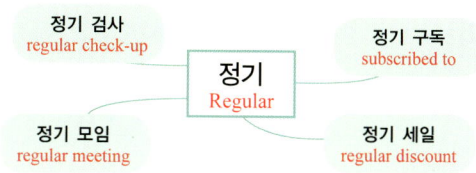

28 정작　　　　　　　　　　　　　　　　부 actually

정작 사과해야 할 사람은 바로 나다.

Actually, I am the one who has to apologize.

29 정치　　　　　　　　　　　　　　　　명 politics

국민들은 정치에 대한 관심을 가져야 합니다.

People should have interest in politics.

 정치가 a politician　　　정치인 statesman
정치학 political science

30 즐겁다 　　　　　　　　　　　　　　　형 enjoy

여가 생활을 즐겁게 보내기 위해 필요한 것은 무엇일까?
What do I need in order to enjoy my free time?

31 진정하다 　　　　　　　　　　　　　동 calm down

그렇게 화만 내지 말고 좀 진정하세요.
Don't get angry, calm down.

32 집안일 　　　　　　　　　　　　　　명 housework

남편이 집안일을 많이 도와주는 편이에요?
Does your husband often help you with the housework?

33 축제 　　　　　　　　　　　　　　　명 festival

한국 대학들은 보통 5월에 축제를 한다.
Usually most of the university in Korea have their festival in May.

TOPIK에서 혼동하기 쉬운 단어

다의어 Polysemy

맡다

❶ get (a seat)

예 시험 기간이라서 도서관 자리 맡기가 쉽지 않다.
It is really hard to get a seat in the library since it is the mid-term season.

❷ smell

예 감기에 걸려서 냄새를 잘 맡을 수가 없어요.
I cannot smell since I have a cold.

❸ care

예 아이를 맡아 줄 시설이 많아지면 좋겠다.
I wish there are many more facilities that provide daycare services.

반의어 Antonym

반대하다 disagree with ↔ 찬성하다 agree with

예 민호 씨 의견에 반대하시는 분 계십니까?
Is there anyone who disagrees with Minho's opinion?

그 의견에 모두 찬성하는 것은 불가능합니다.
It is impossible for all of the members to agree with the opinion.

유의어 Synonym

참을성 endurance ≒ 인내심 patience

예 운동을 통해 아이들에게 참을성을 길러주는 것이 필요합니다.
운동을 통해 아이들에게 인내심을 길러주는 것이 필요합니다.
It is necessary for the adults to teach the children of endurance through sports.

복습해 보세요

 한국어와 영어를 알맞게 연결해 보세요.
Connect the Korean words with the English words of same meaning.

1. 목적 • • a. report
2. 보고서 • • b. goal
3. 분야 • • c. area
4. 서류 • • d. grow
5. 성장하다 • • e. document
6. 영양 • • f. regular
7. 정기적 • • g. ingredient

 다음 빈 칸에 알맞은 단어를 〈보기〉에서 골라 쓰세요.
Pick and write the suitable word among <the options> in the blank space.

〈보기〉
a. 발견했어요   b. 자원봉사를   c. 부담이   d. 설득하는

8. 이번에 병원에서 검사를 받으면서 암을 (   ).
   I found out that I had cancer from the last test I got from the hospital.

9. 부모님이 너무 기대하시고 계시니까 정말 (   ) 커요.
   I feel so much pressure, because my parents have great expectation for me.

10. 반대 의견을 갖고 있던 사람을 (   ) 데 성공했다.
    I was successful to persuade the person with the opposite opinion.

11. 이번 여름 방학 때에는 (   ) 하기로 했다.
    I have decided to do volunteer work for this summer vacation.

정답

1.b 2.a 3.c 4.e 5.d 6.f 7.g 8.a 9.c 10.d 11.b

DAY 13

확인해 보세요

빨간 시트지로 가리고 단어의 뜻을 알면, □ 에 ✓ 해 보세요.
After covering up the words with red cover, please check(✓) the box (□) when you know the meaning of the word.

□ 01	편	piece	□ 13	극복하다	overcome	□ 25	무시하다	look down on
□ 02	포장하다	wrap (up)	□ 14	기름	oil	□ 26	바닷가	the seaside
□ 03	품질	quality	□ 15	먹이	food	□ 27	밤새우다	stay up all night
□ 04	화	angry	□ 16	기본	basic	□ 28	배달	delivery
□ 05	훌륭하다	excellent	□ 17	기사	article	□ 29	벌다	earn
□ 06	이웃	neighbor	□ 18	냄새	smell	□ 30	보관하다	store
□ 07	고등학교	high school	□ 19	다가가다	approach	□ 31	부드럽다	soften
□ 08	가장	head of the household	□ 20	담당하다	be in charge of	□ 32	불러일으키다	cause
□ 09	가져오다	bring (about)	□ 21	도전하다	challenge	□ 33	비율	rate
□ 10	간단하다	simple	□ 22	뛰어나다	fluent			
□ 11	거리	distance	□ 23	면접	interview			
□ 12	구체적	in detail	□ 24	목소리	voice			

DAY 13

 are the words that appeared in the former tests, and you may get a higher grade if you study them together.

01 편   몡 piece

재미있는 영화 한 편 보고 싶은데 시간이 없네요.

I would like to watch an interesting movie but I have no time.

'편'으로 셀 수 있는 것은 뭐가 있을까요?
What can be counted with the word "편(piece)"?
시(poetry), 영화(movie), 소설(novel) 등이 있어요.

02 포장하다   동 wrap (up)

이제 선물을 포장하기만 하면 되니까 조금만 기다리세요.

Can you please wait for a moment, I only need to wrap up the present.

 포장 wrap (up)   포장지 wrapping paper

03 품질   몡 quality

제품의 품질을 높이지 않으면 성공할 수 없어요.

If you don't improve the quality of the product, you won't be able to succeed.

04 화   몡 angry

친구의 심한 장난 때문에 화가 났어요.

I got angry because of my friends' practical jokes.

 화가 나다 get angry   화를 내다 be upset
화를 풀다 blow off steam   화가 풀리다 calm down

05 훌륭하다
[형] excellent

우리 회사에는 **훌륭한** 인재가 많습니다.

There are many excellent employees in our company.

06 이웃
[명] neighbor

아파트에 살다 보니 **이웃**에 누가 사는지조차 모르는 경우가 많아요.

Living in the apartment, we often do not know who our neighbors are.

[관련어]
이웃집 neighbor's house   이웃 사람 a neighbor
이웃 사촌 good neighbor

출제 경향 how this word appears in the test

읽기 영역에서 '불우 이웃 돕기'에 대한 주제로 문제가 출제된 적이 있어요.
There was a question that appeared in the test with the topic of "불우 이웃 돕기(helping unfortunate neighbors)."

다른 사람을 돕는 것에 대한 문제는 꾸준히 나오고 있습니다.
Likewise, the questions that are dealing with helping other people are constantly appearing in the test.

'불우 이웃' 이라는 단어를 기억하세요.
Do not forget to remember the word phrase "불우 이웃(unfortunate neighbors)."

07 고등학교
[명] high school

이 친구는 **고등학교** 다닐 때 만난 친구예요.

This is my good friend from high school.

[관련어]
유치원 kindergarten   초등학교 elementary school
중학교 middle school   대학교 university
대학원 graduate school

08 가장
[명] head of the household

아버지로서 **가장**의 역할을 잘 해야 합니다.

As a father, it is important to partake a good role as the head of the household.

09 가져오다　　　　　　　　　　　　　　　동 bring (about)

핸드폰의 발달은 우리 사회에 큰 변화를 가져왔습니다.
The development of the cell phone has brought a big change in our society.

 가져가다 take away

10 간단하다　　　　　　　　　　　　　　　형 simple

사장님께서 간단한 식사를 준비해 달라고 하셨어요.
My boss asked me for a simple meal.

 간단히 simply

11 거리　　　　　　　　　　　　　　　　　명 distance

저희 회사는 지하철역 2번 출구로 나오시면 5분 거리에 있습니다.
Our company is in 5 minute distance from exit 2 of the subway station.

12 구체적　　　　　　　　　　　　　　　　명 in detail

구체적인 방법을 알려 주십시오.
Please tell me the way in detail.

13 극복하다　　　　　　　　　　　　　　　동 overcome

어려움을 극복하면 반드시 좋은 일이 있을 거예요.
If you overcome your difficulties, good thing will happen.

14 기름　　　　　　　　　　　　　　　　　명 oil

차에 기름 넣을 때가 된 것 같은데요.
I think it is time to fill up the gas tank.

 기름기 greasy

15 먹이　　　　　　　　　　　　　　　　　　　　　　　　　명 food

동물원의 동물한테 아무 먹이나 주면 안 됩니다.
You should not give random food to the animals in the zoo.

 먹잇감 prey　　　　　　　먹을거리 things to eat

Tip 'V-(으)ㄹ거리'의 형태로 쓰이는 것은 또 뭐가 있을까요?
What are the other things that you can express with the form of "V-(으)ㄹ거리(things to V)"?
읽을거리(things to read), 볼거리(things to watch),
놀거리(things to play with), 마실거리(things to drink) 등이 있어요.

16 기본　　　　　　　　　　　　　　　　　　　　　　　　　명 basic

언어를 배우기 위해서는 단어 공부가 기본이 된다고 생각합니다.
I think studying the vocabulary is the basic thing when learning the language.

 기본적 basically　　　　　　기본 요금 basic fee

17 기사　　　　　　　　　　　　　　　　　　　　　　　　　명 article

오늘 아침 신문에 난 기사 보셨어요?
Have you seen the article in the paper this morning?

 기자 a reporter　　　　　　보도 기사 news story

18 냄새　　　　　　　　　　　　　　　　　　　　　　　　　명 smell

이상한 냄새가 나는 것 같아요.
I think there is a strange smell.

19 다가가다　　　　　　　　　　　　　　　　　　　　　　　동 approach

누군가와 친해지고 싶으면 마음을 열고 먼저 다가가세요.
If you want to make friends, then you should open up and approach them first.

 다가오다 come up to

20 담당하다 — 동 be in charge of

저는 은행에서 주로 환전 업무를 담당하고 있어요.
I am mostly in charge of currency exchange in the bank.

 담당자 the person in charge   담당 기관 the agency in charge

21 도전하다 — 동 challenge

그 선수는 이번 대회에서 세계 신기록에 도전합니다.
The athlete is challenging to break the world record in this competition.

 도전 challenge

22 뛰어나다 — 형 fluent

우리 회사는 외국어 실력이 뛰어난 사람을 찾고 있습니다.
Our company is looking for a person who can speak foreign language fluently.

23 면접 — 명 interview

면접을 볼 때 긴장하지 않으려면 어떻게 해야 할까요?
What can I do to not be nervous during the interview?

 면접관 interviewer

24 목소리 — 명 voice

그 사람의 노래하는 목소리는 다른 사람들에게 감동을 준다.
His singing voice deeply moves the listeners.

25 무시하다 — 동 look down on

나이가 어리다고 무시하지 마세요.
Do not look down on me because I am young.

26 바닷가 명 the seaside

바닷가에 가서 수영도 하고 사진도 찍자.
Let's go to the seaside, take pictures and swim.

관련어 바다 sea   바닷물 seawater

Tip 'N가'의 형태로 쓰이는 것은 또 뭐가 있을까요?
What are the other word that has the structure of "N 가(N+side)"?
강가(riverside), 길가(roadside), 물가(waterside), 창가(window) 등이 있어요.

27 밤새우다 동 stay up all night

내일이 휴일이라서 오늘은 밤새워 영화를 볼 생각이에요.
Because tomorrow is a holiday, I am planning to stay up all night and watch movies.

관련어 밤새 all night   밤늦게 late at night
밤새도록 all night long

28 배달 명 delivery

지금 음식 배달이 가능한가요?
Is it possible to get food delivered now?

관련어 배달비 delivery fee   배달되다 be delivered
배달하다 deliver

29 벌다 명 earn

나는 요즘 아르바이트로 돈을 벌고 있다.
I am earning money by working part time these days.

30 보관하다 　　　　　　　　　　　　　　　　　동 store

근처에 짐을 보관할 만한 장소가 있을까요?
Is there any place around here where I can store my luggage.

보관함 storage box

31 부드럽다 　　　　　　　　　　　　　　　　　형 soften

화장품을 바꿨더니 피부가 부드러워졌어요.
After changing my cosmetic products, my the skin softened.

32 불러일으키다 　　　　　　　　　　　　　　　동 cause

그런 수상한 행동은 다른 사람들의 오해를 불러일으킬 수 있으니까 조심하세요.
That kind of strange behavior can cause misunderstanding, so be careful.

33 비율 　　　　　　　　　　　　　　　　　　　명 rate

매년 태어나는 아기들 중에서 남자 아기가 차지하는 비율이 높아지고 있다.
The rate of the male babies that are being born is increasing every year.

> how this word appears in the test
>
> 그래프 정보 읽기 문제에서 'N에 따른 비율'의 형태로 많이 출제가 됩니다.
> This word often appears in the test as a form of "N에 따른 비율(rate according to N)."
>
> 지역에 따른 비율 rate according to the area
> 　　계층에 따른 비율 rate according to the social class
> 　　성별에 따른 비율 rate according to the gender
> 　　연령에 따른 비율 rate according to the age

TOPIK에서 혼동하기 쉬운 단어

다의어 Polysemy

바르다

❶ put on
예) 세수를 하고 얼굴에 화장품을 발랐다.
After washing my face, I put on a makeup.

❷ correct
예) 바른 자세로 앉아서 컴퓨터를 해야 한다.
I should use the computer with the correct posture.

반의어 Antonym

사라지다 disappear ↔ **나타나다** appear

예) 아까 의자 옆에 두었던 가방이 사라졌어요.
The bag I left next to the chair has disappeared.

하늘에 갑자기 큰 별이 나타났다.
Suddenly, a big star appeared in the sky.

유의어 Synonym

참다 bear ≒ **견디다** endure

예) 참기 어려운 통증 때문에 잠에서 깼어요.
견디기 어려운 통증 때문에 잠에서 깼어요.
I woke up because it was too hard to bare the pain.

DAY 13

복습해 보세요

 한국어는 영어로, 영어는 한국어로 써 보세요.
Write Korean in English, and English in Korean.

1. 포장하다 _____
2. 훌륭하다 _____
3. 간단하다 _____
4. 구체적 _____
5. 기본 _____

6. approach _____
7. be in charge of _____
8. challenge _____
9. fluent _____
10. interview _____

 문장이 자연스럽도록 둘 중에서 알맞은 단어를 고르세요.
Choose the proper word that fits the sentence more naturally.

11. 핸드폰의 발달은 우리 사회에 큰 (a.변화를 / b.성화를) 가져왔습니다.
    The development of the cell phone has brought us a big change in our society.

12. 어려움을 (a.극복하면 / b.연기하면) 반드시 좋은 일이 있을 거예요.
    If you overcome your difficulties, good thing will happen.

13. 동물원의 동물한테 아무 (a.거리나 / b.먹이나) 주면 안 됩니다.
    You should not give random food to the animals in the zoo.

14. 나이가 어리다고 (a.무시하지 / b.담당하지) 마세요.
    Do not look down on me because I am young.

15. 매년 태어나는 아기들 중에서 남자 아기가 차지하는 (a.효과가 / b.비율이) 높아지고 있다.
    The rate of the male babies that are being born is increasing every year.

정답

1. wrap (up) 2. excellent 3. simple 4. in detail 5. basic 6. 다가가다 7. 담당하다 8. 도전하다 9. 유창하다 10. 면접 11. a 12. a 13. b 14. a 15. b

DAY 14

확인해 보세요

빨간 시트지로 가리고 단어의 뜻을 알면, □에 ✓해 보세요.
After covering up the words with red cover, please check(✓) the box (□) when you know the meaning of the word.

- □ 01 비판하다 criticize
- □ 02 소설 novel
- □ 03 소재 material
- □ 04 속 inside
- □ 05 승객 passenger
- □ 06 시 poem
- □ 07 시절 time
- □ 08 싸다 pack
- □ 09 쓰레기 waste
- □ 10 아까 a while ago
- □ 11 앞장서다 lead
- □ 12 약하다 weak
- □ 13 에너지 energy
- □ 14 연기하다 act
- □ 15 예상되다 be expected
- □ 16 온도 temperature
- □ 17 원고 manuscript
- □ 18 N위 rank
- □ 19 의심하다 suspect
- □ 20 이어지다 lead
- □ 21 인물 person
- □ 22 인생 life
- □ 23 인식하다 recognize
- □ 24 자유롭다 free
- □ 25 절약하다 save
- □ 26 정책 policy
- □ 27 종류 kinds
- □ 28 종종 often
- □ 29 주장하다 argue
- □ 30 주제 theme
- □ 31 소식 news
- □ 32 중심 main
- □ 33 지나다 pass

DAY 14

 are the words that appeared in the former tests, and you may get a higher grade if you study them together.

01 비판하다　　　　　　　　　　　　　　　　　통 criticize

그 사람은 자주 다른 사람의 생각을 비판하는 경향이 있다.

He has a tendency to criticize other's opinion.

 비판 critique　　　　　　비판적 critical
비판을 받다 be criticized

02 소설　　　　　　　　　　　　　　　　　명 novel

언젠가 기회가 되면 우리 어머니의 삶에 대한 소설을 쓰고 싶다.

When the opportunity comes, I would like to write a novel about my mother's life.

 소설가 novelist

03 소재　　　　　　　　　　　　　　　　　명 material

최근 더 얇고 따뜻한 옷을 만들 수 있는 새로운 소재를 개발했다.

Recently, a new material that can make thinner and warmer clothes was invented.

04 속　　　　　　　　　　　　　　　　　명 inside

그 사람은 겉과 속이 다르다.

He is different inside and out.

05 승객　　　　　　　　　　　　　　　　　명 passenger

지하철이 도착하자 승객들이 내리기 시작했다.

As the subway arrived, passengers started to get off the train.

06 시   명 poem

그 사람은 자연에 대한 시를 많이 쓴 것으로 유명하다.

He is famous with writing many poems on nature.

 시인 poet

07 시절   명 time

이 노래만 들으면 어린 시절 추억이 떠오른다.

When I listen to this song, it reminds me of my childhood.

08 싸다   동 pack

여행을 갈 짐을 싸느라 정신이 없어요.

I am so busy packing for the trip.

09 쓰레기   명 waste

쓰레기를 아무데나 버리지 마세요.

Don't throw wastes just anywhere.

 쓰레기통 waste bin   쓰레기 처리장 waste disposal site

 how this word appears in the test

토픽에 환경 오염에 대한 문제가 자주 출제되는데 그때 쓰레기와 관계 있는 문제가 자주 언급이 됩니다.

TOPIK frequently has questions related to environmental pollution. Often they are related to wastes.

쓰레기와 관계 있는 다양한 주제가 무엇인지 생각해 두면 도움이 되겠지요?

It would be helpful, if you think about diverse issues related to wastes.

 재활용 문제(recycle issues), 음식물 쓰레기 처리 문제(food waste disposals), 바다 쓰레기 문제(sea waste issues), 일회용품 사용 문제(using disposal products)

10 아까 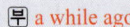 a while ago

아까 어떤 사람이 김 선생님을 찾아 왔었어요.

A person came by to look for Mr. Kim a while ago.

11 앞장서다 lead

그 사람은 다른 사람을 돕는 일이라면 누구보다 앞장서서 열심히 해요.

He leads to help other people.

12 약하다 weak

몸이 약해서 무리하면 안 됩니다.

I can't overwork because I'm weak.

 약화시키다 weaken

13 에너지 energy

요즘 에너지 절약을 위해 불필요한 전기 사용을 줄이려고 노력하고 있다.

Recently, people are trying to lessen the unnecessary use of electricity to save energy.

 에너지원 energy source

 how this word appears in the test

토픽에 출제된 '에너지' 관련 주제는 '에너지 절약' 과 '신에너지 개발' 입니다.
"에너지(Energy)" related topics TOPIK usually deals with are "에너지 절약(saving energy)" and "신에너지 개발(developing new energy)."

이런 지문은 배경 지식이 없으면 이해하기 어려워요.
Some passages are hard to understand without background knowledge.

14 연기하다   동 act

이번 영화에서 연기하면서 가장 힘들었던 장면이 뭐예요?

What was the most challenging scene while you were acting in this movie?

연기 act   연기자 actor/actress

15 예상되다   동 be expected

올해도 청년 실업자가 증가할 것으로 예상된다.

The number of unemployed youths, this year, is expected to rise.

예상 expectation   예상치 expected rate
예상하다 expect

16 온도   명 temperature

여름철 냉방 온도를 1도만 높여도 큰 에너지 절약을 할 수 있다.

Even raising up 1 degree of room temperature in summer will save a large amount of energy.

17 원고   명 manuscript

우리 출판사에 좋은 원고를 주셔서 감사합니다.

Thank you for giving a good manuscript to our company.

원고지 squared manuscript paper
원고료 manuscript fee

18 N위   명 rank

두 사람은 늘 1위를 다투는 라이벌입니다.

Those two are rivals fighting for the number 1 spot in the rank.

19 의심하다   동 suspect

정확한 근거 없이 남을 의심하면 안 된다.

Don't suspect others without accurate grounds.

의심스럽다 suspicious

20 이어지다   lead

작은 충돌 사고가 미끄러운 길 때문에 대형 사고로 이어졌다.

Slippery road has led minor accidents to major ones.

21 인물   person

가장 존경하는 인물은 누구예요?

Who is the person you admire the most?

22 인생   life

직업 선택은 인생에서 가장 중요한 문제 중의 하나입니다.

Choosing an occupation is one of the most important issues in one's life.

23 인식하다  recognize

미래에는 사람의 목소리를 인식할 수 있는 로봇이 실용화될 것이다.

In the future, robots that recognize a human's voice will be commercialized.

 인식 recognition

24 자유롭다   free

현대인들은 누구나 자유로운 생활을 꿈꾼다.

Any modern person dreams about living a free life.

 자유롭게 freely

25 절약하다   save

물을 절약하는 방법으로 뭐가 있죠?

What are the ways to save water?

 절약 save

26 정책 — policy

정부가 서민들을 위한 새로운 정책을 내놓았습니다.

The government has presented a new policy for the people.

27 종류 — kinds

손님, 여기 여러 종류의 핸드폰이 있습니다.

There are many kinds of cellular phones here.

28 종종 — often

돌아가신 할머니가 종종 생각이 난다.

I often think about my grandmother who passed away.

29 주장하다 — argue

자신의 의견만 주장하지 말고 상대방의 의견도 들어야 합니다.

You shouldn't be only arguing your opinions but also listening to what others have to say.

주장 argument

 how this word appears in the test

토픽 듣기에서 누가 주장하는지, 무엇을 주장하는지, 주장하는 태도가 어떠한지를 고르는 문제가 자주 나옵니다. 꼭 알아두세요.

In TOPIK listening part, questions on choosing who is arguing, on what and how one argues are often asked. So don't forget.

30 주제 — theme

이번 글쓰기의 주제는 '나의 인생'입니다.

The topic of this writing assignment is "my life".

31 소식 명 news

고향에 돌아가면 자주 소식을 전해 주세요.

When you go back to your hometown, please send us news frequently.

 소식을 주고받다 exchange news

'소식'과 '소문'은 어떤 차이가 있을까요?
What is the difference between "소식(news)" and "소문(rumor)"?

멀리 있는 사람의 상황을 들으면 '소식'이에요. 반면에 사람들이 많이 이야기하지만 진짜인지 아닌지 모를 때는 '소문'이지요.
"소식(news)" is things you hear about people living a far. Whereas "소문(rumor)" is what many people talk about but they are not sure if it is true or not.

32 중심 명 main

이 글의 중심 생각이 무엇인지 고르십시오.

Choose the main idea of this passage.

33 지나다 동 pass

한국에 온 지 1년이 지나자 향수병이 생겼다.

After living in Korea for about a year I became homesick.

 지나가다 pass   지나오다 pass by

TOPIK에서 혼동하기 쉬운 단어

다의어 Polysemy

번지다

❶ spread around
- 전쟁터에 전염병까지 번지고 있다고 합니다.
  In the battlefield, epidemics are spreading around.

❷ spread around
- 가수 김 모 씨에 대한 소문이 빠른 속도로 인터넷에 번지고 있다.
  The rumors on singer K is spreading around on line very fast.

❸ be smudged
- 잘 그린 그림인데 색깔이 조금 번져서 아쉬워요.
  It is very well-painted picture, but I'm sorry it's a little smudged.

반의어 Antonym

생산하다 produce ↔ 소비하다 consume
- 이 공장에서는 에어컨을 생산하고 있다.
  Air conditioners are produced from this factory.

  현재 우리 회사에서 에너지를 가장 많이 소비하는 부서가 어디입니까?
  Which department in our company is consuming the most energy?

유의어 Synonym

표정 facial expression ≒ 얼굴빛 complexion
- 걱정이 있는지 표정이 어둡다.
  걱정이 있는지 얼굴빛이 어둡다.
  Your bad facial expression says you might have some concerns.

DAY 14

복습해 보세요

 한국어와 영어를 알맞게 연결해 보세요.
Connect the Korean words with the English words of same meaning.

1. 비판하다 •   • a. criticize
2. 소재 •   • b. weak
3. 약하다 •   • c. argue
4. 예상되다 •   • d. kinds
5. 인식하다 •   • e. material
6. 종류 •   • f. be expected
7. 주장하다 •   • g. recognize

 다음 빈 칸에 알맞은 단어를 〈보기〉에서 골라 쓰세요.
Pick and write the suitable word among <the options> in the blank space.

〈보기〉
a. 절약하는   b. 정책을   c. 지나자   d. 의심하면

8. 정확한 근거 없이 남을 (　　) 안 된다.
Don't suspect others without accurate grounds.

9. 물을 (　　) 방법으로 뭐가 있죠?
What are the ways to save water?

10. 정부가 서민들을 위한 새로운 (　　) 내놓았습니다.
The government has presented a new policy for the people.

11. 한국에 온 지 1년이 (　　) 향수병이 생겼다.
After living in Korea for about a year I became homesick.

정답
1.a 2.e 3.b 4.f 5.g 6.d 7.c 8.d 9.a 10.b 11.c

DAY 15

확인해 보세요

빨간 시트지로 가리고 단어의 뜻을 알면, ☐ 에 ✓ 해 보세요.
After covering up the words with red cover, please check(✓) the box (☐) when you know the meaning of the word.

☐ 01 채소	vegetable	☐ 13 공동	commune	☐ 25 당연하다	natural
☐ 02 특성	characteristics	☐ 14 과연	truly	☐ 26 대책	measures
☐ 03 특히	especially	☐ 15 관객	audience	☐ 27 훨씬	way
☐ 04 평가하다	evaluate	☐ 16 규모	size	☐ 28 두렵다	fear
☐ 05 향상시키다	improve	☐ 17 규칙	rule	☐ 29 등장	appear
☐ 06 혹시	perhaps	☐ 18 스스로	by oneself	☐ 30 또한	also
☐ 07 홍보하다	advertise	☐ 19 기부하다	donate	☐ 31 말리다	dry
☐ 08 회원	member	☐ 20 깨다	wake up	☐ 32 맑다	clear
☐ 09 머릿결	hair	☐ 21 나누다	divide	☐ 33 무대	stage
☐ 10 감독	director	☐ 22 뇌	brain		
☐ 11 계단	stairs	☐ 23 눕다	lie		
☐ 12 골고루	balanced	☐ 24 다행이다	fortunate		

DAY 15

 are the words that appeared in the former tests, and you may get a higher grade if you study them together.

01 채소   명 vegetable

싱싱한 **채소**를 세일하고 있습니다.
Fresh vegetables are on sale.

 야채 vegetable   채소류 green grocery
채소 가게 vegetable store

02 특성   명 characteristics

식물을 잘 키우려면 그 식물의 **특성**을 잘 파악해야 합니다.
In order to grow a plant well, you need to know the characteristics of the plant.

03 특히   부 especially

저는 모든 과일을 좋아하지만 **특히** 딸기를 좋아해요.
I like all kinds of fruits but I especially like strawberries.

04 평가하다   동 evaluate

자동차 전문가들이 그 차의 품질을 최고라고 **평가했**다.
Car experts have evaluated the quality of that car as the best.

 평가 evaluation

05 향상시키다   동 improve

한국어 실력을 **향상시키**기 위해 매일 뉴스를 듣고 있습니다.
In order to improve my Korean proficiency, I am listening to the News everyday.

 향상되다 be improved

06 혹시
perhaps

이렇게 늦는 걸 보니 혹시 무슨 일이 생긴 거 아니야?

Being this late, perhaps something happened to him?

07 홍보하다
advertise

새 제품을 홍보하기 위해 무료 쿠폰을 주고 있어요.

We are handing out free coupons to advertise new products.

홍보 advertisement   홍보 행사 advertising event
홍보 모델 advertising model

08 회원
member

인터넷 홈페이지에 회원으로 등록해 주세요.

Please register me as a member in your internet site.

회원모집 recruit members

how this word appears in the test

다양한 분야에서 회원을 모집하는 공고문이 자주 출제되고 있습니다. 회원이 될 수 있는 자격 및 주의 사항 등을 꼼꼼하게 확인해야 합니다.

Often advertisements on recruitments in diverse fields appear on the test. You need to check carefully on requirements and rules of memberships.

09 머릿결
hair

이 샴푸로 머리를 감으면 머릿결이 좋아진대요.

If you wash your hair with this shampoo, your hair will be better.

머리카락 hair

10 감독　　　　　　　　　　　　　　　명 director

감독에 따라 영화 분위기가 달라집니다.

The mood in the films changes depending on directors.

 감독님 director　　　감독하다 direct

 '감독'은 어떤 단어와 같이 사용할까요?
What words can you use "감독(director)" with?

축구 감독(Soccer coach), 시험 감독(Exam Proctor),
영화 감독(Film Director)

11 계단　　　　　　　　　　　　　　　명 stairs

계단에서 뛰지 마십시오.

Don't run in the stairs.

12 골고루　　　　　　　　　　　　　　부 balanced

음식을 골고루 먹었으면 좋겠다.

It would be nice to eat balanced food.

13 공동　　　　　　　　　　　　　　　명 commune

이 하숙집은 부엌을 공동으로 사용해야 합니다.

We need to use the kitchen communally in this foster home.

 공동체 community　　　공동주택 communal house

14 과연　　　　　　　　　　　　　　　부 truly

선의의 거짓말이라고는 하지만 거짓말을 한 것이 과연 잘한 일 일까요?

They call it white lies, but is it truly right to lie?

15 관객

명 audience

영화 개봉 후 관객의 반응이 뜨겁습니다.

After the film was released, the response from the audience was wild.

16 규모

명 size

그 동호회의 규모가 점점 커지고 있어요.

The size the of club is getting bigger.

17 규칙

명 rule

정해진 규칙을 지켜야 합니다.

We need to follow the rules.

규칙적 regular   규칙을 어기다 break the rules
규칙을 지키다 follow the rules

18 스스로

부 by oneself

자기 일은 자기가 스스로 해야 해요.

You need to do your work by yourself.

'스스로'와 '저절로'는 어떤 차이가 있을까요?

What is different between "스스로(by oneself)" and "저절로(by itself)"

'스스로'는 다른 사람의 도움없이 자기 힘으로 한다는 뜻이에요.
그래서 사람에게 쓸 수 있어요.

"스스로(by oneself)" means to have things done without others' help. So you can use it to a person.

 엄마가 깨우지 않아도 스스로 일어날 수 있어요.

I can get up by myself without mom waking me up.

반면에 '저절로'는 외부의 다른 힘이 없이 자동으로 어떤 일이
일어난다는 뜻이에요. 그래서 사람이 아닌 경우에 쓸 수 있어요.

Whereas, "저절로(by itself)" means to have things happen automatically without external force. So it can be used with things other than a person.

 아무도 열지 않았는데 문이 저절로 열렸어요.

The door opened by itself.

19 기부하다　　　　　　　　　　　　　　동 donate

신문에서 전 재산을 기부한 할머니의 기사를 봤어요.

I read an article in the newspaper about an old lady that donated everything she had.

기부 donation　　　　　　　기부금 donation
기부자 donator

20 깨다　　　　　　　　　　　　　　동 wake up

밖이 시끄러워서 잠이 깼어요.

I woke up because it was too noisy outside.

21 나누다　　　　　　　　　　　　　　동 divide

5명이 똑같이 식사비를 나눠서 냈어요.

5 of us divided equally the amount.

나뉘다 be divided　　　　　말씀을 나누다 talk about

22 뇌　　　　　　　　　　　　　　명 brain

인간의 뇌에 대해서 연구를 하고 있습니다.

I am researching on human brain.

23 눕다　　　　　　　　　　　　　　동 lie

침대에 누워서 창 밖을 보니 고향 생각이 난다.

Lying on the bed and looking over the window, it reminded me of my hometown.

24 다행이다　　　　　　　　　　　　　　형 fortunate

선물이 마음에 들어서 다행이에요.

It is fortunate that you like the gift.

다행히 fortunately

25 당연하다 　　　　　　　　　　　　　　　　형 natural

외국 생활이 힘든 것은 당연하다.

It is natural to feel challenged by living in a foreign country.

 당연히 naturally

26 대책 　　　　　　　　　　　　　　　　　　명 measures

실업 문제를 해결하기 위해서 여러 가지 대책을 마련하고 있습니다.

Many different measures are being processed in order to solve the unemployment problem.

27 훨씬 　　　　　　　　　　　　　　　　　　부 way

시장보다 마트가 훨씬 더 비싸서 저는 주로 시장에서 장을 봐요.

Since big markets are way more expensive than traditional markets, I usually go to the traditional markets to shop.

 '훨씬'은 비교하는 문장에서 '더/덜'과 같이 주로 쓰입니다.
"훨씬(way)" is usually used with comparative forms like "더(more)/덜(less)" in the sentene.

28 두렵다 　　　　　　　　　　　　　　　　　형 fear

군인들은 죽음을 두려워하지 않고 싸웠다.

Soldiers fought without the fear of death.

29 등장 　　　　　　　　　　　　　　　　　　명 appear

인터넷의 등장으로 사람들의 생활에 많은 변화가 있었습니다.

There has been many changes in people's lives after the appearance of the internet.

 등장하다 appear

30 또한　　　　　　　　　　　　　　　　　　　　　부 also

전기뿐만 아니라 물 또한 아껴서 사용해야 합니다.

We need to save not only electricity but also water.

31 말리다　　　　　　　　　　　　　　　　　　　동 dry

장마철에는 옷을 말리기가 힘들어요.

It is hard to dry clothes during a rainy season.

32 맑다　　　　　　　　　　　　　　　　　　　　형 clear

호수가 정말 맑고 투명하네요.

The lake is really clear and clean.

33 무대　　　　　　　　　　　　　　　　　　　　명 stage

지금 무대에서 노래 부르고 있는 사람이 누구예요?

Who is the person singing on the stage now?

관련어 무대에 서다 be on the stage

TOPIK에서 혼동하기 쉬운 단어

다의어 Polysemy

뽑다

❶ pull out

예 은행에서 볼 일을 보려면 먼저 번호표를 **뽑아야** 한다.
When you go to the bank, you have to pull out the numbering ticket.

❷ get (coffee or beverage)

예 너무 졸려서 커피를 한 잔 **뽑아** 마셔야겠다.
I need to get some coffee from the vending machine.

❸ hire (person)

예 우리 회사는 능력 있는 직원을 **뽑기** 위한 여러 가지 방법을 생각 중입니다.
Our company is thinking about many different ways to hire competent people.

반의어 Antonym

늘리다 expand ↔ 줄이다 reduce

예 내년에는 회사의 인원을 **늘릴** 계획입니다.
We are planning to expand next year.

이번 달부터 생활비를 **줄일** 수밖에 없습니다.
We have no choice but to reduce the cost of living.

유의어 Synonym

마음껏 as much as one likes ≒ 실컷 as much as one likes

예 다이어트 중이라서 **마음껏** 먹을 수가 없어요.
다이어트 중이라서 **실컷** 먹을 수가 없어요.
I cannot eat as much as I like since I am on a diet.

복습해 보세요

 한국어는 영어로, 영어는 한국어로 써 보세요.
Write Korean in English, and English in Korean.

1. 특성 _____
2. 평가하다 _____
3. 홍보하다 _____
4. 골고루 _____
5. 규칙 _____

6. divide _____
7. measures _____
8. way _____
9. dry _____
10. stage _____

 문장이 자연스럽도록 둘 중에서 알맞은 단어를 고르세요.
Choose the proper word that fits the sentence more naturally.

11. 한국어 실력을 (a.부딪치기 / b.향상시키기) 위해 매일 뉴스를 듣고 있습니다.
    In order to improve my Korean proficiency, I am listening to the News everyday.

12. 이렇게 늦는 걸 보니 (a.혹시 / b.반드시) 무슨 일이 생긴 거 아니야?
    Being this late, perhaps something happened to him?

13. 신문에서 전 재산을 (a.실천한 / b.기부한) 할머니의 기사를 봤어요.
    I read an article in the newspaper about an old lady that donated everything she had.

14. 마음에 들어서 (a.다행이에요 / b.당연해요).
    It is fortunate that you like the gift.

15. 군인들은 죽음을 (a.두려워하지 / b.무시하지) 않고 싸웠다.
    Soldiers fought without the fear of death.

정답

1. characteristics 2. evaluate 3. advertise 4. balanced 5. rule 6. 나누다 7. 대책 8. 방식 9. 말리다 10. 무대 11. b 12. a 13. b 14. a 15. a

주간 복습 day 11 - day 15

아래 단어를 보고 빈 칸에 뜻을 적어 보세요. 그리고 점선대로 접어서 적은 뜻이 맞는지 확인해 보세요. (만일 틀렸다면 뒷면의 단어 앞 □ 에 ✓ 하세요.)

Write down the meaning of the given word in the blank. Also, fold the page along a dotted line and check whether you got it right or wrong. (If you got it wrong check(✓) the box(□) in front of the word in next page.)

▼ 접는선

단어	뜻
평균	
현장	
현상	
낭비하다	
만족하다	
목적	
분야	
성장하다	
설득하다	
자원봉사	
포장하다	
구체적	
다가가다	
뛰어나다	
면접	
비판하다	
약하다	
예상되다	
종류	
주장하다	
평가하다	
골고루	
나누다	
대책	
무대	

청계천

주간 복습 day 11 – day 15

빈 칸에 한국어 단어를 3번 적고 다시 외워 봅시다.
Write down the Korean word 3 times in the blank and try to memorize it again.

뜻	단어		
☐ average	평균		
☐ scene	현장		
☐ phenomenon	현상		
☐ waste	낭비하다		
☐ satisfy	만족하다		
☐ goal	목적		
☐ area	분야		
☐ grow	성장하다		
☐ persuade	설득하다		
☐ volunteer	자원봉사		
☐ wrap (up)	포장하다		
☐ in detail	구체적		
☐ approach	다가가다		
☐ fluent	뛰어나다		
☐ interview	면접		
☐ criticize	비판하다		
☐ weak	약하다		
☐ be expected	예상되다		
☐ kinds	종류		
☐ argue	주장하다		
☐ evaluate	평가하다		
☐ balanced	골고루		
☐ divide	나누다		
☐ measures	대책		
☐ stage	무대		

DAY 16

확인해 보세요

빨간 시트지로 가리고 단어의 뜻을 알면, ☐ 에 ✓ 해 보세요.
After covering up the words with red cover, please check(✓) the box (☐) when you know the meaning of the word.

☐ 01 묻다 — ask
☐ 02 반영하다 — reflect
☐ 03 밝다 — bright
☐ 04 발달 — development
☐ 05 발전 — progress
☐ 06 병 — disease
☐ 07 보호 — protection
☐ 08 부딪치다 — hit
☐ 09 비상구 — emergency exit
☐ 10 사귀다 — get along
☐ 11 사례 — case
☐ 12 상관없이 — regardless of
☐ 13 선호하다 — prefer
☐ 14 소득 — income
☐ 15 손님 — guest
☐ 16 수면 — sleep
☐ 17 순간 — at the moment
☐ 18 시끄럽다 — noise
☐ 19 실력 — ability
☐ 20 직급 — position
☐ 21 실천하다 — practice
☐ 22 심리 — psychology
☐ 23 약속 — promise
☐ 24 업체 — enterprise
☐ 25 여기다 — consider
☐ 26 영업 — business
☐ 27 오염되다 — be polluted
☐ 28 요구되다 — be required
☐ 29 원래 — originally
☐ 30 위하다 — care for
☐ 31 음악 — music
☐ 32 응답자 — respondent
☐ 33 작성하다 — write

DAY 16

 are the words that appeared in the former tests, and you may get a higher grade if you study them together.

01 묻다 동 ask

수업 내용이 잘 이해가 안 되면 선생님께 물어 보세요.

If you do not understand what you learn from the class, ask your teacher.

02 반영하다 동 reflect

이번에 직원들의 의견을 반영해서 회사에 쉴 수 있는 공간을 마련했습니다.

The company has reflected the opinion of the employees and provided the place where they can rest in the building.

 반영되다 be reflected

03 밝다 형 bright

오랜만에 만난 부모님은 얼굴이 밝아 보이셨다.

I met my parents in a while and they looked bright and happy.

 밝기 brightness

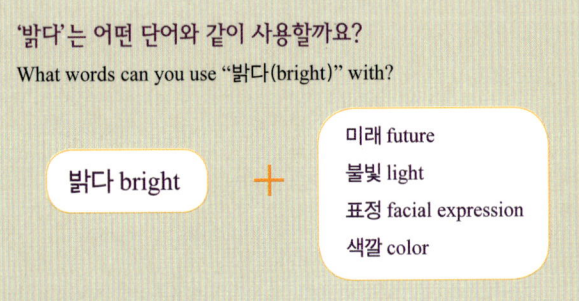

'밝다'는 어떤 단어와 같이 사용할까요?
What words can you use "밝다(bright)" with?

밝다 bright + 미래 future / 불빛 light / 표정 facial expression / 색깔 color

04 발달　　　　　　　　　　　　　　　　　　　　명 development

의학의 발달로 사람들의 평균 수명이 길어졌다.
Due to of the development of the medical technology, the average of life expectancy has lengthened.

발달 development　　　　　　발달되다 be developed
발달하다 develop

05 발전　　　　　　　　　　　　　　　　　　　　명 progress

유은이의 피아노 실력은 작년에 비해 큰 발전을 보이고 있습니다.
Yu Eun's ability to play piano has shown a great progress compared to last year.

발전하다 progress　　　　　　발전시키다 develop (one's ability)

06 병　　　　　　　　　　　　　　　　　　　　　명 disease

병에 걸리면 마음도 약해지는 것 같아요.
It seems that your mind also gets weaker when you get sick.

07 보호　　　　　　　　　　　　　　　　　　　　명 protection

아이는 부모의 보호를 받으며 자란다.
The child grows up under his parents protection.

보호시설 institution　　　　　　보호하다 protect

08 부딪치다　　　　　　　　　　　　　　　　　　동 hit

달려오는 자전거에 부딪칠 뻔했다.
I was almost hit by a bike running toward me.

09 비상구　　　　　　　　　　　　　　　　　　　명 emergency exit

불이 나면 비상구로 빨리 나가야 한다.
When a fire breaks out, you should quickly get yourself out to the emergency exit.

비상금 nest egg　　　　　　비상약 first- aid medicine

10 사귀다 — 동 get along

유학 생활을 하면서 많은 친구를 사귀게 되었다.
While studying abroad, I got along with many friends there.

11 사례 — 명 case

교수님이 여러 가지 사례를 보여 주면서 설명하시니까 이해하기가 쉬웠다.
It was easy for us to understand the lecture since the professor explained with many different cases.

12 상관없이 — 부 regardless of

나이나 국적에 상관없이 누구나 이 일을 할 수 있다.
Regardless of the age or the nationality, anyone can do this work.

상관이 없다 have nothing to do with

13 선호하다 — 동 prefer

요즘 젊은 사람들은 월급보다 복지가 좋은 회사를 선호한다.
The young people these days prefer the company with a better welfare, to the company with a higher salary.

선호도 preference

14 소득 — 명 income

사람들의 소득 수준이 올라가면서 문화비 지출이 늘었다.
As the level of people's income increased people spends more on cultural products.

소득별 for every income

15 손님 — 명 guest

오늘 우리집에 손님이 오셔서 청소를 해야 한다.
Today, we have a guest coming over, therefore we should clean our house.

손 guest

16 수면

명 sleep

아이들이 잘 자라기 위해서는 충분한 수면 시간을 갖는 것이 중요하다.

It is important for the children to get enough hours of sleep in order to grow.

 수면을 취하다 to go to sleep

17 순간

명 at the moment

길이 위험하다고 생각하는 순간 사고가 나 버렸다.

The moment I thought it was dangerous, the accident happened.

 순간적 momentary

18 시끄럽다

형 noise

밖에서 사람들이 싸워서 너무 시끄럽다.

It was so noisy since people were fighting outside.

19 실력

명 ability

모두 그 사람의 실력이 최고라고 인정한다.

Everyone admits that he has the best ability.

20 직급

명 position

직급이 높을수록 책임도 많아져요.

As one's position gets higher, so does one's responsibility.

회사의 직급에는 어떤 것이 있을까요?
What kind of position exists in a company?

인턴 사원(intern), 신입사원(new employee), 대리(deputy section chief), 과장(section chief), 부장(head of department), 사장(CEO) 등이 있어요.

21 실천하다 통 practice

계획을 세웠으면 **실천**하세요.

You should practice your plan.

 실천 practice 실천력 power of execution

22 심리 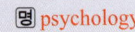 명 psychology

어른들이 아이들의 **심리**를 이해하는 것은 쉬운 일이 아니다.

It is hard for the adults to understand the psychology of the children.

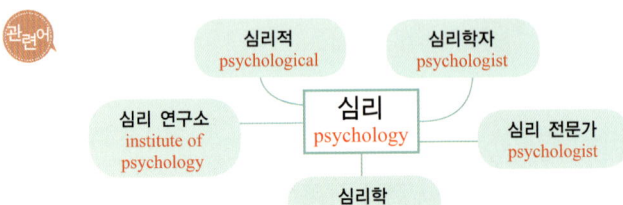

23 약속  명 promise

그 사람은 **약속**을 틀림없이 지키는 사람이다.

He is the person that always keeps his promise.

 약속하다 promise

24 업체 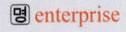 명 enterprise

경쟁 **업체**끼리 너무 심하게 경쟁하면 결국 서로에게 피해만 주게 된다.

When the enterprises are overly competitive they end up harming one another.

25 여기다 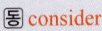 통 consider

나는 내 강아지를 자식처럼 **여기고** 있다.

I consider my dog my child.

26 영업    business

영업 시간이 어떻게 되나요?

What are the business hour?

 영업직 sales job   영업시간 business hour
영업하다 do business

27 오염되다   동 be polluted

오염된 물로 물고기들이 떼죽음을 당했다.

The fishes suffered death en masse because of the polluted water.

 오염 pollution   오염물질 pollutant
오염시키다 contaminate

환경 오염의 종류는 무엇이 있을까요?
What kinds of pollution are there?
'대기오염(air pollution), 수질 오염(water pollution), 토질 오염(land pollution)' 등이 있어요.

28 요구되다   동 be required

지원자에게 요구되는 자격이 어떻게 되지요?

What are the requirements for the applicants?

 요구 demand   요구사항 requirement
요구하다 require

29 원래   부 originally

여기에 원래 병원이 있었어요.

Originally a hospital was located here.

30 위하다 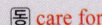 care for

그 사람은 어떤 상황이든 자신보다 남을 위하는 편이다.

That person cares for others more than himself whatever situation he is in.

31 음악 music

저는 한국 전통 음악에 대해 연구하고 있습니다.

I am studying traditional Korean music.

 음악가 musician   음악회 concert

32 응답자 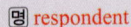 respondent

이번 설문의 응답자 가운데 반 이상이 반대하고 있다.

More than half of the respondents are opposing.

 응답 answer   응답하다 answer

 how this word appears in the test

다양한 분야에서 회원을 모집하는 공고문이 자주 출제되고 있습니다.
회원이 될 수 있는 자격 및 주의 사항 등을 꼼꼼하게 확인해야 합니다.

The questions that contain the statement notification recruiting the members in the various areas are frequently appearing in the actual tests. While taking the test, you should check the qualification, and notice carefully.

설문조사에 자주 나오는 단어들을 정리해서 기억하세요.
이런 단어들은 반복해서 나온답니다.

Be sure to remember the words that often appear in the survey. Words as following appear repeatedly.

응답자(respondent), 응답률(the response rate), 조사 대상(surveying target), 조사 기관(research facility), 조사 결과(the result of the survey)

33 작성하다 write

오늘 5시까지 이력서를 작성해서 보내 주십시오.

Please write your resume and send it by 5 o'clock today.

TOPIK에서 혼동하기 쉬운 단어

다의어 Polysemy

세우다

❶ park (a car)

예 우리 집 앞에 누가 차를 **세워** 놓았어요.
Someone parked his car in front of our house.

❷ set (a plan)

예 휴가 계획을 잘 **세워서** 신나게 놀 거예요.
I will set a great plan for the vacation and have a great time.

❸ build (a building)

예 백화점 옆에 아파트 건물을 **세우는** 중이다.
They are building an apartment building next to the department store.

반의어 Antonym

앞당기다 move up ↔ 늦추다 postpone

예 할아버지 상태가 안 좋아져서 수술 날짜를 **앞당기기로** 했다.
We have decided to move my grandfather's operation date up since his condition is worse.

날씨가 안 좋으면 여행 날짜를 **늦추도록** 해요.
Let's postpone the date of the trip if the weather gets bad.

유의어 Synonym

섭섭하다 be sorry to ≒ 서운하다 be hurt

예 나는 친구에게 **섭섭한** 일이 생기면 바로 이야기를 하는 편이에요.
나는 친구에게 **서운한** 일이 생기면 바로 이야기를 하는 편이에요.
I often tell my friend right away when I am hurt by their words.

DAY 16 ★★

복습해 보세요

 한국어와 영어를 알맞게 연결해 보세요.
Connect the Korean words with the English words of same meaning.

1. 부딪치다 ・　　　　　　・ a. position
2. 선호하다 ・　　　　　　・ b. hit
3. 직급 ・　　　　　　・ c. respondent
4. 오염되다 ・　　　　　　・ d. be required
5. 요구되다 ・　　　　　　・ e. care for
6. 위하다 ・　　　　　　・ f. prefer
7. 응답자 ・　　　　　　・ g. be polluted

 다음 빈 칸에 알맞은 단어를 〈보기〉에서 골라 쓰세요.
Pick and write the suitable word among <the options> in the blank space.

〈보기〉
a. 원래　b. 상관없이　c. 실천하세요　d. 순간

8. 나이나 국적에 (　　) 누구나 이 일을 할 수 있다.
Regardless of the age or the nationality, anyone can do this work.

9. 길이 위험하다고 생각하는 (　　) 사고가 나 버렸다.
The moment I thought it was dangerous, the accident happened.

10. 계획을 세웠으면 (　　).
You should practice your plan.

11. 여기에 (　　) 병원이 있었어요.
Originally a hospital was located here.

정답
1.b 2.f 3.a 4.g 5.d 6.e 7.c 8.b 9.d 10.c 11.a

DAY 17

확인해 보세요

빨간 시트지로 가리고 단어의 뜻을 알면, ☐ 에 ✓ 해 보세요.
After covering up the words with red cover, please check(✓) the box (☐) when you know the meaning of the word.

☐ 01	접수하다	sign up	☐ 13	함부로	indiscreetly	☐ 25	공포감	fear
☐ 02	정서 발달	emotional development	☐ 14	화재	fire	☐ 26	관련되다	be related to
☐ 03	정성	one's heart	☐ 15	화제	issue	☐ 27	그립다	miss
☐ 04	정하다	settle	☐ 16	활발하다	active	☐ 28	그만	stop
☐ 05	제한하다	limit	☐ 17	후회하다	regret	☐ 29	근거	reason
☐ 06	짐	baggage	☐ 18	흔히	usually	☐ 30	기념	commemoration
☐ 07	창업하다	establish a business	☐ 19	부정적	negative	☐ 31	금방	soon
☐ 08	창의력	creativity	☐ 20	연습하다	practice	☐ 32	기뻐하다	be happy
☐ 09	출퇴근하다	commute	☐ 21	상	award	☐ 33	날개	wings
☐ 10	토론하다	discuss	☐ 22	가만히	stay still			
☐ 11	파악하다	figure out	☐ 23	개성	individuality			
☐ 12	평범하다	normal	☐ 24	개최하다	host			

DAY 17

  are the words that appeared in the former tests, and you may get a higher grade if you study them together.

01 접수하다  동 sign up

이 강좌에 접수하려면 무엇이 필요합니까?

I want to sign up for this class, what do I need?

 접수 sign up   접수기간 application period

02 정서 발달  명 emotional development

음악은 아이의 정서 발달에 큰 도움이 된다.

Music greatly helps children with their emotional development.

 정서 emotion   정서적으로 emotionally

03 정성  명 one's heart

그 사람으로부터 정성이 가득 담긴 선물을 받았다.

I received a heartfelt gift from him.

 정성껏 with one's utmost sincerity
정성을다하다 sedulous

04 정하다 동 settle

이번 회의 일정을 다음과 같이 정했습니다.

We have settled the schedule for the meeting as such.

 정해지다 be settled   정해놓다 settle

05 제한하다　　　　　　　　　　　　　　　동 limit

행사장에 음식물 반입을 제한합니다.
Bringing food into the event hall is limited.

제한 limitation　　　　제한시간 limited time

06 짐　　　　　　　　　　　　　　　　명 baggage

무거운 짐을 들고 계단을 오르는 할머니를 도와드렸어요.
I helped an old lady carry heavy baggage up the stairs.

07 창업하다　　　　　　　　　　　동 establish a business

요즘 대학생들은 졸업하기 전에 회사를 창업하기도 한다.
University students these days establish their own business before they graduate.

창업 establish a business
창업지원센터 center that supports to start a business

08 창의력　　　　　　　　　　　　　　명 creativity

창의력이 뛰어난 사람이 예술가가 될 수 있다.
People with great creativity can be an artist.

창의성 creativity　　　　창의적 creative

09 출퇴근하다　　　　　　　　　　　　동 commute

출퇴근하는 데에 보통 얼마정도 걸리세요?
How long does it take for you to commute?

출근 Go to work	퇴근 Leave from office
출근길 on the way to office	퇴근길 on one's way home
출근 시간 the office-open hours	퇴근시간 the closing hours
출퇴근 Commute	

10 토론하다 　　　　　　　　　　　　　　　　　　　　　　　　　동 discuss

두 사람은 책을 읽고 내용에 대해 토론하고 있었다.
Two people are discussing the details of the book after reading it.

 토론 discussion　　　　　　토론회 debate
토론문화 discussing culture

 how this word appears in the test

토픽 듣기 지문에 토론하는 상황이 자주 출제됩니다.
주장의 내용, 주장하는 태도, 주장의 근거가 되는 내용을 찾는 것이 중요합니다.
In the listening section of the test, the situation where people are having a discussion often appears on the test. It is important to figure out what the speaker is insisting, what kind of attitude the speaker is taking, and what kind of proof the speaker is suggesting to support his claim.

11 파악하다 　　　　　　　　　　　　　　　　　　　　　　　　　동 figure out

그 사고의 원인을 파악하기 위해 노력하고 있다.
We are trying hard to figure out the cause of the accident.

 파악 figuration　　　　　　파악되다 be figured out

12 평범하다 　　　　　　　　　　　　　　　　　　　　　　　　　형 normal

외모는 평범하지만 그가 가진 실력은 놀랍습니다.
His appearance is normal, but his ability is spectacular.

13 함부로 　　　　　　　　　　　　　　　　　　　　　　　　　부 indiscreetly

사람의 첫인상을 보고 함부로 판단하지 마세요.
Do not indiscreetly judge him only based on the first impression.

14 화재 　　　　　　　　　　　　　　　　　　　　　　　　　명 fire

어젯밤 화재로 인해 많은 피해가 있었어요.
Last night, there was much damage done because of the fire.

 소방서 fire station　　　　　　소방차 fire truck
소방관 fire fighter　　　　　　화재가 나다 there is a fire

15 화제
명 issue

대화의 화제를 잘 찾아야 해요.

We should choose the topic of our conversation very well.

 화제가 되다 become an issue

16 활발하다
형 active

그는 활발하고 외향적인 사람입니다.

He is an active and outgoing person.

17 후회하다
형 regret

지금까지 살면서 가장 후회하는 일이 뭐예요?

What are the things you regret the most so far?

 후회 regret

18 흔히
부 usually

이 꽃은 흔히 볼 수 있는 꽃이 아닙니다.

This flower is not the one that you can usually see.

19 부정적
명 negative

부정적인 생각은 가능한 한 하지 말고 좋게 생각하세요.

You should not think about negativity as much as possible but you should think positively.

> **Tip**
> 'N적'의 형태로 쓰이는 성격은 또 뭐가 있을까요?
> What are the words that ends with "N 적(–tive)"?
>
> 부정적(negative), 긍정적(positive), 외향적(outgoing), 내성적(passive), 개방적(open-minded), 보수적(conservative) 등이 있어요.

20 연습하다   동 practice

아무리 어려운 발음도 연습하다보면 좋아질 거예요.
No matter how hard it is, you will get better practicing the hard pronunciation.

연습 practice

21 상   명 award

이번대회에서 상을 받으면 친구들에게 한턱내려고 한다.
If I get an award on this competition, I will buy a meal for my friends.

 how this word appears in the test

토픽에는 상을 받은 인물이나 기업에 대한 지문이 출제되곤 합니다.
The passage from the past test often was related to the person or the firm that was given awards.

이미 출제된 상의 종류로는
The rewards that was on the test were

환경상(environmental awards), 공로상(achievement award), 대상(grand prize), 상품개발상(a product development award) 등이 있습니다.

22 가만히   부 stay still

가만히 앉아 있지만 말고 빨리 와서 도와 줘.
Don't just stay still but come here quickly and help me!

23 개성   명 individuality

앞으로는 개성이 중요한 시대가 될 것입니다.
I think it will be an important time for one's individuality.

24 개최하다   동 host

강원도 평창에서 2018년 동계올림픽을 개최하게 되었습니다.
Pyungchang, the city of Kangwon province, has been decided to host the Olympics in 2018.

개최 host   개최되다 be held

25 공포감 명 fear

그 뉴스 기사는 사람들에게 공포감을 주었습니다.

The article on the news scared people.

공포 fear

26 관련되다 동 be related to

그 사건과 관련된 사람들을 모두 만나야 할까요?

Do I have to meet all the people who are related to the case?

관련 relation   관련하다 relate

27 그립다 형 miss

고향을 떠나온 지 20년이 넘었지만 아직도 고향이 그립습니다.

I still miss my hometown even after it has been 20 years.

그리워하다 miss

28 그만 부 stop

벌써 10시야! 그만 자고 일어나!

It's already 10! Stop sleeping and wake up!

29 근거 명 reason

그렇게 말씀하시는 근거가 있습니까?

What is the reason for you saying that?

30 기념 명 commemoration

지금부터 기념 사진을 찍겠습니다.

We will now take the commemoration picture.

기념일 commemoration day   기념하다 commemorate
기념행사 commemorate event

31 금방　　　　　　　　　　　　　　　　　　　　　　　　　부 soon

기차가 금방 도착할 테니까 내릴 준비를 하세요.

The train will soon arrive, so please get ready to get off.

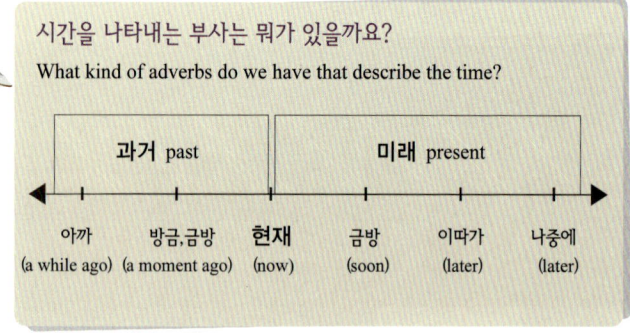

시간을 나타내는 부사는 뭐가 있을까요?
What kind of adverbs do we have that describe the time?

과거 past		미래 present
아까 (a while ago)　방금,금방 (a moment ago)	현재 (now)	금방 (soon)　이따가 (later)　나중에 (later)

32 기뻐하다　　　　　　　　　　　　　　　　　　　　　　　형 be happy

제가 대학에 합격했다는 소식을 듣고 부모님께서 기뻐하셨습니다.

My parents were happy to hear the news that I got an admission from the university.

33 날개　　　　　　　　　　　　　　　　　　　　　　　　　명 wings

새들이 날개를 활짝 펴고 높이 날아올랐다.

The birds flew up the sky spreading their wings.

 날갯짓 flapping

TOPIK에서 혼동하기 쉬운 단어

다의어 Polysemy

쏟다

❶ pour water
예) 컵 안에 들어 있던 물을 모두 **쏟아** 버렸다.
I poured all the water out of the cup.

❷ put life in to something
친구가 정성을 **쏟아** 만든 케이크를 선물해 줘서 너무 기뻤어요.
I was so happy that my friend gave me a cake that she put her life in.

반의어 Antonym

어둡다 dark ↔ **환하다** bright

예) 방이 너무 **어두워서** 불을 켰다.
It was too dark in the room, so I turned on the light.

빛이 **환하게** 들어오는 집이 좋습니다.
A sunny house would be better.

유의어 Synonym

염려하다 feel anxious about ≒ **걱정하다** be worry about

예) 이번 시험은 망쳤지만 앞으로 열심히 공부할 테니까 **염려하지** 마세요.
이번 시험은 망쳤지만 앞으로 열심히 공부할 테니까 **걱정하지** 마세요.
Even though I failed this test, I will study harder from now on so do not feel anxious about it.

복습해 보세요

 한국어는 영어로, 영어는 한국어로 써 보세요.
Write Korean in English, and English in Korean.

1. 정성 _____ 6. active _____

2. 제한하다 _____ 7. usually _____

3. 토론하다 _____ 8. individuality _____

4. 평범하다 _____ 9. host _____

5. 함부로 _____ 10. reason _____

 문장이 자연스럽도록 둘 중에서 알맞은 단어를 고르세요.
Choose the proper word that fits the sentence more naturally.

11. 이 강좌에 (a.접수하려면 / b.변경하려면) 무엇이 필요합니까?
    I want to sign up for this class, what do I need?

12. 이번 회의 일정을 다음과 같이 (a.놓았습니다 / b.정했습니다).
    We have settled the schedule for the meeting as such.

13. 그 사고의 원인을 (a.파악하기 / b.관련되기) 위해 노력하고 있다.
    We are trying hard to figure out the cause of the accident.

14. 지금까지 생활하면서 가장 (a.오염되는 / b.후회되는) 일이 뭐예요?
    What are the things you regret the most so far?

15. (a.가만히 / b.원래) 앉아 있지만 말고 와서 빨리 와서 도와 줘.
    Don't just stay still but come here quickly and help me!

정답

1.one's heart 2.limit 3.discuss 4.normal 5.indiscreetly 6.활동적이다 7.흔히 8.개성 9.개최하다 10.근거 11.a 12.b 13.a 14.b 15.a

DAY 18

확인해 보세요

빨간 시트지로 가리고 단어의 뜻을 알면, □ 에 ✓ 해 보세요.
After covering up the words with red cover, please check(✓) the box (□) when you know the meaning of the word.

□ 01 날다	fly	□ 13 마라톤	marathon	□ 25 사물	object
□ 02 낮추다	turn down	□ 14 아무	anyone	□ 26 사업	business
□ 03 넘치다	flood	□ 15 막	just	□ 27 사정	excuse
□ 04 놀라다	be surprised	□ 16 면	(many) ways	□ 28 속도	speed
□ 05 승진	promotion	□ 17 모	anonymous	□ 29 시기	timing
□ 06 대표	representative	□ 18 모기	mosquito	□ 30 신설하다	create
□ 07 독자	readers	□ 19 미끄럽다	slippery	□ 31 시대	age
□ 08 돌보다	take care of	□ 20 반복	repeat	□ 32 심다	plant
□ 09 동아리	club	□ 21 법	law	□ 33 쌀	rice
□ 10 등산객	mountain climber	□ 22 벽	wall		
□ 11 땀	sweat	□ 23 불가	not allowed to		
□ 12 로봇	robot	□ 24 비밀	secret		

DAY 18

 are the words that appeared in the former tests, and you may get a higher grade if you study them together.

01 날다   동 fly

비행기가 바다 위를 날고 있다.

The plane is flying over the sea.

 날아가다 fly to   날아다니다 fly around

02 낮추다   동 turn down

음악 소리를 좀 낮춰 주세요.

Please turn down the volume.

관련어 몸을 낮추다 lower the body

03 넘치다   동 flood

비 때문에 강물이 넘쳤다고 합니다.

The heavy rain flooded the river.

 넘쳐나다 overflow

04 놀라다   동 be surprised

갑자기 소리를 질러서 깜짝 놀랐어요.

I was so surprised when you screamed out of blue.

05 승진   명 promotion

이번에 승진했다고 들었는데 한턱 내셔야지요?

I heard that you got a promotion, you should treat us big?

06 대표
명 representative

축구 국가 대표가 되려고 매일 연습하고 있어요.

I am practicing every day in order to be one of the players in the national football team.

 대표팀 national team   대표하다 represent
대표적이다 representative

07 독자
명 readers

이 책을 읽고 많은 독자들이 감동했다.

Many readers were moved by this book.

08 돌보다
동 take care of

부모님이 안 계실 때는 제가 동생을 돌봐요.

When my parents are away, I take care of my younger brother.

09 동아리
명 club

나는 연극 동아리에 가입하고 싶어.

I want to sign up for the drama club.

10 등산객
명 mountain climber

가을이 되면 산은 단풍을 구경하려는 등산객으로 가득하다.

In autumn the mountain is usually crowded with people enjoying the change of leaves.

 등산화 hiking boots

'N객'의 형태로 쓰이는 것은 또 뭐가 있을까요?
What is the other word that has the form of "N객(N-er)"?

관객(audience), 방청객(observer), 승객(passenger), 관람객(spectator) 등이 있어요.

11 땀 sweat

아까 **땀**을 많이 흘렸더니 옷에서 냄새가 난다.
After sweating for just a moment, I stink.

12 로봇 robot

앞으로는 **로봇**이 사람을 대신해서 많은 일을 하게 될 거예요.
The robots in the future will be doing many things instead of human.

13 마라톤 marathon

마라톤 대회에 참가해 본 적 있어요?
Have you ever run in the marathon?

14 아무 anyone

그 사람은 아이처럼 **아무**나 쉽게 믿어요.
He trusts anyone just like a child.

 아무거나 whatever   아무데나 wherever
아무때나 whenever

> **Tip**
>
> '아무나' 와 '아무도' 는 어떤 차이가 있을까요?
> What is the difference between "아무나(whoever)" and "아무도(no one)"?
>
> '아무나'는 누구나 상관없이 괜찮을 때 사용해요.
> "아무나(whoever)" is used when it does not matter who the subject is.
>
> 교실 청소는 아무나 해도 괜찮아요.
> It doesn't matter whoever cleans the classroom.
>
> 반면에 '아무도'는 보통 '안/못 A/V'과 같이 쓰고 한 명도 없다는 것을 강조할 때 사용해요.
> whereas, "아무도(no one)" is used with the form of "안/못 + A/V(not + A/V)" and emphasizing that there is no one available.
>
> 일요일에 학교에 갔더니 아무도 없었어요.
> There was no one at school when I went there on Sunday.

15 막
부 just

집에 막 들어오니까 전화가 왔다.

Just as I entered my house, the phone rang.

16 면
명 (many) ways

집을 살 때는 위치, 주변환경 등 여러가지 면을 고려해 봐야 한다.

When you are buying a house, you should consider many things such as the location, the surroundings, etc.

17 모
명 anonymous

연예인 김 모 씨가 오늘 경찰서에서 조사를 받았다.

Anonymous celebrity was investigated at the police station.

출제 경향 how this word appears in the test

읽기나 듣기에서 뉴스기사가 자주 출제됩니다. 뉴스 기사에서는 실명을 거론하면 곤란한 경우가 자주 있기 때문에 이름을 밝히지 않고 '김 모 씨, 박 모 씨' 등과 같이 성만 사용해서 나타냅니다.

The news article often appears in the reading and listening section. Since there are many awkward case when the name is revealed, therefore they indicate the person only by saying "김 모 씨(anonymous Kim)," "박 모 씨(anonymous Park)."

18 모기
명 mosquito

모기 때문에 잠을 잘 수가 없어요.

I cannot sleep because of the mosquitoes.

19 미끄럽다
형 slippery

눈이 와서 길이 너무 미끄럽네요.

The road is slippery since it snowed.

 관련어

미끄럼틀 slide   미끄러지다 slip

20 반복 repeat

외국어를 공부할 때는 반복하는 게 제일 좋아요.

Repeating is the best way to learn foreign language.

 반복적 repeatedly　　　반복하다 repeat

21 법 law

법을 지키지 않으면 처벌을 받는다.

You get punished if you do not abide by the law.

 법률 legislation

22 벽 wall

벽에 그림이 걸려 있었다.

There is a painting hanging on the wall.

 벽걸이 tapestry

23 불가  not allowed to

그 영화는 폭력적인 장면이 많아서 19세 미만은 관람 불가다.

There are many violent scenes in the movie, so people under 19 years old are not allowed.

 불가하다 impossible　　　불가능 impossible

24 비밀 secret

이건 비밀인데, 너한테만 말해 줄게.

It is a secret but I'm only telling you.

 비밀번호 password　　　비밀스럽다 secret
비밀을 지키다 keep a secret

25 사물 명 object

그 예술가는 사물에 대해 자세히 관찰하고 개성있게 표현하는 것으로 유명하다.

The artist is famous for observing the object indetails and expressing it in a unique way.

26 사업 명 business

친구가 새로 사업을 시작했는데 너무 바빠서 통 얼굴을 볼 수가 없다.

My friend just started a new business and he is too busy, I don't get to see him at all.

사업가 businessman

27 사정 명 excuse

사정이 있어서 그동안 학교에 못 나왔다.

There were circumstances that wouldn't allow me to come to school so far.

사정이 생기다 unforeseen circumstance

28 속도 명 speed

일을 하면 할수록 속도가 빨라진다.

The move I work, the faster it gets.

29 시기 명 timing

병에 걸렸을 때 치료 시기를 놓치면 치료하기 어렵다.

It would be hard for you to treat the illness if you miss the proper timing.

30 신설하다 통 create

우리 대학에 인터넷 관련 학과를 신설했다.

My university created a new major related to the internet.

31 시대 — 명 age

요즘같은 정보화 **시대**에는 인터넷을 모르면 일을 할 수 없다.

In the information age, you cannot do anything without the internet.

 시대가 변하다 change of the times

 how this word appears in the test

시대의 변화에 따라 달라지는 문화 현상에 대한 지문이 출제됩니다.
The passage that is related to the cultural phenomenon that changed along with the change of the times appears in the test.

예 남녀의 지위(the status of the male and female),
　 이혼율의 증가(increasing divorce rate),
　 저출산 문제(the problem of the low birth rate),
　 고령화 사회(the aging society)

32 심다 — 동 plant

산에 나무를 많이 **심어야** 해요.

You should plant more trees in the mountain.

33 쌀 — 명 rice

쌀 소비량이 점차 줄고 있어서 농사짓는 사람들이 힘들어하고 있어요.

The consumption of the rice is decreasing so the farmers are going through a hard time.

TOPIK에서 혼동하기 쉬운 단어

다의어 Polysemy

잡다

❶ make (an appointment)
- 예 친구가 너무 바빠서 약속 한번 잡기도 힘들다.
  My friend is too busy even to meet once in a while.

❷ get (the chance)
- 예 준비된 사람만이 기회를 잡을 수 있습니다.
  Only one who prepared will get the chance.

반의어 Antonym

이기다 win ↔ 지다 lose

- 예 이번 축구 경기는 꼭 이겼으면 좋겠어요.
  I hope we win this soccer game.

  경기를 하다보면 질 때도 있으니 속상해하지 마세요.
  When you play games, there are times you lose.

유의어 Synonym

적다 jot down ≒ 쓰다 write

- 예 수첩에 친구들의 전화번호를 적어 놓았어요.
  수첩에 친구들의 전화번호를 써 놓았어요.
  I have written my friends' phone number on the notebook.

DAY 18

복습해 보세요

 한국어와 영어를 알맞게 연결해 보세요.
Connect the Korean words with the English words of same meaning.

1. 낮추다 • • a. object
2. 넘치다 • • b. flood
3. 놀라다 • • c. take care of
4. 돌보다 • • d. create
5. 반복 • • e. repeat
6. 사물 • • f. turn down
7. 신설하다 • • g. be surprised

 다음 빈 칸에 알맞은 단어를 〈보기〉에서 골라 쓰세요.
Pick and write the suitable word among <the options> in the blank space.

〈보기〉
a. 사정이   b. 속도가   c. 시기를   d. 심어야

8. (　　　) 있어서 그동안 학교에 못 나왔다.
There were circumstances that wouldn't allow me to come to school so far.

9. 병에 걸렸을 때 치료 (　　　) 놓치면 치료하기 어렵다.
It would be hard for you to treat the illness if you miss the proper timing.

10. 산에 나무를 많이 (　　　) 해요.
You should plant more trees in the mountain.

11. 일을 하면 할수록 (　　　) 빨라진다.
The move I work, the faster it gets.

정답

1.f 2.b 3.g 4.c 5.e 6.a 7.d 8.a 9.c 10.d 11.b

DAY 19

확인해 보세요

빨간 시트지로 가리고 단어의 뜻을 알면, ☐ 에 ✓ 해 보세요.
After covering up the words with red cover, please check(✓) the box (☐) when you know the meaning of the word.

☐ 01	아무래도	somehow	☐ 13	이사하다	move	☐ 25	절대로	never
☐ 02	양심	conscience	☐ 14	예매하다	get a ticket	☐ 26	조정하다	rearrange
☐ 03	연주하다	performance	☐ 15	이익	profit	☐ 27	졸업	graduation
☐ 04	과소비	overconsumption	☐ 16	이제	now	☐ 28	졸음	sleepy
☐ 05	예술가	artist	☐ 17	자랑하다	brag	☐ 29	주고받다	exchange
☐ 06	예의	manner	☐ 18	저렴하다	cheap	☐ 30	증정하다	give out
☐ 07	외	but also	☐ 19	전공하다	major	☐ 31	최고	the best
☐ 08	외모	appearance	☐ 20	전국	all over the country	☐ 32	출연하다	appear
☐ 09	외출하다	go out	☐ 21	전기	electricity	☐ 33	취소되다	be canceled
☐ 10	우수하다	superb	☐ 22	전자	electronic	☐ 34	가꾸다	grow
☐ 11	위기	crisis	☐ 23	전체	whole			
☐ 12	이내	in	☐ 24	전혀	not at all			

DAY 19

 are the words that appeared in the former tests, and you may get a higher grade if you study them together.

01 아무래도   부 somehow

오늘 일은 아무래도 내 잘못인 것 같다.

What happened today somehow seems to be my fault.

02 양심   명 conscience

요즘에는 양심이 없는 사람들이 많아지는 것 같다.

There seems to be more people with no conscience these days.

 양심적 conscience

03 연주하다   동 performance

무슨 악기든 악기 하나쯤은 연주할 줄 알았으면 좋겠어요.

Whatever the instrument it may be, I would like to know how to play it.

04 과소비   명 overconsumption

젊은 세대들의 과소비가 늘고 있다.

The overconsumption of the younger generation is increasing.

05 예술가 　　　　　　　　　　　　　　　　　　　명 artist

고흐는 죽은 후에 비로소 예술가로서 인정받았다.
Vincent Van Gogh was finally accepted as an artist after he was dead.

예술 art　　　　　　　　　예술 회관 art center

06 예의 　　　　　　　　　　　　　　　　　　　명 manner

친한 친구일수록 아무리 사소한 예의라도 지켜야 한다.
You should still keep manners even when you are with your best friends.

예의 바르다 keep the manner

07 외 　　　　　　　　　　　　　　　　　　　명 but also

우리 회사는 현직 근무자 외에 퇴직자에게도 동일한 보험 혜택을 드립니다.
Our firm provides same insurance benefits not only to the current workers but also to the retired ones.

08 외모 　　　　　　　　　　　　　　　　　　　명 appearance

최근 조사에 의하면 취업하는 데에 외모의 영향도 크다고 한다.
According to the recent survey, the applicants' has a crucial influence in getting the job.

09 외출하다 　　　　　　　　　　　　　　　　　　　동 go out

얼마 전 다리를 다쳐 혼자 외출하는 것이 힘들어졌다.
Few days ago, I got my leg injured so it has been harder to go out alone.

외출 go out

10 우수하다 　　　　　　　　　　　　　　　　　　　형 superb

그 친구는 우수한 성적으로 졸업했고 취업에도 성공했다.
He graduated with a superb grade, and also succeeded in getting a job.

우수성 superiority　　　　　　　우수 사원 the best employee

11 위기 　　　　　　　　　　　　　　　　　　　　　　　　명 crisis

어려운 상황일 때는 **위기**를 기회로 삼으라는 말을 떠올렸다.
When I am in trouble, I remembered the saying that says "You should make the opportunity out of you crisis."

12 이내 　　　　　　　　　　　　　　　　　　　　　　　　명 in

이 일을 3일 **이내**로 끝내주실 수 있나요?
Can you finish this work in 3 days?

13 이사하다 　　　　　　　　　　　　　　　　　　　동 move

이사하는 날 비가 안 왔으면 좋겠어요.
I hope it does not rain on our moving day.

이삿짐 moving boxes　　　　이삿짐 센터 moving company
이사가다 move to someplace else

14 예매하다 　　　　　　　　　　　　　　　　　　　동 get a ticket

인터넷으로 표를 **예매하면** 할인을 받을 수 있다.
If you get a ticket online, you may get a discount.

예매율 ticket sales

'예약하다' 와 '예매하다' 는 어떤 차이가 있을까요?
What is the difference between "예약하다(make a reservation)" and "예매하다(buy in advance)"?

'예매하다'는 주로 표로 구입 가능한 것에 대해서만 사용합니다.
"예매하다(buy in advance)" is mostly used in situations to purchase it as a ticket.

 영화표/비행기표를 예매했어요.
　　　I bought the movie/airline ticket in advance.

반면에 '예약하다'는 표 이외에도 호텔이나 식당에 대해서도 사용 가능합니다.
However, "예약하다(make a reservation)" can be used in the situation not only when you are getting a ticket but also when you are booking a seat in the hotel or the restaurant.

 비행기표/호텔/식당을 예약했어요.
　　　I reserved an airline ticket/a room/a seat/a table at the restaurant.

15 이익　　　　　　　　　　　　　　　　　　　　　명 profit

회사 입장에서는 큰 **이익**을 보는 것이 가장 큰 목표지요.
From the firm's point of view, the biggest goal is to make a large profit.

 손해 loss

16 이제　　　　　　　　　　　　　　　　　　　　　부 now

아이를 낳아 보니 **이제** 부모님의 마음을 잘 알게 되었어요.
After having my own baby, I now know how my parents felt.

17 자랑하다　　　　　　　　　　　　　　　　　　　형 brag

윌슨 씨가 이번에 토픽 시험에 합격했다고 **자랑했다**.
Mr. Wilson bragged about passing TOPIK.

자랑 boast　　　　　　　자랑거리 something to boast about
자랑스럽다 be proud of

18 저렴하다　　　　　　　　　　　　　　　　　　　형 cheap

생필품을 **저렴하게** 살 수 있는 곳이 어디에 있어요?
Where can I buy things cheap?

19 전공하다　　　　　　　　　　　　　　　　　　　동 major

대학에서 무엇을 **전공할지** 못 정했다.
I haven't decided what to major in college.

전공 major　　　　　　　전공자 a student majoring in
전공 서적 textbook

20 전국　　　　　　　　　　　　　　　　　명 all over the country

전국에 비가 내린 지 벌써 일주일째다.
It has already been raining all over the country for a week.

21 전기　　　　　　　　　　　　　　　　　명 electricity

폭우로 전기마저 끊겨 버렸다.
The heavy rain has shut down the electricity.

 전기 밥솥 electric rice cooker　　전기 소비량 consuming rate of electricity
전기 요금 고지서 electricity bill

22 전자　　　　　　　　　　　　　　　　　명 electronic

이 회사에서 생산되는 전자 제품은 세계로 수출되고 있다.
Electronic products produced by this company are being exported to the world.

23 전체　　　　　　　　　　　　　　　　　명 whole

그 사람의 죽음으로 나라 전체가 슬픔에 빠졌다.
The whole country is mourning of his death.

 전체적 overall

24 전혀　　　　　　　　　　　　　　　　　명 not at all

냉장고가 고장이 났는지 전혀 작동되지 않고 있다.
The refrigerator is not at all working, it must be broken.

25 절대로　　　　　　　　　　　　　　　　부 never

이번 회의에는 절대로 늦으면 안 돼요.
You can never be late for this meeting.

 절대 never

26 조정하다   동 rearrange

출근 시간을 아침 7시로 조정했다.

We rearranged the time we go to work at 7 am.

27 졸업   명 graduation

입학한 지가 엊그제 같은데 벌써 졸업이네요.

It seems like it has only been a couple of days since I entered the university, but I am already graduating.

졸업하다 graduate   졸업식 a graduation ceremony
졸업생 a university graduate

28 졸음   명 sleepy

따뜻한 우유를 먹으니 졸음이 오기 시작했다.

I feel sleepy after drinking hot milk.

졸음 운전 drive while drowsy

29 주고받다   동 exchange

선물을 주고받으면서 즐거운 크리스마스를 보낸다.

We had a happy Christmas while exchanging the presents with one another.

30 증정하다   동 give out

30만원 이상 구입하시면 사은품을 증정합니다.

We give out free gifts to the customers who purchase more than three hundred thousand won.

증정 give out   증정품 free gifts
증정 장소 a place they give out freebies

31 최고　　　　　　　　　　　　　　　　　명 the best

우리 나라 최고의 과학자를 소개합니다.

I introduce you the best scientist in our country.

최하 the worst　　　　최초 the first
최종 the final　　　　최신 the latest
최장 the longest

32 출연하다　　　　　　　　　　　　　　동 appear

오늘 프로그램에 좋아하는 연예인이 출연한다고 해서 기대하고 있습니다.

I am looking forward to seeing the celebrity who is planning to appear on today's program.

출연자 cast

33 취소되다　　　　　　　　　　　　　동 be canceled

비가 와서 등산 계획이 취소되었습니다.

The plan to climb the mountain was canceled due to the heavy rain.

취소하다 cancel

34 가꾸다　　　　　　　　　　　　　　　동 grow

우리 할아버지께서는 꽃을 가꾸시는 게 취미다.

My grandfather's hobby is to grow flowers.

TOPIK에서 혼동하기 쉬운 단어

다의어 Polysemy

지내다

❶ close
- 예) 친하게 지내던 친구가 고향으로 돌아가서 섭섭하다.
  I was sad to see my close friend go back to his hometown.

❷ spend time
- 예) 생일이었지만 아무에게도 연락하지 않고 조용하게 가족들과 지냈습니다.
  Even though it was my birthday, I did not call anyone. Instead I spent the day with my family.

❸ work as
- 예) 우리 아버지는 고등학교 축구 대표팀의 감독을 지내셨다.
  My father worked as a coach on a high school soccer team.

반의어 Antonym

이륙하다 departure(take off) ↔ **착륙하다** land
- 예) 10분 후에 비행기가 이륙할 예정입니다.
  The plane is about to take off in 10 minutes.

  비행기가 착륙할 때 반드시 안전벨트를 하세요.
  While the plane lands on the ground, please be sure to fasten your seatbelt.

유의어 Synonym

하락하다 drop (fall) ≒ **감소하다** decrease
- 예) 경제가 어려워서 의류 제품 판매량이 하락하였다.
  경제가 어려워서 의류 제품 판매량이 감소하였다.
  Due to the adverse economy, the number of the clothes that has been sold decreased.

DAY 19 ★★

복습해 보세요

한국어는 영어로, 영어는 한국어로 써 보세요.
Write Korean in English, and English in Korean.

1. 과소비 _____
2. 예의 _____
3. 우수하다 _____
4. 예매하다 _____
5. 자랑하다 _____

6. major _____
7. not at all _____
8. rearrange _____
9. move _____
10. appear _____

문장이 자연스럽도록 둘 중에서 알맞은 단어를 고르세요.
Choose the proper word that fits the sentence more naturally.

11. 요즘에는 (a.양심 / b.적성)이 없는 사람들이 많아지는 것 같다.
    There seems to be more people with no conscience these days.

12. 어려운 상황일 때는 (a.보호 / b.위기)를 기회로 삼으라는 말을 떠올렸다.
    When I am in trouble, I remembered the saying that says "You should make the opportunity out of you crisis."

13. 우리 나라 (a.최고 / b.최저)의 과학자를 소개합니다.
    I introduce you the best scientist in our country.

14. 30만원 이상 구입하시면 사은품을 (a.증정합니다 / b.선호합니다).
    We give out free gifts to the customers who purchase more than three hundred thousand won.

15. 회사 입장에서는 큰 (a.유익 / b.이익)을 보는 것이 가장 큰 목표이지요.
    From the firm's point of view, the biggest goal is to make a large profit.

정답
1.overconsumption 2.manner 3.superb 4.get a ticket 5.brag 6.장점화다 7.전혀 8.조정하다 9.이사하다 10.출연하다 11.a 12.b 13.a 14.a 15.b

DAY 20

확인해 보세요

빨간 시트지로 가리고 단어의 뜻을 알면, ☐ 에 ✓ 해 보세요.
After covering up the words with red cover, please check(✓) the box (☐) when you know the meaning of the word.

- ☐ 01 친하다 — close
- ☐ 02 파괴하다 — destroy
- ☐ 03 피로 — fatigue
- ☐ 04 한꺼번에 — at once
- ☐ 05 화려하다 — fancy
- ☐ 06 화면 — screen
- ☐ 07 화장품 — cosmetics
- ☐ 08 횡단보도 — crosswalk
- ☐ 09 효율성 — efficiency
- ☐ 10 휴식 — rest, break time
- ☐ 11 흔하다 — common
- ☐ 12 켜다 — turn on
- ☐ 13 가정 — family
- ☐ 14 감각 — sense
- ☐ 15 강화하다 — improve
- ☐ 16 갖추다 — possess
- ☐ 17 거짓말 — lie
- ☐ 18 검사 — examination
- ☐ 19 겨우 — barely
- ☐ 20 계산 — calculation
- ☐ 21 고속도로 — expressway
- ☐ 22 공지 — announcement
- ☐ 23 공통되다 — overlap
- ☐ 24 구조하다 — rescue
- ☐ 25 국가 — nation
- ☐ 26 궁금하다 — be curious
- ☐ 27 귀찮다 — tiresome
- ☐ 28 그치다 — stop
- ☐ 29 깜빡 — slip out
- ☐ 30 깜짝 — be startled
- ☐ 31 깨닫다 — realize
- ☐ 32 꺼내다 — bring up
- ☐ 33 이혼 — divorce

DAY 20

 are the words that appeared in the former tests, and you may get a higher grade if you study them together.

01 친하다　　　　　　　　　　　　　　　　　　　　　형 close

이번 주말에 친한 친구들과 여행을 가려고 한다.
I am planning to go on a trip this weekend with my close friends.

02 파괴하다　　　　　　　　　　　　　　　　　　　동 destroy

환경을 파괴하는 개발은 멈춰져야 합니다.
The development that destroys the environment should be stopped.

 파괴 destroy　　　　　　파괴되다 be destroyed

03 피로　　　　　　　　　　　　　　　　　　　　　명 fatigue

피로를 푸는 데에는 목욕이 좋잖아요.
Taking a bath is good for relieving fatigue.

04 한꺼번에　　　　　　　　　　　　　　　　　　　부 at once

다이어트를 하다가 한꺼번에 많이 먹으면 건강에 안 좋다.
Eating a lot of food while you are on a diet is bad for your health.

05 화려하다　　　　　　　　　　　　　　　　　　　형 fancy

그 배우의 옷이 정말 화려하네요.
That actor's outfit is so fancy.

06 화면
명 screen

텔레비전 화면이 보이지 않아요.
I cannot see the television screen.

07 화장품
명 cosmetics

지금 사용하는 화장품이 어떤 거예요?
Which of cosmetic products are you using now?

08 횡단보도
명 crosswalk

신호등이 바뀌기 전까지 횡단보도를 건너지 마세요.
Do not cross the street before the traffic light changes.

09 효율성
명 efficiency

효율성을 높이면 일을 빨리 끝낼 수 있어요.
If you foster the efficiency, you may finish the work earlier than you planned.

관련어
효율 efficiency   효율적 efficient

10 휴식
명 rest, break time

지금부터 30분 동안 휴식 시간입니다.
Now, we will take a break for 30 minutes.

11 흔하다
형 common

그 옷은 어디에서나 살 수 있는 흔한 옷입니다.
That clothes is common so that you can get it anywhere.

DAY 20 ★★

12 켜다 turn on

텔레비전을 켜자마자 뉴스 속보가 나왔다.
As soon as I turned the TV on, the news was on.

 끄다 turn off   틀다 turn on

13 가정 명 family

최근 한국에는 다문화 가정이 늘어나고 있다.
Recently, the number of multicultural family is increasing.

 가정 문제 home problem   가정 상담사 family consultant

'다문화 가정'은 무엇을 의미하는 걸까요?
What does the multicultural family mean?

서로 다른 국적, 문화를 가진 남녀가 이룬 가정을 말합니다. 한국 사회에서 다문화 가정의 수가 급격히 늘어나고 있기 때문에 관련 주제에 대한 지문이 출제될 가능성이 있습니다.

It means a family that consist of a man and a woman who have different nationality and culture. Since the number of the multicultural family in our society is explosively increasing, it is possible that there will be passaged related to this topic.

14 감각 명 sense

감각 기관에 문제가 생긴 것 같습니다.
I think something is wrong with my senses.

15 강화하다 동 improve

어휘력을 강화하기 위해서 하루에 30개씩 어휘를 외우고 있습니다.
In order to improve my vocabulary, I am memorizing 30 words a day.

 강화 improve   강화시키다 be improved

16 갖추다   동 possess

그 회사에 취직하기 위해서는 실력뿐만 아니라 인성도 갖추어야 합니다.

In order to get a job in that company, you should not only have the good ability but also a good personality.

17 거짓말   명 lie

어떤 조사에 의하면 거짓말을 할 때 사람들은 머리를 자주 만진다고 합니다.

According to the survey, people tend to touch their head when they lie.

18 검사   명 examination

건강을 위해서 2년에 한 번씩은 종합 검사를 받으세요.

Please get your medical check-up once every 2 years for your health.

관련어   검사하다 examine   검사(를) 받다 have an examination

19 겨우   부 barely

밤을 새워서 그 일을 겨우 끝냈습니다.

I was up all night, and just barely finished the work.

20 계산   명 calculation

계산이 틀린 것 같은데 다시 한 번 확인해 주세요.

I'm afraid the calculation is wrong, can you please check that again?

관련어   계산하다 calculate

Tip 계산하는 방법을 같이 읽어 볼까요?
Why don't we read together how we calculate?

더하기(addition) ➕   빼기(subtraction) ➖

곱하기(multiplication) ✖   나누기(division) ➗

21 고속도로  expressway

고속도로가 하도 막혀서 다른 길로 갔습니다.

I took the different path since the expressway was too jammed with cars.

 고속열차 express train   고속버스터미널 express bus terminal

22 공지 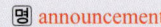 announcement

오늘까지 다른 분들에게 공지를 부탁 드립니다.

Please announce that to the other members of the group by today.

 공지하다 announce   공지 사항 announcement

 how this word appears in the test

읽기 문제에 공지문이 자주 등장합니다.
공지사항을 나타낼 때 자주 사용하는 표현은 다음과 같습니다.
The announcement often appears in the reading section of the test.
The expressions that are often used are as following.

 아래 공지사항을 확인하시고 ……-기 바랍니다.
Please check the announcement below and~

다음과 같이 공지하오니 ……-기 바랍니다.
We announce as following, so please~

변경된 공지사항을 확인해 주시기 바랍니다.
Please check the changed information on the announcement.

23 공통되다 overlap

공통된 부분은 말씀드리지 않도록 하겠습니다.

I won't go over the part that was overlapped.

 공통적 in common   공통점 something in common

24 구조하다   동 rescue

불이 난 건물 안에서 사람들을 구조했다.

We rescued people from the burning building.

구조 rescue   구조대 rescue team
구조대원 a rescue worker   구조되다 be rescued

25 국가   명 nation

유럽에는 많은 국가가 서로 연합하고 있습니다.

In Europe, many nations are united with one another.

국가적 national   국가 이미지 global image

26 궁금하다   형 be curious

저는 궁금한 것을 참지 못하는 성격이에요.

I cannot bear it when I am curious about something.

27 귀찮다   형 tiresome

몸이 아프니까 모든 것이 다 귀찮아졌어요.

I am so sick that I don't feel like doing anything.

28 그치다   동 stop

비가 그칠 때까지 기다렸다가 출발합시다.

Let's wait until it stops raining and then go.

29 깜빡   부 slip out

깜빡 잊고 숙제를 안 가져왔어요.

I guess it slipped out of my mind to bring my homework.

깜빡하다 forget

30 깜짝　　　　　　　　　　　　　　　　부 be startled

고양이가 갑자기 튀어나와서 깜짝 놀랐어요.

I was startled when the cat jumped out of no where.

31 깨닫다　　　　　　　　　　　　　　　동 realize

이제야 실수를 깨닫게 되었습니다.

I finally realized my mistake.

32 꺼내다　　　　　　　　　　　　　　　동 bring up

그는 아주 조심스럽게 이야기를 꺼냈다.

He brought up the subject very carefully.

33 이혼　　　　　　　　　　　　　　　　명 divorce

요즘 이혼을 하는 사람들이 많아지고 있어요.

Lately, the couples who are getting a divorce are increasing.

Tip

'결혼'이나 '이혼'과 관련된 단어는 뭐가 있을까요?

What kinds of words are related to the word "결혼(marriage)" or "이혼(divorce)"?

결혼 marriage	이혼 divorce
결혼 연령 the age of marriage	이혼율 divorce rate
결혼 대상 person to marry with	이혼 사유 reason to get divorce
결혼 준비 prepare for the marriage	이혼 신청 file for divorce
결혼 자금 a marriage fund	

TOPIK에서 혼동하기 쉬운 단어

다의어 Polysemy

지다

❶ (sun) set
- 바다에서 해가 지는 모습을 바라보았다.
  I watched the sunset at the sea.

❷ carry (the bag)
- 산에 올라가는 사람들을 대신해서 짐을 지는 직업이 있어요.
  There is a job that carries the bags up on the mountain instead of the climbers.

❸ take (responsibility)
- 누구든지 그 일에 대한 책임을 져야지요.
  There should be a person who takes the responsibility for the result.

반의어 Antonym

진하다 dark ↔ 연하다 light

- 잠이 와서 진한 커피를 계속 마셔요.
  I am constantly taking dark coffee because I am so sleepy.

  화장을 연하게 하는 것이 낫지 않아요?
  Isn't it better to put on less make up?

유의어 Synonym

연기하다 postpone ≒ 미루다 delay

- 이번 주 토요일 예정이었던 체육대회를 일주일 연기한대요.
  이번 주 토요일 예정이었던 체육대회를 일주일 미룬대요.
  The athletic meeting which was planned on coming Saturday was postphone for another week.

복습해 보세요

 한국어와 영어를 알맞게 연결해 보세요.
Connect the Korean words with the English words of same meaning.

1. 효율성 •   • a. announcement
2. 감각 •   • b. be curious
3. 겨우 •   • c. sense
4. 공지 •   • d. bring up
5. 공통되다 •   • e. barely
6. 궁금하다 •   • f. efficiency
7. 꺼내다 •   • g. overlap

 다음 빈 칸에 알맞은 단어를 〈보기〉에서 골라 쓰세요.
Pick and write the suitable word among <the options> in the blank space.

〈보기〉
a. 흔한 b. 갖추어야 c. 깨닫게 d. 한꺼번에

8. 이제야 실수를 (　　　) 되었습니다.
I finally realized my mistake.

9. 다이어트를 하다가 (　　　) 많이 먹으면 건강에 안 좋다.
Eating a lot of food while you are on a diet is bad for your health.

10. 그 회사에 취직하기 위해서는 실력뿐만 아니라 인성도 (　　　) 합니다.
In order to get a job in that company, you should not only have the good ability but also a good personality.

11. 그 옷은 어디에서나 살 수 있는 (　　　) 옷입니다.
That clothes is common so that you can get it anywhere.

정답

1.f 2.c 3.e 4.a 5.g 6.b 7.d 8.c 9.d 10.b 11.a

주간 복습 day 16 - day 20

아래 단어를 보고 빈 칸에 뜻을 적어 보세요. 그리고 점선대로 접어서 적은 뜻이 맞는지 확인해 보세요. (만일 틀렸다면 뒷면의 단어 앞 □ 에 ✓ 하세요.)

Write down the meaning of the given word in the blank. Also, fold the page along a dotted line and check whether you got it right or wrong. (If you got it wrong check(✓) the box(□) in front of the word in next page.)

▼접는선

단어	뜻
부딪치다	
선호하다	
요구되다	
위하다	
응답자	
제한하다	
토론하다	
흔히	
개성	
근거	
낮추다	
넘치다	
돌보다	
반복	
신설하다	
전혀	
전공하다	
조정하다	
증정하다	
출연하다	
흔하다	
공통되다	
궁금하다	
깨닫다	
겨우	

경복궁

주간복습 | 223

주간 복습 day 16 - day 20

빈 칸에 한국어 단어를 3번 적고 다시 외워 봅시다.
Write down the Korean word 3 times in the blank and try to memorize it again.

◀ 접는선

뜻	단어		
☐ hit	부딪치다		
☐ prefer	선호하다		
☐ be required	요구되다		
☐ care for	위하다		
☐ respondent	응답자		
☐ limit	제한하다		
☐ discuss	토론하다		
☐ usually	흔히		
☐ individuality	개성		
☐ reason	근거		
☐ turn down	낮추다		
☐ flood	넘치다		
☐ take care of	돌보다		
☐ repeat	반복		
☐ create	신설하다		
☐ not at all	전혀		
☐ major	전공하다		
☐ rearrange	조정하다		
☐ give out	증정하다		
☐ appear	출연하다		
☐ common	흔하다		
☐ overlap	공통되다		
☐ be curious	궁금하다		
☐ realize	깨닫다		
☐ barely	겨우		

DAY 21

확인해 보세요

빨간 시트지로 가리고 단어의 뜻을 알면, □ 에 ✓ 해 보세요.
After covering up the words with red cover, please check(✓) the box (□) when you know the meaning of the word.

□ 01 꽤	quite	□ 13 독창성	creativity	□ 25 부럽다	envy
□ 02 끊임없이	endlessly	□ 14 돌	first birthday	□ 26 부부	couple
□ 03 노동	labor	□ 15 동화책	fairy tale book	□ 27 불쾌하다	(be) unpleasant
□ 04 강조되다	be emphasized	□ 16 마치	as if	□ 28 비치다	be reflected (in)
□ 05 길이	length	□ 17 못지않다	as (adjective) as	□ 29 사연	story
□ 06 논리적	logical	□ 18 무척	really	□ 30 성과	accomplishment
□ 07 누르다	push	□ 19 미치다	affect	□ 31 상하다	go bad
□ 08 닦다	brush	□ 20 별	not much	□ 32 성분	ingredient
□ 09 단위	unit	□ 21 배	be doubled	□ 33 세상	world
□ 10 대기하다	stand by	□ 22 벗어나다	get out of	□ 34 세제	detergent
□ 11 대하다	treat	□ 23 보험	insurance		
□ 12 남기다	leave	□ 24 복사	copy		

DAY 21

 관련어 are the words that appeared in the former tests, and you may get a higher grade if you study them together.

01 꽤   🔹 quite

그 학교가 생각보다 **꽤** 유명한 학교라고 하던데요.

I heard that school is quite more famous than we had thought.

02 끊임없이   🔹 endlessly

학생들한테 **끊임없이** 전화가 걸려왔다.

Endless phone calls came from the students.

 끊임없다 endless

03 노동   🔹 labor

그 회사는 **노동** 시간이 긴 편입니다.

The working hour of that company is quite long.

- 노동자 worker
- 노동량 manshift
- 노동 labor
- 노동 시장 labor market
- 노동 환경 working environment

04 강조되다   🔹 be emphasized

미래의 환경을 위해 녹색 에너지 개발이 **강조되고** 있다.

The green energy development is being emphasized for the sake of the future environment.

출제 경향 how this word appears in the test

최근 한국에서는 '녹색 성장'이 화제가 되고 있습니다. '녹색 성장'이란 환경을 파괴하지 않으면서도 경제를 발전시킬 수 있는 것에 관한 모든 걸 말합니다. 관련 어휘로는 '녹색 에너지, 녹색 공간, 녹색 공원' 등이 있습니다.

Recently, the green development is a popular issue. Green development refers to every thing related to economic development without destroying the environment. Related vocabularies are "녹색 에너지(green energy)", "녹색 공간(green space)", "녹색 공원(green park)" etc.

05 길이　　　　　　　　　　　　　　　명 length

머리 길이가 너무 길어서 자르려고요.

I am planning to cut my hair because it is too long.

> **Tip** '길이'와 같은 단위는 또 뭐가 있을까요?
> What kind of basic unit is there that is similar to "길이(length)"?
> 높이(height), 넓이(width), 크기(size), 무게(weight), 깊이(depth) 등이 있어요.

06 논리적　　　　　　　　　　　　　명 logical

저희 할아버지는 논리적이신 분이세요.

My grandfather is logical.

07 누르다　　　　　　　　　　　　　동 push

이쪽 버튼을 누르면 문이 열립니다.

Push this button, and the door will be open.

08 닦다　　　　　　　　　　　　　　동 brush

하루에 세 번 이를 닦아야 합니다.

You should brush your teeth three times a day.

09 단위　　　　　　　　　　　　　　명 unit

한국어에는 물건을 세는 단위가 많아요.

There are many units in Korea that count the number of the goods.

10 대기하다　　　　　　　　　　　　동 stand by

여기서 잠깐 대기하시다가 이름을 부르면 진찰실로 들어오세요.

Please stand by here and enter the doctor's office when your name is called.

 대기 stand by　　　　대기실 waiting room

11 대하다   동 treat

진심으로 사람을 대하는지 아닌지는 금방 알 수 있어요.

It can easily be told whether you are treating the person sincerely or not.

12 남기다   동 leave

우리의 추억을 사진으로 남겨 두었어요.

The time we had together was left in the picture.

Tip

'남기다' 는 어떤 단어와 같이 사용할까요?

What words can you use "남기다(leave)" with?

남기다 leave + 메모 memo / 음식 the food / 추억 memory / 유산 an asset

13 독창성   명 creativity

예술 분야에서 독창성은 아주 중요하다.

Creativity is important in the fields of art.

14 돌   명 first birthday

한국에서는 아이가 태어난 지 1년이 된 날을 돌이라고 불러요.

In korea, people call a child's first birthday "Dol".

관련어 돌잔치 first- birthday party

15 동화책   명 fairy tale book

아이들이 읽을 만한 동화책 좀 추천해 주세요.

Can you please recommend a book on fairy tales that my children can read?

 동화 fairy tales

16 마치　　　　　　　　　　　　　　　부 as if

동생은 내 옷을 **마치** 자기 옷처럼 자주 입는다.

My sister wears my clothes as if they were hers.

17 못지않다　　　　　　　　　　　형 as (adjective) as

이 집 빵도 유명한 가게 **못지않게** 맛있어요.

This place's breads are as delicious as the breads from the famous bakery.

18 무척　　　　　　　　　　　　　　부 really

우리 아버지는 예전에 음악을 **무척** 좋아하셨다고 들었습니다.

I heard that my father really liked music before.

19 미치다　　　　　　　　　　　　　동 affect

인터넷의 발달이 우리 생활에 아주 큰 영향을 **미치고** 있다.

The development of internet greatly affects our daily life.

20 별　　　　　　　　　　　　　　　관 not much

두 제품을 다 사용해 봤는데 **별** 차이는 없었어요.

After using both products, there was not much of a difference.

'별 N' 뒤에는 주로 '없다', '아니다' 가 와요.
"별 N(not much + N)" are followed by "없다(no)" of "아니다(wrong)".

 어머니께서는 별 말씀이 없었어요.
My mom had not much of things to say.

그건 별 일이 아니네요.
It is not of a big deal.

21 배   명 be doubled

돼지고기 가격이 지난 달에 비해서 2배 정도 오른 것 같다.

The pork price has doubled compare to last month.

22 벗어나다   동 get out of

꼭 1등을 해야 한다는 부담감에서 벗어날 수가 없다.

I cannot get out of the pressure that I must win first place.

23 보험   명 insurance

만일의 경우를 대비해서 보험에 가입했어요.

Preparing for the emergency I got an insurance.

 보험료 insurance fee   보험을 들다 get an insurance

24 복사   명 copy

복사 용지가 떨어졌나 봐요.

I guess there is no more paper in the copy machine.

 복사기 copy machine

25 부럽다   형 envy

회사 동료가 과장이 됐는데 솔직히 말하면 부러워 죽겠다.

My colleague got a promotion and became a section chief, and to tell you the truth I envy him so much.

26 부부   명 couple

부부는 살면서 서로 닮아가게 된다.

Couples resemble one another as they live together.

27 불쾌하다　　　　　　　　　　　　　　형 (be) unpleasant

내 사생활에 대해 다른 사람에게 말을 하다니 정말 불쾌하다.

It is really unpleasant to hear that you told something about my personal life to other people.

관련어 불쾌감 displeasure

28 비치다　　　　　　　　　　　　　　동 be reflected (in)

거울에 비친 내 모습을 보고 너무 피곤해 보여서 깜짝 놀랐다.

I was surprised to see myself looking so tired on the mirror.

29 사연　　　　　　　　　　　　　　명 story

라디오에 그 사람과의 사연을 써서 보냈다.

I sent the story of me and him to the radio station.

30 성과　　　　　　　　　　　　　　명 accomplishment

그 사람은 지금까지의 성과에 만족하지 않고 계속 열심히 노력하고 있다.

He is not satisfy with the accomplishment that he has made until now, and is constantly working hard.

31 상하다　　　　　　　　　　　　　　동 go bad

여름철에는 날씨가 더워서 음식이 상하기 쉬우니까 냉장고에 보관해야 한다.

In the summer, it is easy for food to go bad, therefore you should keep the food in the refrigerator.

Tip '상하다'는 여러가지 뜻이 있습니다.
There are many meanings to the word "상하다(go bad)".

 음식이 상하다　The food gone bad
　　　기분이 상하다　be distressed
　　　옷이 상하다　　the clothed get rotten

32 성분
명 ingredient

많은 사람들이 식중독에 걸리자 그 라면 재료의 성분에 대한 조사가 시작되었다.

As many people got food poisoned, there was an investigation on Ramen's ingredients.

33 세상
명 world

이 세상에는 이해할 수 없는 일들이 많이 있다.

There are many incomprehensible things in the world.

34 세제
명 detergent

한국에서는 집들이 때 세제를 많이 선물한다.

In Korea, many people give detergents as a present for the housewarming party.

TOPIK에서 혼동하기 쉬운 단어

다의어 Polysemy

찌다

❶ (be) steamed
예) 저는 **찐** 만두를 좋아해요.
I enjoy eating steamed dumplings.

❷ steamy (heat)
예) 이렇게 푹푹 **찌는** 날씨에는 더위를 먹을 수도 있어요.
In this kind of steamy heat, one may suffer from a heat stroke.

❸ gain (weight)
예) 살이 너무 많이 **쪄서** 다이어트를 하려고요.
I am trying to go on a diet since I gained too much weight.

반의어 Antonym

참석하다 attend ↔ **빠지다** drop out

예) 바쁘신데도 불구하고 **참석해** 주셔서 정말 감사합니다.
We really thank you for your attendance in spite of your busy schedule.

부상 때문에 이번 대회는 **빠져야** 할 것 같아요.
I am afraid I should drop out from the competition because of the injury.

유의어 Synonym

늘어나다 grow ≒ **증가하다** increase

예) 작년에 비해서 인구가 15% **늘어났습니다**.
작년에 비해서 인구가 15% **증가했습니다**.
The population increased by 15 percent compared to last year.

DAY 21 ★

복습해 보세요

 한국어는 영어로, 영어는 한국어로 써 보세요.
Write Korean in English, and English in Korean.

1. 강조되다 _____   6. labor _____
2. 독창성 _____   7. story _____
3. 상하다 _____   8. accomplishment _____
4. 벗어나다 _____   9. (be) unpleasant _____
5. 성분 _____   10. leave _____

 문장이 자연스럽도록 둘 중에서 알맞은 단어를 고르세요.
Choose the proper word that fits the sentence more naturally.

11. 만일의 경우를 대비해서 (a.보람 / b.보험)에 가입했어요.
    Preparing for the emergency I got an insurance.

12. 동생은 내 옷을 (a.무척 / b.마치) 자기 옷처럼 자주 입는다.
    My sister wears my clothes as if they were hers.

13. 인터넷의 발달이 우리 생활에 아주 큰 영향을 (a.미치고 / b.그치고) 있다.
    The development of internet greatly affects our daily life.

14. 회사 동료가 과장이 됐는데 솔직히 말하면 (a.부러워 / b.부끄러워) 죽겠다.
    My colleague got a promotion and became a section chief, and to tell you the truth I envy him so much.

15. 이쪽 버튼을 (a.누르면 / b.대하면) 문이 열립니다.
    Push this button, and the door will be open.

정답

1.be emphasized 2.creativity 3.go bad 4.get out of 5.ingredient 6.노동 7.사연 8.성과 9.불쾌하다 10.물러가다 11.b 12.b 13.a 14.a 15.a

DAY 22

확인해 보세요

빨간 시트지로 가리고 단어의 뜻을 알면, □ 에 ✓ 해 보세요.
After covering up the words with red cover, please check(✓) the box (□) when you know the meaning of the word.

□ 01 소극장	small theater	□ 13 씹다	chew	□ 25 유리창	window
□ 02 수상하다	be awarded	□ 14 아쉽다	feel sorry for~	□ 26 유익하다	beneficial
□ 03 숨	breath	□ 15 악화되다	get worse	□ 27 이	teeth
□ 04 시장	mayor	□ 16 애쓰다	make (put) an effort	□ 28 입다	get (damaged)
□ 05 식품	food	□ 17 애완동물	pet	□ 29 잊다	forget
□ 06 신제품	new product	□ 18 양보하다	yield	□ 30 자꾸	often
□ 07 신체	body	□ 19 얼른	hurry	□ 31 자라다	grow up
□ 08 주인공	main character	□ 20 연말	the end of the year	□ 32 자세하다	in detail
□ 09 신호	signal	□ 21 완성되다	be completed	□ 33 저축하다	save
□ 10 실외	outdoor	□ 22 외면	ignore	□ 34 N별	distinction
□ 11 심장	heart	□ 23 운영하다	operate, run		
□ 12 교사	teacher	□ 24 위험하다	threaten		

DAY 22

관련어 are the words that appeared in the former tests, and you may get a higher grade if you study them together.

01 소극장 · small theater

저는 대학로에 있는 소극장에서 연극을 보는 것을 좋아해요.
I enjoy going to the plays in a small theaters located at Deahangno.

02 수상하다 · be awarded

내 친구는 이번 대회에서 대상을 수상하였다.
My friend was awarded the grand prize in this competition.

 수상 award   수상자 prize winner

03 숨 · breath

빨리 달리고 나니까 숨이 차서 아무 말도 할 수 없었다.
After running fast, I could not say anything because I was short of breath.

숨을 쉬다 breathe

04 시장 · mayor

서울시 시장의 연설을 들으러 사람들이 모였다.
People gathered to hear the mayor's speech.

05 식품 · food

전염병을 막기 위해 외국에서 들어오는 식품을 엄격하게 검사하고 있다.
We are strictly examining the food from outer countries to prevent the outbreak of contagious disease.

 식품 매장 food market

06 신제품   명 new product

최근에 나온 신제품 광고를 TV에서 볼 수 있어요.

You may see the commercial of the recently released product on TV.

신형 new model   신기술 new technology

07 신체   명 body

신체가 건강해야 정신도 건강하다.

Your mind is healthy only when your body is healthy.

신체적 physical   신체 언어 body language
신체 증상 physical symptom

08 주인공   명 main character

이 소설은 실제 인물을 주인공으로 하고 있습니다.

This novel's main character is based on a real person.

Tip

'주인공'과 '주연'은 어떤 차이가 있을까요?

What is the difference between "주인공(main character)" and "주연 (leading role)"?

'주인공'은 드라마나 공연 뿐만 아니라 소설 등의 문학 작품에 나오는 등장인물에게도 사용해요. 반면에 '주연'은 드라마나 공연의 등장인물에게만 사용해요.

We use the term "주인공(main character)" to indicate the role in a drama, play and also in the novel, whereas we only use the term "주연(leading role)" only to indicate the character in a drama or a play.

09 신호   명 signal

신호등의 신호가 바뀌자 차들이 출발했다.

As the traffic signal changed, the cars departed.

10 실외 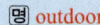 명 outdoor

여름에는 실외 수영장에 가는 사람이 많아요.

There are many people in the summer that go to outdoor swimming pools.

 실내 indoor　　　　야외 outside

11 심장 명 heart

내가 좋아하는 사람을 보자 심장이 빨리 뛰기 시작했다.

When I saw the person that I like, my heart started to beat fast.

 심장병 heart disease

12 교사 명 teacher

교사들을 위한 워크숍을 개최하도록 하겠습니다.

We will hold a workshop for the teachers.

 '교사'와 '선생님'은 어떤 차이가 있을까요?
What is the difference between "교사(teacher)" and "선생님(Mr. someone)"?
'교사'는 직업의 종류고, 교사를 부르는 말이 '선생님'이에요.
"교사(teacher)" is one of the occupations, and "선생님(Mr.someone)" is how you call your teacher.

13 씹다 동 chew

수업시간에는 껌을 씹지 마세요.

Do not chew gum during the class.

14 아쉽다  형 feel sorry for~

오랜만에 동창을 만났는데 이야기할 시간이 많지 않아서 아쉬웠다.

I felt sorry for not having much time to talk with my old friend who I haven't met in a long time.

15 악화되다 — 동 get worse

추운 날씨에도 밖에서 운동했더니 감기가 악화되었다.
My cold got worse because I exercised outdoor in the cold weather.

 악화시키다 aggravate

16 애쓰다 — 동 make (put) an effort

우리 부모님은 나를 위해 항상 애쓰신다.
My parents always put a great effort for me.

17 애완동물 — 명 pet

요즘에는 애완동물을 키우는 노인들이 증가하고 있다.
These days the number of older people raising pets are increasing.

 애완견 pet dog

 how this word appears in the test

최근 한국에서는 반려 동물로서의 '애완동물(pet)'이 주목을 받고 있습니다.
Recently, people are paying more and more attention to the "애완동물(pet)" animals as a companion animal.

특히 고령화 사회가 되면서 노인들이 애완동물을 키우는 경우가 늘고 있습니다.
Especially, the case of the older people raising pet is increasing since the average age of the population is getting older and older.

따라서 읽기나 듣기 지문으로 출제될 가능성이 있습니다.
Therefore, it is possible for this topic to appear on the test.

18 양보하다 — 동 yield

지하철에서는 나이 많으신 분들에게 자리를 양보해야 해요.
You should yield your seat to the elders while you are on the subway.

 양보 yield

19 얼른　　　　　　　　　　　　　　　　　　　　　　㉾ hurry

날씨가 추우니까 **얼른** 집에 들어와서 쉬세요.

It is cold, so you should hurry back home and take a rest.

20 연말　　　　　　　　　　　　　　　　　　　　　㉾ the end of the year

연말에 모임이 많아지는데 과음하지 않도록 해야겠습니다.

There are many social gatherings at the end of the year, I should try not to drink too much.

21 완성되다　　　　　　　　　　　　　　　　　　　　㉾ be completed

이제 조금만 더 하면 **완성되니** 기다려 주십시오.

Now it is almost done, so please wait.

　　관련어　완성도 completeness　　　완성하다 complete

22 외면　　　　　　　　　　　　　　　　　　　　　　㉾ ignore

그 사람에게 도와 달라고 여러 번 말했지만 **외면**을 당했어요.

I cried for help many times, but he just ignored me.

　　관련어　외면 받다 be ignored

23 운영하다　　　　　　　　　　　　　　　　　　　㉾ operate, run

10년 안에 작은 가게를 **운영하는** 것이 저의 꿈입니다.

It is my dream to run a small store in 10 years.

　　관련어　운영 operation

24 위협하다　　　　　　　　　　　　　　　　　　　　㉾ threaten

지나친 흡연은 건강을 **위협한다**.

Too much smoking threatens one's health.

　　관련어　위협 threat

25 유리창 　　　　　　　　　　　　　　　　　　　명 window

이 방의 유리창은 방음 효과가 뛰어나요.

The window in this room is highly soundproofed.

26 유익하다 　　　　　　　　　　　　　　　　　형 beneficial

그 사람은 아이들과 유익한 시간을 보내기 위해 노력한다.

He is trying to spend quality time with the children.

27 이 　　　　　　　　　　　　　　　　　　　　명 teeth

사람마다 이의 개수가 다를 수도 있다고 한다.

Each person may have different number of teeth. .

> **출제 경향** how this word appears in the test
>
> '이'에 대한 지문으로는 치아 건강, 껌을 씹는 이유 등 과학 관련 지문이 출제가 되었습니다.
>
> The passage that related to "이(teeth)" has been about science such as dental health, the reason why people chew gum.

28 입다 　　　　　　　　　　　　　　　　　　동 get (damaged)

이번 홍수로 농촌에서 많은 피해를 입었습니다.

Many rural areas were damaged because of this flood.

29 잊다 　　　　　　　　　　　　　　　　　　　동 forget

중요한 날을 잊지 않기 위해 달력에 미리 표시해 둡시다.

Let's mark the important days on the calendar in order not to forget about it.

DAY 22 ★

30 자꾸   🟦 often

자꾸 보고 싶은 걸 보니까 그 사람을 사랑하는게 분명해요.
I am sure that I love her since I often miss her.

31 자라다   🟦 grow up

아이들이 **자랄수록** 부모의 책임이 더 커지기 마련이다.
The responsibility of the parents becomes bigger as the child grows older.

32 자세하다   🟦 in detail

이 사용설명서는 설명이 **자세해서** 쉽게 이해할 수 있어요.
This instruction is explained in detail so that it is easy to understand.

33 저축하다   🟦 save

집 마련을 위해 월급의 반 이상을 **저축하고** 있다.
I am saving more than half of my salary in order to get a house.

 저축 savings

34 N별   🟦 distinction

성별과 상관없이 모든 사람이 동등한 기회를 가져야 한다.
All people should be granted with same opportunity without distinction of sex.

> **Tip**
> 'N별'의 형태로 쓰이는 것은 또 뭐가 있을까요?
> What are the expression that uses the form of "N별(distinction of N)"?
> 국가별(distinction of country), 연령별(distinction of age), 나이별(distinction of age), 성별(distinction of sex) 등이 있어요.

TOPIK에서 혼동하기 쉬운 단어

다의어 Polysemy

차다

❶ cold
> 낮에는 따뜻하지만 아침 저녁으로는 공기가 찹니다.
> It is warm during the day, but it is cold at night.

❷ be filled with
> 술잔에 술이 가득 차 있는데도 계속 술을 붓습니다.
> Even though the glass was filled with drink, he kept on pouring it.

❸ kick
> 아이들이 공을 차며 이리저리 뛰어다닙니다.
> The kids are running around kicking the ball.

반의어 Antonym

특별하다 special ↔ 평범하다 common

> 오늘은 친구들과 아주 특별한 하루를 보냈다.
> I spent a special day with my friends.

> 아주 평범해 보이는 그 사람이 연예인이라고요?
> Are you telling me that he is a celebrity even though he looks so common?

유의어 Synonym

다투다 argue ≒ 싸우다 fight

> 아파트간 소음 문제로 이웃끼리 다투는 일이 자주 일어난다.
> 아파트간 소음 문제로 이웃끼리 싸우는 일이 자주 일어난다.
> Often people argue with their neighbors over the noise problem.

DAY 22

복습해 보세요

 한국어와 영어를 알맞게 연결해 보세요.
Connect the Korean words with the English words of same meaning.

1. 수상하다 •   • a. New product
2. 입다 •   • b. be awarded
3. 신제품 •   • c. get (damaged)
4. 주인공 •   • d. make (put) an effort
5. 아쉽다 •   • e. be completed
6. 애쓰다 •   • f. main character
7. 완성되다 •   • g. feel sorry for~

 다음 빈 칸에 알맞은 단어를 〈보기〉에서 골라 쓰세요.
Pick and write the suitable word among <the options> in the blank space.

〈보기〉
　　a. 운영하는　 b. 자세해서　 c. 양보해야　 d. 유익한

8. 이 사용설명서는 설명이 (　　　) 쉽게 이해할 수 있어요.
This instruction is explained in detail so that it is easy to understand.

9. 그 사람은 아이들과 (　　　) 시간을 보내기 위해 노력한다.
He is trying to spend quality time with the children.

10. 10년 안에 작은 가게를 (　　　) 것이 저의 꿈입니다.
It is my dream to run a small store in 10 years.

11. 지하철에서는 나이 많으신 분들에게 자리를 (　　　) 해요.
You should yield your seat to the elders while you are on the subway.

정답
1.b 2.c 3.a 4.f 5.g 6.d 7.e 8.b 9.d 10.a 11.c

DAY 23

확인해 보세요

빨간 시트지로 가리고 단어의 뜻을 알면, □에 ✓해 보세요.
After covering up the words with red cover, please check(✓) the box (□) when you know the meaning of the word.

□ 01 적성 aptitude	□ 13 치우다 clean	□ 25 흥미 interest
□ 02 적절하다 proper	□ 14 내 in	□ 26 일상생활 daily life
□ 03 조언 advice	□ 15 통행 pass by	□ 27 특정 certain
□ 04 좌석 seat	□ 16 튼튼하다 olid	□ 28 두통 headache
□ 05 중소기업 smaller firms	□ 17 퍼센트 percent	□ 29 이상 more than
□ 06 지구 the earth	□ 18 한자 chinese character	□ 30 간식 snack
□ 07 슬프다 sad	□ 19 한참 (for) a while	□ 31 감동적 emotional
□ 08 지적하다 point out	□ 20 허락하다 give one a permission	□ 32 거칠다 rough
□ 09 첫인상 the first impression	□ 21 혜택 benefit	□ 33 건설 construction
□ 10 초 candle	□ 22 호기심 curiosity	□ 34 경향 tendency
□ 11 최대한 at most	□ 23 흘러가다 pass	
□ 12 추천하다 recommend	□ 24 늙다 get older	

DAY 23

 are the words that appeared in the former tests, and you may get a higher grade if you study them together.

01 적성 — 명 aptitude

적성에 맞는 직업을 찾는 것이 중요하다.
It is important for you to get a job that fits your aptitude.

관련어 적성 검사 aptitude test

02 적절하다 — 형 proper

지위에 맞는 적절한 옷차림이 필요하다.
You need to wear clothes that fits your position.

03 조언 — 명 advice

친구의 조언이 큰 도움이 됐다.
My friend's advice helped me a lot.

04 좌석 — 명 seat

좌석 번호를 확인하고 탑승하시기 바랍니다.
Please check your seat number before you go aboard.

05 중소기업 — 명 smaller firms

중소기업에 취직하려는 젊은이들이 많아지고 있다.
More and more youth are trying to get a job in the smaller firms.

관련어 대기업 conglomerate

06 지구   명 the earth

지구에는 많은 종류의 생물들이 있다.

There are many kinds of living creatures on the earth.

07 슬프다   형 sad

오랫동안 정이 든 친구와 이별을 해야 하다니 너무 슬프다.

I am sad to say goodbye to my old friend.

 슬픔 sadness

> '슬프다-슬픔'처럼 'A/V-(으)ㅁ'의 형태로 쓰이는 것은 또 뭐가 있을까요?
>
> What kind of words do we have that uses the form of "슬프다-슬픔(sad- sadness)"?
>
> 기쁘다(Happy)-기쁨(happiness), 죽다(die)-죽음(death), 울다(cry)-울음(crying), 졸다(sleepy)-졸음(sleepiness), 자다(sleep)-잠(sleep), 살다(live)-삶(life), 걷다(walk)-걸음(walk) 등이 있어요.

08 지적하다   동 point out

김 과장님이 지적한 문제들을 다 수정했어요?

Did you change all the part that Mr.Kim pointed out?

 지적 pointing out

09 첫인상   명 the first impression

첫인상은 쉽게 바뀌지 않아요.

The first impression does not easily change.

10 초 · candle

생일 케이크의 **초**는 몇 개가 필요하세요?
How many candles do you need for your cake?

11 최대한 · at most

손님, **최대한** 빠른 시간 안에 고쳐드리겠습니다.
Sir, I will fix it as fast as I can.

 최대 maximum   최소한 at least
최소 minimum

12 추천하다 · recommend

이 일에 적당한 사람을 좀 **추천해** 주시겠습니까?
Can you recommend someone who is suitable for this job?

 추천 recommendation   추천서 recommendation letter

13 치우다 · clean

손님들이 오기 전에 집을 좀 **치워야겠어요**.
I should clean up my house before the guest comes.

14 내 · in

시간 **내**에 끝내 주시기 바랍니다.
Please finish the work in time.

'N 내'는 어떤 단어와 같이 사용할까요?
What words can you use "N 내(in~)" with?

아파트 in my apartment
지역 in my area
회사 in my company

➕ 내 in

15 통행   명 pass by

공사로 인해 차들의 통행을 금지하고 있습니다.

We are prohibiting cars to pass by because of the construction.

 통행금지 no passing   통행료 toll

16 튼튼하다   형 solid

저 건물은 정말 튼튼하게 지어진 것 같습니다.

That building was solidly built.

17 퍼센트   명 percent

유학생의 30퍼센트 이상이 장학금을 받고 있습니다.

More than thirty percent of the students studying abroad are receiving scholarship.

 how this word appears in the test

'퍼센트'는 그래프 문제에서 항상 등장하는 어휘입니다.
The word "퍼센트(percent)" always appears in the question with graphs.
'퍼센트'를 비교하고 분석해야 정보를 잘 찾을 수 있습니다.
You should be good at comparing and analyzing the "퍼센트(percentages)" in order to solve the questions better.

18 한자   명 chinese character

한자를 알면 한국어를 배우기가 쉽습니다.

It is easy for you to learn Korean if you know many Chinese characters.

19 한참   명 (for) a while

한참 기다려도 친구가 오지 않았어요.

I waited for a while, but my friend didn't show up.

20 허락하다   통 give one a permission

부모님께서 유학가는 것을 허락해 주셨다.
My parents gave me permission to go abroad and study.

허락 permission

21 혜택   명 benefit

이 보험을 가입하면 어떤 혜택을 받을 수 있어요?
What kinds of benefit can I get if I sign up for this insurance?

22 호기심   명 curiosity

그 아이는 호기심이 많아요.
The kid is filled with curiosity.

23 흘러가다   통 pass

시간이 정말 빠르게 흘러갑니다.
Time passes very fast.

24 늙다   통 get older

오랜만에 뵌 부모님이 많이 늙으신 것 같아 가슴이 아파요.
Seeing my parents in a while, it is sad to realize that they are getting old.

출제경향 how this word appears in the test

'늙다'는 형용사가 아니라 동사라는 것을 주의하세요.
Do not forget the fact that "늙다(get older)" is a verb and not an adjective.

동사와 형용사를 활용하는 문법 질문에서 실수가 많은 단어입니다.
Many people make many mistakes on its grammatical use.

25 흥미　　　　　　　　　　　　　　　　　　　　　　명 interest

그는 새로운 것보다는 전통적인 것들에 흥미가 있어요.

He is more interested in traditional things rather than new things.

26 일상생활　　　　　　　　　　　　　　　　　　　명 daily life

바쁜 일상생활 속에서 여유를 가지기가 쉽지 않다.

It is hard to relax during your busy days.

27 특정　　　　　　　　　　　　　　　　　　　　　명 certain

비행기를 탈 때 몇 가지 특정 용품을 가지고 들어갈 수 없다.

There are certain things that you are not allowed to take when you get on the plane.

28 두통　　　　　　　　　　　　　　　　　　　　　명 headache

두통이 심하면 약이라도 좀 먹어 보세요.

Try some pills if you have severe headache.

치통 toothache　　　　　　　복통 stomachache

29 이상　　　　　　　　　　　　　　　　　　　　　명 more than

한 달에 50만원 이상을 용돈으로 사용하고 있어요.

I spend more than five hundred thousand won in a month as an allowance.

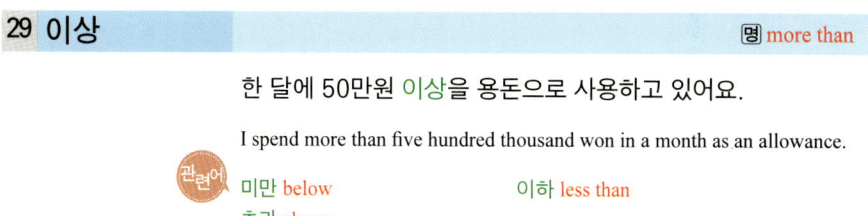
미만 below　　　　　　　　　이하 less than
초과 above

30 간식　　　　　　　　　　　　　　　　　　　　　명 snack

군대에서 인기 있는 간식은 초코파이래요.

The popular snack in the military is Choco-pie.

31 감동적   명 emotional

한 아버지의 감동적인 이야기가 영화로 만들어졌다.

One emotional story of a father has been made into a movie.

 감동 emotion   감동을 주다 move one's heart

32 거칠다   형 rough

나이가 들수록 피부가 거칠어지는 것 같아요.

I am afraid that my skin is getting rougher as I am getting older.

33 건설   명 construction

건설 회사들 간의 경쟁이 치열하다.

The competition among construction companies is high.

34 경향   명 tendency

토픽 출제 경향을 알고 싶으시면 이 책을 보십시오.

You may read this book if you want to know the tendency of the TOPIK test.

경향이 있다 have a tendency to

TOPIK에서 혼동하기 쉬운 단어

다의어 Polysemy

타다

❶ (get) burned

예) 휴가를 갔다가 피부가 까맣게 탔어요.
My skin got burned while I was on my vacation.

❷ get (allowance)

예) 취직을 못해서 아직 부모님께 용돈을 타고 있습니다.
I am still getting allowance from my parents since I don't have a job.

❸ get (cold)

예) 저는 다른 사람들보다 추위를 잘 타는 편이에요.
Compared to others I easily feel cold.

반의어 Antonym

틀다 turn on ↔ 잠그다 turn off

예) 샤워할 때 물을 계속 틀어놓지 마세요.
You should not keep the water on while you are taking a shower.

수도꼭지를 잘 잠가야 물이 새지 않아요.
You should turn off the water tap well in order not to have a leak.

유의어 Synonym

수리하다 repair ≒ 고치다 fix

예) 컴퓨터가 고장이 나서 수리하려고요.
컴퓨터가 고장이 나서 고치려고요.
I am trying to get my computer repaired since it is broken.

복습해 보세요

 한국어는 영어로, 영어는 한국어로 써 보세요.
Write Korean in English, and English in Korean.

1. 조언 _____
2. 지적하다 _____
3. 최대한 _____
4. 한참 _____
5. 혜택 _____

6. smaller firms _____
7. get older _____
8. clean _____
9. emotional _____
10. rough _____

 문장이 자연스럽도록 둘 중에서 알맞은 단어를 고르세요.
Choose the proper word that fits the sentence more naturally.

11. (a.적성 b.적용)에 맞는 직업을 찾는 것이 중요하다.
    It is important for you to get a job that fits your aptitude.

12. 토픽 출제 (a.경향 b.경험)을 알고 싶으시면 이 책을 보십시오.
    You may read this book if you want to know the tendency of the TOPIK test.

13. 부모님께서 유학가는 것을 (a.방해해 b.허락해) 주셨다.
    My parents gave me permission to go abroad and study.

14. 이 일에 적당한 사람을 좀 (a.추천해 b.체험해) 주시겠습니까?
    Can you recommend someone who is suitable for this job?

15. 지위에 맞는 (a.제한한 b.적절한) 옷차림이 필요하다.
    You need to wear clothes that fits your position.

정답

1.advice 2.point out 3.at most 4.(for) a while 5.benefit 6.중소기업 7.늙다 8.깨끗하다 9.감동적 10.거칠다 11.a 12.a 13.b 14.a 15.b

DAY 24

확인해 보세요

빨간 시트지로 가리고 단어의 뜻을 알면, ☐ 에 ✓ 해 보세요.
After covering up the words with red cover, please check(✓) the box (☐) when you know the meaning of the word.

☐ 01	곧	soon	☐ 13	기운	energy	☐ 25	당일	on that day
☐ 02	골목	street	☐ 14	기존	existing	☐ 26	대비	prepare
☐ 03	곱다	pretty	☐ 15	깎다	cut	☐ 27	덜다	take (out)
☐ 04	공격적	offensive	☐ 16	깨지다	be broken	☐ 28	동네	neighborhood
☐ 05	공급하다	supply	☐ 17	미루다	delay	☐ 29	순서	turn
☐ 06	명절	holiday	☐ 18	껌	gum	☐ 30	동시	at the same time
☐ 07	공모하다	invite public participation	☐ 19	꼽다	pick	☐ 31	동의하다	agree with
☐ 08	공사	construction	☐ 20	남녀노소	men and women of all ages	☐ 32	둘러보다	look around
☐ 09	과정	process	☐ 21	널리	widely	☐ 33	뚜렷하다	clear
☐ 10	구독	subscription	☐ 22	단체	group	☐ 34	마감	deadline
☐ 11	금지되다	be prohibited	☐ 23	달리다	run			
☐ 12	기관	organization	☐ 24	답답하다	stuffy			

DAY 24

 관련어 are the words that appeared in the former tests, and you may get a higher grade if you study them together.

01 곧 — 부 soon

곧 돌아올테니까 여기서 기다려.
I will come back soon so wait here.

02 골목 — 명 street

신당동 떡볶이 골목이 얼마나 유명한데요!
You can't imagine how famous Sindangdongddukbokgi street is?

03 곱다 — 형 pretty

디자인도 예쁠 뿐만 아니라 색도 아주 곱군요.
Not only the design but also the color is very pretty.

04 공격적 — 명 offensive

컴퓨터 게임을 많이 한 아이일수록 공격적인 성향을 보입니다.
A more offensive attitude is shown from the child who played more computer games.

관련어
공격 offense 공격력 striking power
공격수 the offense 공격하다 offend

05 공급하다 — 동 supply

우리 농장에서는 여러 식당에 신선한 재료를 공급합니다.
Our farm supplies fresh materials to many different restaurants.

06 명절　　　　　　　　　　　　　　　　　　　　　명 holiday

명절이 되면 많은 사람들이 고향으로 돌아가서 가족과 시간을 보낸다.

When it is the holiday season, many people visit their hometown and spend much time with their family.

Tip 한국의 대표적인 명절로
설(음력 1월 1일)과 추석(음력 8월 15일)이 있어요.
The most famous holiday in Korea is 설(Lunar New year's day (January 1st in lunar calendar)) and 추석(thanks giving (August 15th in lunar calendar)).

07 공모하다　　　　　　　　　　　　　　　동 invite public participation

서울시에서 서울 로고 디자인을 공모하고 있습니다.

The city of seoul is inviting public participation for a new designed logo of Seoul.

공모 contest　　　　　　　　공모전 contest exhibit

08 공사　　　　　　　　　　　　　　　　　　　명 construction

건물을 지을 때 기초 공사를 꼼꼼하게 해 두어야 합니다.

When new structure is built, you should always solidify the ground work.

공사 중 under construction

09 과정　　　　　　　　　　　　　　　　　　　　명 process

저희 학교의 교육 과정을 소개하겠습니다.

Let me introduce the educational process of our school.

10 구독　　　　　　　　　　　　　　　　　　　　명 subscription

작년부터 이 잡지를 정기 구독하게 되었습니다.

I signed up for a subscription of this magazine starting from last year.

구독료 subscription fee

11 금지되다　　　　　　　　　　　　　　图 be prohibited

수업 시간에는 핸드폰 사용이 금지됩니다.
Using cell phones during the class is prohibited.

관련어　금지 prohibition　　　금지시키다 prohibit

12 기관　　　　　　　　　　　　　　图 organization

한국어 교육 기관이 늘어나고 있습니다.
The number of the organizations that teach Korean is increasing.

13 기운　　　　　　　　　　　　　　图 energy

밥을 먹었더니 기운이 나는 것 같아요.
After having a meal, I feel like having more energy.

관련어　감기 기운 a slight cold

14 기존　　　　　　　　　　　　　　图 existing

기존 계획대로 하겠습니다.
We will go with the existing plan.

15 깎다　　　　　　　　　　　　　　图 cut

수염을 깎았더니 깔끔해 보이네요.
After shaving myself, I look better.

16 깨지다　　　　　　　　　　　　　　图 be broken

그릇이 깨질 수도 있으니까 조심하세요.
Be careful not to break the bowl.

17 미루다   동 delay

급한 일이 생겨서 친구와의 약속을 다음날로 미뤘어요.

I delayed the appointment with my friend since something urgent came up.

Tip

'미루다'와 '연기하다'는 어떤 차이가 있을까요?
What is the difference between "미루다(delay)" and "연기하다(postpone)"?

'약속 시간, 회의 시간'의 경우 '미루다'와 '연기하다'를 모두 사용할 수 있지만 '할 일, 숙제'는 '미루다'만 사용할 수 있어요.
When we are talking about time of an appointment or a meeting both "미루다(delay)" and "연기하다(postpone)" can be used. However, only "미루다(delay)" is used when we are referring to chore or homework.

18 껌   명 gum

껌을 씹은 후에는 종이에 싸서 버려야지요.

You should wrap the gum with paper when you throw it away.

출제 경향 how this word appears in the test

토픽에서 '껌'을 주제로 '껌을 씹는 이유', '치아 건강' 등의 지문이 출제되었습니다.
The past question that dealt with "껌(gum)" was a topic about "껌을 씹는 이유(the reason why people chew gum)" or "치아 건강(dental health)".

19 꼽다   동 pick

외국 사람들은 한국 요리 중에서 불고기를 최고로 꼽는다.

Foreigners pick Bulgogi as their favorite Korean food.

20 남녀노소   명 men and women of all ages

떡볶이는 남녀노소 누구나 좋아하는 음식입니다.

Ddukbokgi is the food that men and women of all ages like.

21 널리　　　　　　　　　　　　　　　　　　　　　　부 widely

저는 한국 음식을 **널리** 알리고 싶습니다.
I want to widely spread the merit of the Korean food.

22 단체　　　　　　　　　　　　　　　　　　　　　　명 group

오늘 **단체** 사진을 찍는 줄 몰랐어요.
I didn't know that we are taking a group picture today.

23 달리다　　　　　　　　　　　　　　　　　　　　동 run

요즘 새벽마다 공원을 **달리면서** 운동하고 있습니다.
Lately, I am running in the park every morning.

 달리기 running

24 답답하다　　　　　　　　　　　　　　　　　　　형 stuffy

교실이 너무 덥고 **답답한데** 에어컨을 켤까요?
The classroom feels very stuffy and hot, should I turn on the air conditioner?

25 당일　　　　　　　　　　　　　　　　　　　　　명 on that day

이 표로는 **당일** 공연만 관람이 가능합니다.
This is a day ticket which allows you to see on that particular day.

 how this word appears in the test

이 어휘는 '쿠폰'이나 '티켓'에서 볼 수 있는데 주로 다음과 같은 표현이 많습니다.
This word appears often on the coupon or a ticket, and you may also see the following expression.

 당일 취소는 불가능합니다. You may not cancel your ticket on that day.
당일 예매만 가능합니다. Only ticketing on the day is allowed.

26 대비　　　　　　　　　　　　　　　　　　　　　　명 prepare

자연 재해의 피해를 줄이려면 대비가 필요합니다.

You should well prepare for the natural disaster in order to prevent the damage.

27 덜다　　　　　　　　　　　　　　　　　　　　　　동 take (out)

밥이 많아서 빈 그릇에 덜었다.

I took out some rice to an empty bowl since the quantity was too much.

28 동네　　　　　　　　　　　　　　　　　　　　　　명 neighborhood

우리 동네에는 공원이 많아서 참 좋아요.

There are many parks in my neighborhood and I really like it.

29 순서　　　　　　　　　　　　　　　　　　　　　　명 turn

사람들이 모두 줄을 서서 자기 순서를 기다리고 있다.

People are standing in line waiting for their turn.

관련어　순서대로 in turn

'순서'와 '차례'는 어떤 차이가 있을까요?
What is the difference between "순서(order)" and "차례(in turn)"?

'순서'와 '차례'는 바꿔서 사용할 수 있어요.
the word "순서(order)" and "차례(in turn)" can replace one another.

　예　순서대로 표를 사세요.
　　= 차례대로 표를 사세요.
　　　Please buy the ticket in turn.

반면에 '차례'에는 '순서'에는 없는 '-번'의 뜻도 있어요.
Whereas in the word "in turn," it includes the meaning of "-번(~times)"

　예　여러 차례 전화했지만 받지 않았어요.
　　= 여러 번 전화했지만 받지 않았어요.
　　　I made a call many times, however, he did not answer.

이때는 '순서'와 '차례'를 바꿔서 사용할 수 없으니까 조심하세요.
You cannot use the word "순서(order)" instead of the word "차례(in turn)"
Therefore, you should always be careful.

30 동시   명 at the same time

두 가지 일을 **동시**에 하는 것은 무리입니다.
Working on two works at the same time is too much to handle.

31 동의하다   동 agree with

그 사람의 의견에 **동의하기** 힘듭니다.
It is hard to agree with his opinion.

관련어   동의 agreement

32 둘러보다   동 look around

옷을 살 때는 여러 매장을 **둘러보고** 비교해 본 다음에 사는 것이 좋아요.
It is good for you to buy your clothes after looking around many shops and comparing the price.

33 뚜렷하다   형 clear

민호는 자신의 의견이나 주관이 **뚜렷한** 편이다.
Minho has a very clear view on his opinion.

34 마감   명 deadline

마감 시간까지 원고를 보내드리지 못할 것 같은데 어떡하죠?
I am afraid I won't be able to send you the document before the deadline.

TOPIK에서 혼동하기 쉬운 단어

다의어 Polysemy

풀다

❶ solve (the problem)
- 예) 이 문제를 푸는 데에 얼마나 시간이 걸릴까요?
  How long do you think it will take for you to solve the problem?

❷ relieve (the stress)
- 예) 스트레스를 푼다는 핑계로 다른 사람에게 피해를 주는 행동을 하지 마세요.
  You should not interfere others with the excuse that that you are relieving your stress.

❸ unwrap (the package)
- 예) 내 이름으로 온 소포를 룸메이트가 풀어 버렸다.
  My roommate unwrapped the package that was sent for me.

반의어 Antonym

승차하다 get on ↔ 하차하다 get off
- 예) 손님들이 전원 승차할 때까지 버스는 출발하면 안 됩니다.
  The bus should not depart until all the passengers are on the bus.

  버스에서 하차할 때 넘어지지 않게 조심하세요.
  Be careful while you are getting off the bus.

유의어 Synonym

중단하다 stop ≒ 멈추다 stop
- 예) 하던 일을 중단하고 라디오에서 나오는 이야기에 귀를 기울였다.
  하던 일을 멈추고 라디오에서 나오는 이야기에 귀를 기울였다.
  I stopped what I was doing, and listened carefully to the story from of the radio.

DAY 24

복습해 보세요

 한국어와 영어를 알맞게 연결해 보세요.
Connect the Korean words with the English words of same meaning.

1. 골목 • • a. holiday
2. 명절 • • b. street
3. 공급하다 • • c. organization
4. 구독 • • d. subscription
5. 기관 • • e. supply
6. 미루다 • • f. take (out)
7. 덜다 • • g. delay

 다음 빈 칸에 알맞은 단어를 〈보기〉에서 골라 쓰세요.
Pick and write the suitable word among <the options> in the blank space.

> 〈보기〉
> a. 답답한데   b. 공모하고   c. 뚜렷한   d. 동의하기

8. 서울시에서 서울 로고 디자인을 (   ) 있습니다.
   The city of seoul is inviting public participation for a new designed logo of Seoul.

9. 교실이 너무 덥고 (   ) 에어컨을 켤까요?
   The classroom feels very stuffy and hot, should I turn on the air conditioner?

10. 그 사람의 의견에 (   ) 힘듭니다.
    It is hard to agree with his opinion.

11. 민호는 자신의 의견이나 주관이 (   ) 편이다.
    Minho has a very clear view on his opinion.

정답
1.b 2.a 3.e 4.d 5.c 6.g 7.f 8.b 9.a 10.d 11.c

DAY 25

확인해 보세요

빨간 시트지로 가리고 단어의 뜻을 알면, ☐ 에 ✓ 해 보세요.
After covering up the words with red cover, please check(✓) the box (☐) when you know the meaning of the word.

- ☐ 01 마땅하다 — suitable
- ☐ 02 마지막 — last
- ☐ 03 만 — american age
- ☐ 04 약 — approximately
- ☐ 05 멈추다 — stop
- ☐ 06 명함 — business card
- ☐ 07 몰리다 — be accused of
- ☐ 08 무늬 — pattern
- ☐ 09 무역 — trade
- ☐ 10 민속 — folk
- ☐ 11 바닥 — floor
- ☐ 12 바람직하다 — desirable
- ☐ 13 반사되다 — be reflected
- ☐ 14 발송 — send
- ☐ 15 방안 — option
- ☐ 16 버릇 — habit
- ☐ 17 벌이다 — start
- ☐ 18 범죄 — crime
- ☐ 19 변경하다 — change
- ☐ 20 보람 — worthwhile
- ☐ 21 보수 — pay
- ☐ 22 보상 — compensate
- ☐ 23 입원 — enter a hospital
- ☐ 24 부상 — injury
- ☐ 25 부작용 — side effects
- ☐ 26 부지런하다 — diligent
- ☐ 27 불가능하다 — impossible
- ☐ 28 빨다 — wash
- ☐ 29 빼다 — without
- ☐ 30 상승하다 — increase
- ☐ 31 서투르다 — unskilled
- ☐ 32 선거 — election
- ☐ 33 선발하다 — select
- ☐ 34 재학생 — registered student

DAY 25

 are the words that appeared in the former tests, and you may get a higher grade if you study them together.

01 마땅하다 형 suitable

마땅한 일자리를 찾는 것이 쉽지가 않네요.

It is hard to find a suitable job.

02 마지막 명 last

누가 교실에서 마지막으로 나왔어요?

Who was the last to come out of the classroom?

03 만 명 american age

제 남동생은 올해로 만 27세입니다.

My younger brother is 27 in American age.

04 약 관 approximately

그 공연을 보기 위해 약 5천 명의 사람들이 모였다.

Approximately five thousand people gathered to watch the show.

 Tip

'약' 과 비슷한 뜻을 가진 단어는 뭐가 있을까요?
What kind of word is there that has similar meaning of "약(approximately)"?

쯤(around), 정도(about), 한 N(almost N), N 여(over N) 등이 있어요.

5천 명쯤	around 5 thousand people
5천 명정도	about 5 thousand people
한 5천 명	almost 5 thousand people
5천여 명	over 5 thousand people

05 멈추다
stop

하던 일을 멈추고 뉴스를 봤다.

I stopped what I was doing and watched the news.

06 명함
business card

혹시 명함이 있으시면 한장 주시겠어요?

Can you give me your business card if you have one?

07 몰리다
be accused of

민호는 자신이 도둑으로 몰리자 화를 내면서 나가 버렸다.

When Minho was accused of stealing, he got angry and went out.

관련어: 몰다 accuse

08 무늬
pattern

미영이는 오늘 물방울 무늬 원피스를 입고 왔어요.

Miyoung came wearing a polka-dot dress.

09 무역
trade

지금은 어느 나라도 무역을 하지 않고는 살 수 없는 상황이다.

We are in the situation where no country can survive without internationally trading with other countries.

관련어: 무역 전시관 trade exhibition center

10 민속
folk

명절이면 사람들은 민속놀이를 즐기며 시간을 보낸다.

When it is a traditional holiday, people spend time playing folk games.

관련어: 민속품 folk-craft article

11 바닥 　　　　　　　　　　　　　　　　　　　　　명 floor

오랫동안 청소를 안 했더니 바닥이 더러워요.
Since I have not cleaned for a long time, the floor is dirty.

12 바람직하다 　　　　　　　　　　　　　　　　형 desirable

건강을 위해서 금연을 하는 것이 바람직하다.
It is desirable for your health not to smoke.

13 반사되다 　　　　　　　　　　　　　　　　동 be reflected

창문에 반사된 햇빛 때문에 눈을 뜰 수가 없어요.
I cannot open my eyes because of the sunlight reflected on the window.

관련어 반사하다 reflect

14 발송 　　　　　　　　　　　　　　　　　　　　명 send

주문하신 상품은 내일까지 발송이 가능할 것 같습니다.
The product that you ordered will be sent until tomorrow.

관련어 발송하다 send

15 방안 　　　　　　　　　　　　　　　　　　　　명 option

문제를 해결하기 위한 여러 가지 방안이 논의되고 있다.
Many options are being discussed in order to solve the problem.

16 버릇 　　　　　　　　　　　　　　　　　　　　명 habit

오래된 버릇은 고치기가 어렵다.
Old habits are hard to fix. (Old habits die hard)

17 벌이다 　　　　　　　　　　　　　　　　　동 start

내 친구가 이번에 또 새로운 사업을 벌인다고 해요.

My friend is trying to start a new business.

18 범죄 　　　　　　　　　　　　　　　　　명 crime

올해는 작년에 비해 청소년의 범죄가 많이 줄었다고 합니다.

It is known that the number of crimes commited by teenagers this year was decreased.

19 변경하다 　　　　　　　　　　　　　　　동 change

이번 주말에 비가 온다고 해서 여행 일정을 조금 변경할 거예요.

The travel plan will somewhat change since it has been told that it will rain this weekend.

 변경되다 be changed

20 보람 　　　　　　　　　　　　　　　　　명 worthwhile

이번에 봉사 활동을 하면서 많은 보람을 느꼈다.

This volunteer activity was worthwhile to do.

21 보수 　　　　　　　　　　　　　　　　　명 pay

내일이면 일주일 동안 아르바이트한 보수를 받을 거예요.

I will be paid tomorrow for the work I have done for the past one week.

Tip '보수'와 비슷한 표현에는 또 뭐가 있을까요?
What kind of words do we have that has similar meaning like "보수(pay)"?
월급(salary), 봉급(pay), 임금(wage) 등이 있어요.

22 보상 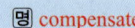 compensate

공장의 매연 때문에 피해를 입었지만 보상을 받지 못했다.
Even though I suffered harm because of the exhaust from the factory, I was never compensated.

 보상하다 compensate

23 입원 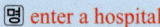 enter a hospital

입원 후에는 의사의 지시에 잘 따라야 합니다.
After you enter the hospital, you should obey what doctor says.

'입원'과 관련된 단어는 뭐가 있을까요?
What are the words that are related to "입원(enter a hospital)"?

퇴원(leave the hospital), 문병(visit somebody who is sick), 병문안(visit someone in the hospital), 환자(patient) 등이 있어요.

24 부상 명 injury

농구하다가 다리에 부상을 입었어요.
I got injured on my leg while playing basketball.

25 부작용 명 side effects

모든 약을 먹을 때는 부작용을 조심해야 한다.
No matter what medicine you take, you should always be cautious of side effects.

26 부지런하다 형 diligent

내 친구는 부지런한 성격 때문에 매일 집을 깨끗이 청소한다.
My friend is so diligent that he cleans his room everyday.

27 불가능하다   혱 impossible

차가 많이 막혀서 비행기 시간 안에 공항에 도착하는 것은 불가능할 것 같다.

It is impossible for me to arrive at the airport in time because of the traffic jam.

 불가능 impossible   불가능에 가깝다 it is almost impossible

28 빨다   동 wash

이 옷은 망가지기 쉬우니까 손으로 빨아야 해요.

These clothes are easy to get ruined so you should wash it with your hands.

29 빼다   동 without

저는 매운 음식을 안 좋아하니까 고추는 빼고 요리해 주세요.

I don't like spicy food, so can you please cook without using any hot pepper?

30 상승하다   동 increase

요즘 물가가 상승해서 생활비가 많이 든다.

Lately, the price has increased and therefore living expenses also increased.

31 서투르다   혱 unskilled

아직은 운전이 서툴러서 차가 막힐 때는 운전하기 힘들다.

I am an unskilled driver and it is hard for me to drive when traffic is jammed.

 서툴다 be poor at

32 선거   명 election

모든 사람들이 이번 선거는 깨끗하게 치러지기를 바라고 있다.

Everyone wants this election to be done clearly.

 선거 운동 election campaign   선거일 election date

33 선발하다 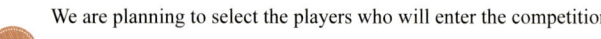 select

다음달에 세계 대회에 나갈 선수들을 선발할 예정이다.

We are planning to select the players who will enter the competition.

 선발되다 be selected   선발 방법 how they are selected

34 재학생 ⓜ registered student

도서 대출은 재학생만 가능합니다.

Only the registered students can borrow the books from the library.

'재학생' 과 관련된 단어는 뭐가 있을까요?
What words do we have that are related to the word "재학생(registered students)"?

복학생(student returning to school after taking time off),
자퇴생(drop out), 퇴학생(expelled student),
휴학생(student on a leave of absence) 등이 있어요.

TOPIK에서 혼동하기 쉬운 단어

다의어 Polysemy

붓다

① pour

예) 컵라면은 요리할 필요없이 뜨거울 물만 **부으면** 된다.
You can eat Kupramen only by pouring the hot water without cooking.

② be puffy

예) 어젯밤에 물을 많이 마시고 잤더니 오늘 아침에 얼굴이 많이 **부었다**.
My face is puffy this morning since I drank too much water before I went to bed.

반의어 Antonym

단순하다 simple ↔ 복잡하다 complex

예) 그 업무는 알고보면 **단순하다**.
You will realize that the task is simpler than you think.

사정이 **복잡하니까** 다음에 설명 드릴게요.
I am in a complexed situation, so I will explain it later.

유의어 Synonym

부끄럽다 be embarrased ≒ 창피하다 be ashamed

예) 사람이 많은 계단에서 넘어져서 **부끄러워** 죽겠다.
사람이 많은 계단에서 넘어져서 **창피해** 죽겠다.
I fell from the stairs where there were many people, so I am embarrased.

DAY 25

복습해 보세요

 한국어는 영어로, 영어는 한국어로 써 보세요.
Write Korean in English, and English in Korean.

1. 마땅하다 _____
2. 마지막 _____
3. 명함 _____
4. 변경하다 _____
5. 부지런하다 _____

6. trade _____
7. wash _____
8. be reflected _____
9. floor _____
10. option _____

 문장이 자연스럽도록 둘 중에서 알맞은 단어를 고르세요.
Choose the proper word that fits the sentence more naturally.

11. 민호는 자신이 도둑으로 (a.몰리자 / b.당하자) 화를 내면서 나가 버렸다.
    When Minho was accused of stealing, he got angry and went out.

12. 이번에 봉사 활동을 하면서 많은 (a.준비를 / b.보람을) 느꼈다.
    This volunteer activity was worthwhile to do.

13. 차가 많이 막혀서 비행기 시간 안에 공항에 도착하는 것은 (a.불가능할 / b.충분할) 것 같다.
    It is impossible for me to arrive at the airport in time because of the traffic jam.

14. 다음달에 세계 대회에 나갈 선수들을 (a.선발할 / b.연장할) 예정이다.
    We are planning to select the players who will enter the competition.

15. 저는 매운 음식을 안 좋아하니까 고추는 (a.빼고 / b.팔고) 요리해 주세요.
    I don't like spicy food, so can you please cook without using any hot pepper?

정답
1.suitable 2.last 3.business card 4.change 5.diligent 6.무역 7.씻다 8.반사되다 9.바닥 10.선택 11.a 12.b 13.a 14.a 15.a

주간 복습 day 21 - day 25

아래 단어를 보고 빈 칸에 뜻을 적어 보세요. 그리고 점선대로 접어서 적은 뜻이 맞는지 확인해 보세요. (만일 틀렸다면 뒷면의 단어 앞 □ 에 ✓ 하세요.)

Write down the meaning of the given word in the blank. Also, fold the page along a dotted line and check whether you got it right or wrong. (If you got it wrong check(✓) the box(□) in front of the word in next page.)

▼접는선

단어	뜻
강조되다	
마치	
벗어나다	
성과	
상하다	
수상하다	
아쉽다	
양보하다	
완성되다	
운영하다	
적성	
조언	
추천하다	
한참	
경향	
공급하다	
미루다	
답답하다	
동의하다	
뚜렷하다	
마땅하다	
명함	
변경하다	
무역	
빨다	

명동

주간 복습 day 21 - day 25

빈 칸에 한국어 단어를 3번 적고 다시 외워 봅시다.
Write down the Korean word 3 times in the blank and try to memorize it again.

◀ 접는선

뜻	단어		
☐ be emphasized	강조되다		
☐ as if	마치		
☐ get out of	벗어나다		
☐ accomplishment	성과		
☐ go bad	심하다		
☐ be awarded	수상하다		
☐ feel sorry for~	아쉽다		
☐ yield	양보하다		
☐ be completed	완성되다		
☐ operate, run	운영하다		
☐ aptitude	적성		
☐ advice	조언		
☐ recommend	추천하다		
☐ (for) a while	한참		
☐ tendency	경향		
☐ supply	공급하다		
☐ delay	미루다		
☐ stuffy	답답하다		
☐ agree with	동의하다		
☐ clear	뚜렷하다		
☐ suitable	마땅하다		
☐ business card	명함		
☐ change	변경하다		
☐ trade	무역		
☐ wash	빨다		

DAY 26

확인해 보세요

빨간 시트지로 가리고 단어의 뜻을 알면, □에 ✓해 보세요.
After covering up the words with red cover, please check(✓) the box (□) when you know the meaning of the word.

- ☐ 01 세기 — century
- ☐ 02 소화 — digest
- ☐ 03 손쉽다 — easy (to do)
- ☐ 04 근무 — work
- ☐ 05 수분 — water
- ☐ 06 수출 — export
- ☐ 07 시급하다 — urgent
- ☐ 08 시키다 — make (someone to do)
- ☐ 09 신고하다 — report
- ☐ 10 신분증 — identification
- ☐ 11 심사 — screening
- ☐ 12 언어 — language
- ☐ 13 여부 — whether
- ☐ 14 열람 — reading
- ☐ 15 열쇠 — key
- ☐ 16 열차 — train
- ☐ 17 영수증 — receipt
- ☐ 18 내놓다 — release
- ☐ 19 예 — old times
- ☐ 20 올라가다 — rise
- ☐ 21 올바르다 — right
- ☐ 22 욕심 — greed
- ☐ 23 용도 — use
- ☐ 24 음료수 — beverage
- ☐ 25 의무 — duty
- ☐ 26 의사소통 — communicate
- ☐ 27 이성 — opposite sex
- ☐ 28 넘어지다 — fall
- ☐ 29 자극하다 — stimulate
- ☐ 30 자동 — automatically
- ☐ 31 잠시 — for a moment
- ☐ 32 자율 — autonomy
- ☐ 33 장난 — joke

DAY 26

 are the words that appeared in the former tests, and you may get a higher grade if you study them together.

01 세기   명 century

21세기는 인터넷의 발달로 사람들이 빠르게 정보를 공유할 수 있게 되었다.

The 21st century is the era when people can quickly share information with each other.

02 소화   명 digest

요즘 소화가 잘 안 되는데 병원에 한번 가 봐야 할 것 같다.

Lately, I have trouble digesting, so I should go to hospital.

 소화되다 be digested   소화제 digestive medicine

03 손쉽다   형 easy (to do)

컴퓨터가 있으면 사람이 하기 어려운 일을 손쉽게 끝낼 수 있다.

If you have the computer with you, you can do a difficult work easy.

04 근무   명 work

그 회사는 근무 조건이 아주 좋습니다.

That company's working condition is really good.

 근무하다 work   근무 환경 working condition

보통 중요하게 생각하는 '근무 조건'으로는 뭐가 있을까요?

What is the important "근무 조건(working condition)" in general?

월급(salary), 연봉(annual income), 근무 시간(working hours), 휴가 일수(vacation days), 복지(welfare), 보너스(bonus) 등이 있어요.

05 수분　　　　　　　　　　　　　　　　명 water

여름철을 건강하게 보내려면 충분한 수분을 섭취해야 한다.

In order to be healthy during the summer, you should drink plenty of water.

06 수출　　　　　　　　　　　　　　　　명 export

수입보다 수출이 증가하면서 나라 경제가 좋아지고 있다.

Even though the export is higher than the import, the national eoconomy is getting better.

관련어　수입 emport

07 시급하다　　　　　　　　　　　　　　형 urgent

그 문제의 원인을 찾는 것보다 그 문제를 해결하는 것이 더 시급하다.

Solving the problem is more urgent than finding the cause of the problem.

08 시키다　　　　　　　　　　　　명 make (someone to do)

할아버지께서 심부름을 시키셨다.

Grandfather made me run errands.

09 신고하다　　　　　　　　　　　　　　동 report

수상한 사람을 보면 경찰에 신고해야 한다.

If you see a suspicious person, you should report it to the police.

관련어　신고를 받다 be informed

10 신분증　　　　　　　　　　　　　명 identification

외부인이 우리 회사에 들어오려면 신분증을 보여줘야 한다.

When people try to enter the building, they should show their identificaiton.

11 심사 — 명 screening

논문 **심사**를 통과해서 이제 곧 졸업할 거예요.
The thesis was passed after the defense so he will soon graduate.

관련어: 심사 위원 judge

12 언어 — 명 language

인간은 동물과 달리 **언어**가 있다.
Human beings have language unlike animals.

관련어: 언어 치료사 speech therapist

13 여부 — 명 whether

지진이 일어나자 많은 사람들이 가족의 생사 **여부**를 확인하기 위해 애쓰고 있다.
When the earthquake happened, many people were trying hard to know whether their family members were dead or alive.

14 열람 — 명 reading

도서관 **열람** 시간은 오전 9시부터 오후 6시까지입니다.
You can read in the library from 9 in the morning to 6 in the evening.

관련어: 열람실 reading room

15 열쇠 — 명 key

요즘은 **열쇠**보다는 카드키나 번호키를 이용합니다.
Lately, people are using more card key or passwords than a regular key.

16 열차 — 명 train

서두르지 않으면 **열차**를 놓치겠어요.
We will miss the train if we do not hurry.

17 영수증
명 receipt

교환이나 환불을 할 경우 영수증을 지참해 주십시오.

When trying to exchange or to get a refund, please bring the receipt with you.

18 내놓다
동 release

작가들이 이번 전시회에서 많은 작품을 내놓았다.

The artists released many works during this exhibition.

> **Tip**
> '내놓다'는 어떤 단어와 같이 사용할까요?
> What words can you use "내놓다(release)" with?
>
> 대책 release a countermeasure
> 작품 works
> 신제품 a new product
> 아이디어 an idea
>
> ＋ 내놓다 release

19 예
명 old times

예로부터 한국 사람들은 노인에 대한 공경심이 강했다.

Korean people strongly respected the elders from the old times.

20 올라가다
동 rise

지구 온난화 현상으로 극지방의 온도가 매년 올라간다고 한다.

Because of the global warming, the temparature of the polar regions are rising annually.

21 올바르다
형 right

어린 아이들은 올바른 행동이 무엇인지 때로는 모를 수 있다.

Youngsters may not know what is the right behavior from time to time.

22 욕심 　　　　　　　　　　　　　　　　　　　　　　명 greed

자기의 욕심만 생각하면 남을 배려하기 어렵다.

When you only think of your own benefit, it is hard to care for others.

 욕심을 내다 be greedy

23 용도 　　　　　　　　　　　　　　　　　　　　　　명 use

이 물건은 여러 가지 용도로 쓰일 수 있어 실용적인 것 같아요.

It is practical since it can be used for many uses.

24 음료수 　　　　　　　　　　　　　　　　　　　　　명 beverage

운동 후에는 음료수보다 물이 수분 보충에 좋다.

Drinking water after you worked out is better than drinking a beverage for hydration.

 음료 광고 beverage commercial

25 의무 　　　　　　　　　　　　　　　　　　　　　　명 duty

선생님과 학생 사이에 서로 지켜야 할 의무가 있다.

There is a duty that must be followed between teacher and students.

 의무제 policy of duty

26 의사소통 　　　　　　　　　　　　　　　　　　　　명 communicate

외국에 가면 의사소통 문제가 가장 힘들어요.

There would be a communicating problem when you go abroad.

27 이성 　　　　　　　　　　　　　　　　　　　　　명 opposite sex

청소년들의 이성 교제에 대해 무조건 반대하는 것은 옳지 않다.

Simply objecting to teenagers dating is not right.

28 넘어지다   동 fall

스키를 타다가 넘어져서 크게 다쳤어요.

I fell while skiing and hurt myself greatly.

Tip

'넘어지다'와 비슷한 뜻을 가진 단어는 뭐가 있을까요?
What is the words that has a similar meaning as the word "넘어지다 (fall)"?

| 쓰러지다 Faint | 예 | 민호 씨가 3일 동안 잠도 안 자고 일하더니 결국 쓰러졌다.
Minho finally fainted down after working three days without getting any sleep. |
| 미끄러지다 Slip | 예 | 눈이 쌓인 길을 걷다가 미끄러졌어요.
I slipped while walking on the snowy road. |

29 자극하다   동 stimulate

요즘 들어 호기심을 자극하는 유아 장난감이 많아졌다.

These days, there are many toys that stimulate my curiosity.

30 자동   명 automaticallly

방 안에 사람이 없으면 자동으로 꺼지는 에어컨이 발명됐다.

The air conditioner that turns off automatically when there is no people in the room has been invented.

 자동 응답 answering machine   자동문 automatic door

31 잠시   부 for a moment

잠시 길 좀 여쭤봐도 될까요?

May I ask you about the direction for a moment?

32 자율   명 autonomy

1월부터 승용차 자율 요일제를 실시한다고 합니다.

From January, the policy allowing the drivers to choose the day of not driving will be executed.

 자율적 freely

 how this word appears in the test

토픽에서 '승용차 자율 요일제'가 주제로 출제된 적이 있습니다. '승용차 자율 요일제'란 운전자가 요일을 정해서 일주일에 한 번 정한 요일에는 본인의 차를 운전하지 않는 제도를 가리킵니다.

There is time when this concept appeared in the TOPIK test. This policy lets the drivers to choose one day in a week and freely not drive their cars on that particular day.

33 장난   명 joke

장난도 심하게 치면 남의 기분을 망칠 수 있다.

A joke can hurt other people's feelings if they are harsh.

 장난감 toy

TOPIK에서 혼동하기 쉬운 단어

다의어 Polysemy

내다

❶ submit
- 예) 모든 회원은 회비를 **내야** 합니다.
  All the members should pay their membership fee.

❷ submit
- 예) 이번 주말까지 보고서를 **내** 주세요.
  Please submit your reports by this weekend.

❸ make (sound)
- 예) 도서관에서는 큰 소리를 **내지** 말고 작은 소리로 대화해야 한다.
  You should not make any big sounds in the library, so please speak quietly.

반의어 Antonym

달리 different ↔ 마찬가지로 likewise

- 예) 그는 첫인상과는 **달리** 매우 친절한 사람이었습니다.
  He was very friendly unlike his first impression.

  한국도 독일과 **마찬가지로** 통일을 이룰 것이다.
  Korea will unify just like Germany did.

유의어 Synonym

분명하다 be clear ≒ 확실하다 be sure

- 예) 지금까지 연락이 없는 것을 보니 무슨 일이 생긴 것이 **분명하다**.
  지금까지 연락이 없는 것을 보니 무슨 일이 생긴 것이 **확실하다**.
  It is sure that something must have happened since there was no contact at all.

DAY 26

복습해 보세요

 한국어와 영어를 알맞게 연결해 보세요.
Connect the Korean words with the English words of same meaning.

1. 소화   • a. for a moment
2. 시급하다   • b. whether
3. 여부   • c. urgent
4. 욕심   • d. duty
5. 넘어지다   • e. fall
6. 의무   • f. greed
7. 잠시   • g. digest

 다음 빈 칸에 알맞은 단어를 〈보기〉에서 골라 쓰세요.
Pick and write the suitable word among <the options> in the blank space.

〈보기〉
　　a. 올바른　b. 손쉽게　c. 자극하는　d. 신분증을

8. 컴퓨터가 있으면 사람이 하기 어려운 일을 (　　) 끝낼 수 있다.
   If you have the computer with you, you can do a difficult work easy.

9. 외부인이 우리 회사에 들어오려면 (　　) 보여줘야 한다.
   When people try to enter the building, they should show their identificaiton.

10. 어린 아이들은 (　　) 행동이 무엇인지 때로는 모를 수 있다.
    Youngsters may not know what is the right behavior from time to time.

11. 요즘 들어 호기심을 (　　) 유아 장난감이 많아졌다.
    These days, there are many toys that stimulate my curiosity.

정답

1.g 2.c 3.b 4.f 5.e 6.d 7.a 8.b 9.d 10.a 11.c

DAY 27

확인해 보세요

빨간 시트지로 가리고 단어의 뜻을 알면, □ 에 ✓ 해 보세요.
After covering up the words with red cover, please check(✓) the box (□) when you know the meaning of the word.

□ 01	장사	business	□ 13	조절하다	control	□ 25	가전제품	home appliances
□ 02	재능	talent	□ 14	존경하다	respect	□ 26	취하다	get
□ 03	적용하다	apply	□ 15	주택	house	□ 27	친밀하다	friendly
□ 04	전 N	all	□ 16	중요성	importance	□ 28	택배	parcel service
□ 05	적응하다	adapt	□ 17	지르다	shout out	□ 29	통화하다	talk on the phone
□ 06	절반	half	□ 18	진심	sincerity	□ 30	표시하다	mark
□ 07	늘	always	□ 19	차지하다	occupy	□ 31	풍부하다	abundant
□ 08	접종	vaccination	□ 20	비롯하다	including	□ 32	프린터	printer
□ 09	접하다	access	□ 21	챙기다	take	□ 33	피부	skin
□ 10	제거하다	remove	□ 22	최신	latest	□ 34	협조하다	cooperate
□ 11	제안하다	suggest	□ 23	추가하다	add			
□ 12	제작하다	produce	□ 24	출입	enter			

DAY 27

 are the words that appeared in the former tests, and you may get a higher grade if you study them together.

01 장사   명 business

그 사람은 다니던 회사를 그만두고 장사를 시작하였다.
He quit his job and started his own business.

02 재능   명 talent

자녀의 재능을 찾아 키워주는 것이 가장 중요하다.
The most important thing is to find your children's talent and support it.

03 적용하다   동 apply

이 방법을 적용해서 문제를 풀어 보세요.
Please apply this method and solve the problems.

 적용되다 be applied to

04 전 N   명 all

이번 선거는 전 학생들의 투표 참가를 목표로 합니다.
This election aims to have all students participate in voting.

 how this word appears in the test

읽기에서 '전 학생, 전 국민, 전 기업' 등과 같은 '전 N'의 표현을 자주 볼 수 있습니다. 이 때 지문과 일치하는 내용을 찾는 문제가 자주 출제되곤 합니다. 이 때 이것이 '모든 학생, 모든 국민, 모든 기업'이라는 뜻을 알아야 오답을 피할 수 있습니다.

In reading, "전 N(all +noun)" such as "전 학생, 전 국민, 전 기업(all students, all people, all companies)" appears frequently. They come with questions that ask about finding correct information from the passage. You need to know it means "모든 학생, 모든 국민, 모든 기업(all students all people, all companies)" so that you can avoid choosing incorrect answers.

05 적응하다　　　　　　　　　　　　　통 adapt

이제 혼자 사는 것에 적응해서 별로 외롭지 않아요.
Now that I have adapted to living alone, I don't feel lonely.

06 절반　　　　　　　　　　　　　　명 half

학생들이 절반 정도밖에 오지 않았다.
Only half of the students showed up.

07 늘　　　　　　　　　　　　　　　부 always

늘 바쁘다는 핑계로 부모님을 찾아뵙지 못하고 있습니다.
I haven't been able to visit my parents; always the same excuse of being too busy.

> **Tip**
> '늘'과 같은 빈도 부사는 또 뭐가 있을까요?
> What other frequent adverbs are there?
> 전혀(never), 가끔(sometimes), 자주(often), 항상(always) 등이 있어요.

08 접종　　　　　　　　　　　　　　명 vaccination

아이의 예방 접종을 위해 병원을 찾았다.
I went to the hospital to have my child vaccinated.

 접종비 vaccination fee

09 접하다　　　　　　　　　　　　　통 access

고향에서는 한국 문화를 접할 기회가 별로 없었어요.
I don't have many chances to access Korean culture back in my hometown.

접촉 contact

10 제거하다   图 remove

악취를 **제거하는** 데에 양파를 이용할 수 있다.

In order to remove stench, you can use onions.

11 제안하다   图 suggest

그 친구에게 이번 여행을 함께 가자고 **제안했다**.

I suggested my friend to go on a trip together.

 제안 suggestions

12 제작하다   图 produce

작은 영화사에서 **제작한** 영화가 큰 성공을 거두었다.

The film produced by a small film company had a great success.

 제작 produce   제작진 production crew
제작되다 be produced

13 조절하다   图 control

건강을 위해 음식을 **조절해야** 합니다.

You need to control what you eat for your health.

14 존경하다   图 respect

내가 가장 **존경하는** 분은 바로 우리 아버지시다.

The person I respect the most is my father.

 존경받다 be respected

15 주택   图 house

아이들을 키우기에는 아파트보다는 **주택**이 낫다고 생각해요.

I think it is better to raise children in houses than in apartments.

16 중요성   명 importance

교육의 중요성을 생각할 때 더 많은 교육비가 투자되어야 합니다.

To think of the importance of education, much more money should be invested.

 중요하다 it is important

17 지르다   동 shout out

산에 올라가 소리를 크게 지르고 나면 마음이 시원해진다.

When you climb up the mountain and shout out loud, you feel much better.

18 진심   명 sincerity

편지를 통해 그 사람의 진심을 느낄 수 있었어요.

I could feel his sincerity from his letter.

19 차지하다   동 occupy

방의 대부분을 침대가 차지하고 있다.

The bed occupies most of the space in the room.

20 비롯하다   동 including

사장님을 비롯한 모든 직원들이 열심히 일을 하고 있다.

All employees including the CEO is working hard.

'비롯하다'가 '처음으로 시작한다'는 의미를 가질 때는 '비롯되다'로 바꿔 쓸 수 있어요.

"비롯하다" could be changed to "비롯되다" when it means to "start for the first time".

 그 싸움은 작은 오해에서 비롯한 것이다.
= 그 싸움은 작은 오해에서 비롯된 것이다.
    The fight was started from the small misunderstandings.

21 챙기다 동 take

짐을 잘 **챙겨서** 나오세요.

Please don't forget to take your luggage out with you.

22 최신 명 latest

저는 **최신** 가요를 즐겨 듣습니다.

I like listening to the latest pop music.

23 추가하다 동 add

사람이 더 와서 삼겹살 3인분을 **추가했습니다**.

More people came, so I added 3 more dishes of Samgyupsal.

 추가 addition   추가 비용 additional cost

24 출입 명 enter

이 건물은 사람들의 **출입**을 통제하고 있습니다.

We are forbidding people from entering the building.

 출입하다 enter

25 가전제품 명 home appliances

요즘에 결혼 준비를 하는데 오늘은 **가전제품**을 사러 가려고 한다.

I'm preparing for my wedding these days; I'm planning to go buy home appliances today.

> '가전제품'에는 뭐가 있을까요?
> What are "가전제품(home appliances)"?
>
> 전자레인지(They are microwave), 냉장고(refrigerator),
> 세탁기(washing machine), 에어컨(air conditioner),
> 공기청정기(air purifier) 등이 있어요.

26 취하다   동 get

깊은 수면을 **취하기** 위해 잠자는 습관을 고쳐야 합니다.

In order to get enough sleep, you need to change your sleep habits.

27 친밀하다   형 friendly

개는 인간과 가장 **친밀한** 동물 중의 하나입니다.

Dogs are one of the friendliest animals to humans.

관련어   친밀감 intimacy   친밀도 level of intimacy

28 택배   명 parcel service

오늘 **택배**를 보내면 내일 받을 수 있나요?

If I send the package with the parcel service today, can they get it tomorrow?

29 통화하다   동 talk on the phone

지금 **통화하는** 사람이 누구예요?

With whom are you talking on the phone now?

30 표시하다   동 mark

중요한 것은 빨간색으로 **표시해** 주세요.

Please mark something important in red.

관련어   표시 mark

31 풍부하다   형 abundant

그 나라는 자원이 **풍부합니다**.

The country is abundant in resources.

32 프린터 printer

이 컴퓨터와 연결된 프린터가 고장난 것 같아요.

The printer connected to this computer seems to be out of order.

사무용품에는 뭐가 있을까요?
What are office supplies?
컴퓨터(They are computer), 프린터(printer), 팩스(fax), 복사기(copier) 등이 있습니다.

33 피부 skin

피부가 정말 부드럽네요.

Your skin is very soft.

 피부과 dermatology

34 협조하다 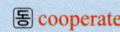 cooperate

자원봉사자들의 지시에 협조하고 있습니다.

I am cooperating with the volunteer's direction.

 협조 cooperation

TOPIK에서 혼동하기 쉬운 단어

다의어 Polysemy

들다

❶ take one's fancy
- 그 옷이 마음에 들었지만 비싸서 못 샀어요.
  The cloth took my fancy, but it was too expensive to buy.

❷ be in
- 핸드폰이 가방에 들어 있는지 확인해 보세요.
  Please check your bag to see if your cellular phone is in there.

❸ (the thought) hit someone
- 집에 가기 전에 잠깐 병원에 가야겠다는 생각이 들었다.
  It (the thought) hit me that I need to stop by the hospital before I go home.

반의어 Antonym

데우다 heat up ↔ 식히다 cool down
- 찬 음식은 전자레인지에 데워 드세요.
  You should heat cold food up in the microwave.

  뜨거운 음식을 잘 못 먹어서 항상 식혀 먹어요.
  I can't eat hot food, so I always cool them down before I eat them.

유의어 Synonym

우선 above all ≒ 먼저 first
- 식사를 하기 전에 우선 손을 씻으세요.
  식사를 하기 전에 먼저 손을 씻으세요.
  Before the meal, please wash your hands above all.

DAY 27

복습해 보세요

 한국어는 영어로, 영어는 한국어로 써 보세요.
Write Korean in English, and English in Korean.

1. 적용하다 _____
2. 늘 _____
3. 접종 _____
4. 접하다 _____
5. 제안하다 _____

6. control _____
7. importance _____
8. occupy _____
9. parcel service _____
10. abundant _____

 문장이 자연스럽도록 둘 중에서 알맞은 단어를 고르세요.
Choose the proper word that fits the sentence more naturally.

11. 이제 혼자 사는 것에 (a.적응해서 / b.적당해서) 별로 외롭지 않아요.
    Now that I have adapted to living alone, I don't feel lonely.

12. 산에 올라가 소리를 크게 (a.부르고 / b.지르고) 나면 마음이 시원해진다.
    When you climb up the mountain and shout out loud, you feel much better.

13. 자녀의 (a.단점 / b.재능)을 찾아 키워주는 것이 가장 중요하다.
    The most important thing is to find your children's talent and support it.

14. 편지를 통해 그 사람이 (a.진심 / b.명함)을 느낄 수 있었어요.
    I could feel his sincerity from his letter.

15. 개는 인간과 가장 (a.친밀한 / b.친절한) 동물 중의 하나입니다.
    Dogs are one of the friendliest animals to humans.

정답
1. apply 2. always 3. vaccination 4. access 5. suggest 6. 조절하다 7. 중요성 8. 차지하다 9. 택배 10. 풍부하다 11. a 12. b 13. b 14. a 15. a

DAY 28

확인해 보세요

빨간 시트지로 가리고 단어의 뜻을 알면, ☐에 ✓해 보세요.
After covering up the words with red cover, please check(✓) the box (☐) when you know the meaning of the word.

☐ 01	형식	format	☐ 13	해당되다	apply to	☐ 25	고집	stubborn
☐ 02	대여하다	lend	☐ 14	해소하다	alleviate	☐ 26	도구	tool
☐ 03	아예	at all	☐ 15	까다롭다	particular	☐ 27	고통	pain
☐ 04	오해	misunderstanding	☐ 16	곁	on someone's side	☐ 28	공개	open
☐ 05	원망스럽다	blame	☐ 17	가리다	choose over	☐ 29	공고	notice
☐ 06	응모	enter	☐ 18	간편하다	easy	☐ 30	과장되다	exaggerate
☐ 07	이동하다	move	☐ 19	강요하다	force	☐ 31	관점	perspective
☐ 08	인류	human	☐ 20	객관적	objective	☐ 32	괜히	in vain
☐ 09	현금	cash	☐ 21	건조하다	dry	☐ 33	괴롭다	painful
☐ 10	저장하다	store	☐ 22	겉	out[side]	☐ 34	교과서	textbook
☐ 11	정체	congestion	☐ 23	경조사비	gratuity (for family events)			
☐ 12	체조	stretching	☐ 24	고유하다	original			

DAY 28

 are the words that appeared in the former tests, and you may get a higher grade if you study them together.

01 형식   명 format

보고서를 쓸 때는 형식에 맞게 써야 해요.
When writing a report, you need to follow the formats.

 형식적 formal

02 대여하다   동 lend

집 앞에 DVD를 대여해 주는 가게가 없어졌어요.
The shop across from my home, from where I used to rent DVDS, is gone.

대여 rental   대여 기간 rental period

03 아예   부 at all

담배처럼 몸에 나쁜 것은 아예 시작하지 않는 게 좋다.
It's better not to start something that's bad for your health at all, like smoking.

04 오해   명 misunderstanding

서로 오해가 있어서 조금 말다툼을 했지만 곧 풀었어요.
We misunderstood each other and had an argument but we soon solved it.

05 원망스럽다   형 blame

퇴근 시간이 지나도록 일을 시키는 부장님이 정말 원망스럽다.
I blame the head of our department for making me stay late working.

06 응모   명 enter

이 이벤트에는 누구나 응모가 가능합니다.
Anybody can enter for this event.

 응모 대상 target group   응모 기간 a period for entry

 출제 경향 how this word appears in the test

읽기에서 '응모'와 관련된 공고문이 자주 출제됩니다. 이 때 '응모 자격'을 꼼꼼히 살펴볼 필요가 있습니다. '응모 자격'을 나타내는 표현으로는 'N으로 제한하다', 'N을 포함하다' 등이 있습니다.
In reading, there frequently appears notice posters that are related to "응모(entering for an event)." It is necessary to read carefully of "응모 자격(entry eligibilities)." Some of the expressions that are used in "응모 자격(entry eligibilities)" are "N으로 제한하다(limits to N)" and "N을 포함하다(includes N)" etc.

07 이동하다   동 move

다음 장소로 이동하기 전에 인원을 점검하겠습니다.
We'll do the headcount before we move to the next location.

08 인류   명 human

인류 문명의 발전은 여가 시간의 증가를 가져왔다.
The development of human civilization has brought the increase of leisure times.

09 현금   명 cash

현금이 없는데 카드로 계산해도 될까요?
I don't have any cash; can I pay with my credit card?

 **Tip** '현금'과 관련된 단어는 또 뭐가 있을까요?
What other words are related to "현금(cash)"?

수표(They are check), 신용카드(credit card), 체크카드(debit card), 지폐(bill), 동전(coin) 등이 있어요.

DAY 28

10 저장하다　　　　　　　　　　　　　　　　　통 store

USB에는 많은 자료를 저장할 수 있다.
We can store a lot of data in the USB.

> '저장하다'는 어떤 단어와 같이 사용할까요?
> What kinds of words can be used with "저장하다(store)"?
>
> 파일 File
> 김치 Kimchi　＋　저장하다 store
> 와인 Wine

11 정체　　　　　　　　　　　　　　　　　　명 congestion

출근 시간이라서 교통 정체가 심하네요.
Traffic congestions in the morning make rush hours heavy.

12 체조　　　　　　　　　　　　　　　　　　명 stretching

아침 운동으로 간단히 할 만한 체조가 있는데 가르쳐 줄까?
I know a basic stretching routine you can do in the morning, would you like to learn?

13 해당되다　　　　　　　　　　　　　　　　통 apply to

영화표 할인은 평일만 가능하고 주말은 해당되지 않습니다.
The ticket discounts are only applied to weekdays. It is not applied to the weekends.

 해당 appropriate

14 해소하다　　　　　　　　　　　　　　　　통 alleviate

빈부격차를 해소하기 위해 어떤 노력을 하고 있습니까?
What kind of efforts are you putting in to alleviate the gap between the rich and the poor?

 해소 alleviation

15 까다롭다   형 particular

그 회사는 입사 조건이 까다로워서 들어가기가 어렵다.

The recruiting qualifications for the company are so particular that it is very hard to get in.

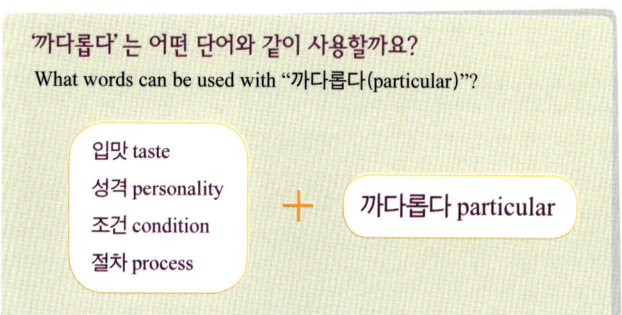

16 곁   명 on someone's side

부모는 아이들 곁에서 조용히 지켜봐 주는 것이 필요합니다.

Parents need to be on their children's side and calmly watch them.

 옆 side

17 가리다   동 choose over

음식을 가려서 먹는 것을 편식이라고 합니다.

When you are choosing over food, that is called being picky on food.

18 간편하다   형 easy

휴대가 간편한 노트북이 인기를 끌고 있어요.

Laptops that are easy to carry around are being more popular.

19 강요하다   동 force

누구든지 다른 사람에게 선택을 강요할 수는 없습니다.

Nobody can force others to choose against their wills.

20 객관적 　　　　　　　　　　　　　　　　　　　　명 objective

객관적인 자료를 제시해 주십시오.

Please provide objective data.

 주관적 subjective

21 건조하다 　　　　　　　　　　　　　　　　　　　　형 dry

히터 때문에 눈이 너무 건조해요.

My eyes are too dry because of the heater.

 건조시키다 dry

22 겉 　　　　　　　　　　　　　　　　　　　　명 out[side]

겉과 속이 다른 사람을 조심해야 한다.

You need to be cautious about people who are different in[side] and out[side].

 겉모양 appearance　　　　겉으로 outwardly

23 경조사비 　　　　　　　　　　　　　　　　명 gratuity (for family events)

경조사비 지출이 가계에 부담이 되고 있습니다.

Expenses for gratuities are burdening my household budget.

 '경조사비'에는 어떤 것이 있을까요?
What are the kinds of "경조사비(gratuity)"?
축의금(money gift for weddings),
부의금,조의금(condolence money for the funerals) 등이 있어요.

24 고유하다 　　　　　　　　　　　　　　　　　　　　형 original

우리의 고유한 전통 문화를 세계에 알리도록 합시다.

Let's introduce our original traditional culture to the world.

25 고집 — 명 stubborn

그 아이가 이렇게 고집이 센 줄 몰랐어요.

I didn't know he is this stubborn.

관련어 고집하다 be stubborn

26 도구 — 명 tool

이 도구는 어디에 쓰는 거예요?

Where will you be using the tool?

27 고통 — 명 pain

고통 받는 이웃을 위해 기도해 주세요.

Please pray for the neighbors in pain.

관련어 고통스럽다 be in pain

28 공개 — 명 open

지난 주말에 좋아하는 가수가 나온다고 해서 공개 방송에 갔습니다.

I went to the open broadcasting show last weekend to see my favorite singer.

관련어 공개하다 open to public   공개적 openly
공개 모집 open recruitment

29 공고 — 명 notice

신입 사원 모집 공고를 보고 왔습니다.

I came about the notice on hiring.

30 과장되다 — 동 exaggerate

과장된 광고에 속았던 것 같아요.

I think I was fooled by the exaggerated advertisement.

31 관점   명 perspective

사람에 따라 관점의 차이는 있을 수밖에 없다.
There must be differences in perspectives depending on people.

32 괜히   부 in vain

어차피 지각인데 괜히 뛰어왔나 봐요.
I was obviously late, I had to run in vain.

33 괴롭다   형 painful

친구가 내 마음을 몰라 주니까 괴롭다.
It is painful that my friend misunderstands my intentions.

34 교과서   명 textbook

교과서에 없는 내용도 알아야 합니다.
You should know things not in the textbook.

TOPIK에서 혼동하기 쉬운 단어

다의어 Polysemy

떨어지다

❶ separate
예) 가족과 **떨어져** 지낸 지 벌써 2년이 넘었네요.
It has been over 2 years since I've been separated from my family.

❷ get worse
예) 시력이 자꾸만 **떨어져서** 병원에 갔어요.
I went to the hospital since my eye sight is getting worse.

❸ fall
예) 지하철 선로에 **떨어진** 아이를 구한 청년의 인터뷰를 봤어요.
I saw an interview of the man who saved a child who fell down the subway track.

❹ lack
예) 이 영화는 작품의 완성도가 **떨어집니다**.
This film lacks artistic perfection.

반의어 Antonym

삼키다 swallow ↔ 뱉다 spit

예) 침을 **삼키기** 힘들 정도로 목이 아파요.
My throat is too sore even to swallow without pain.

거리에서 침을 **뱉으면** 벌금을 내야 합니다.
If you spit on the street, you need to pay the fine.

유의어 Synonym

전망 prospect ≒ 예측 prediction

예) 기후 변화에 대한 다양한 **전망**이 나오고 있습니다.
기후 변화에 대한 다양한 **예측**이 나오고 있습니다.
There are many different prospects coming out on the climate change.

DAY 28

복습해 보세요

 한국어와 영어를 알맞게 연결해 보세요.
Connect the Korean words with the English words of same meaning.

1. 아예 • • a. in vain
2. 저장하다 • • b. choose over
3. 까다롭다 • • c. perspective
4. 가리다 • • d. store
5. 겉 • • e. particular
6. 관점 • • f. at all
7. 괜히 • • g. on someone's side

 다음 빈 칸에 알맞은 단어를 〈보기〉에서 골라 쓰세요.
Pick and write the suitable word among <the options> in the blank space.

〈보기〉
a. 간편한   b. 해당되지   c. 이동하기   d. 형식에

8. 보고서를 쓸 때는 (   ) 맞게 써야 해요.
   When writing a report, you need to follow the formats.

9. 다음 장소로 (   ) 전에 인원을 점검하겠습니다.
   We'll do the headcount before we move to the next location.

10. 영화표 할인은 평일만 가능하고 주말은 (   ) 않습니다.
    The ticket discounts are only applied to weekdays. It is not applied to the weekends.

11. 휴대가 (   ) 노트북이 인기를 끌고 있어요.
    Laptops that are easy to carry around are being more popular.

정답

1.f 2.d 3.e 4.b 5.g 6.c 7.a 8.d 9.c 10.b 11.a

DAY 29

확인해 보세요

빨간 시트지로 가리고 단어의 뜻을 알면, ☐ 에 ✓ 해 보세요.
After covering up the words with red cover, please check(✓) the box (☐) when you know the meaning of the word.

☐ 01 굽다	roast	☐ 13 녹다	melt	☐ 25 당분간	for a while
☐ 02 권리	rights	☐ 14 놀랍다	amaze	☐ 26 당하다	be caught in~
☐ 03 귀가	returning home	☐ 15 놀이터	play ground	☐ 27 당황스럽다	be embarrassed
☐ 04 동쪽	east	☐ 16 곤란하다	it will be difficult to ~	☐ 28 대우	treatments
☐ 05 그늘	shade	☐ 17 굳이	obstinately	☐ 29 더구나	besides
☐ 06 기온	temperature	☐ 18 다	everything	☐ 30 어버이날	parent's day
☐ 07 까닭	reason	☐ 19 다림질하다	iron	☐ 31 데려다 주다	take someone home
☐ 08 껍질	skin	☐ 20 석식	dinner	☐ 32 도입하다	introduce
☐ 09 끼다	cloud over	☐ 21 다수	majority	☐ 33 도저히	not..at all
☐ 10 나름	depend on	☐ 22 닫다	close	☐ 34 동참하다	take part in
☐ 11 날마다	everyday	☐ 23 달하다	reach		
☐ 12 내내	throughout	☐ 24 당당하다	confident		

DAY 29

 are the words that appeared in the former tests, and you may get a higher grade if you study them together.

01 굽다 동 roast

오늘은 고기를 구워 먹읍시다.
Let's roast some meat for dinner.

02 권리 명 rights

누구에게나 사랑 받을 권리가 있다.
Everyone has rights to be loved.

03 귀가 명 returning home

딸의 귀가 시간이 점점 늦어지고 있어서 걱정입니다.
I am worried since the time of my daughter's returning home is getting late.

 귀가하다 return home

04 동쪽 명 east

해는 동쪽에서 뜬다.
The sun rises in the east.

 또 어떤 방향이 있을까요?
What other directions are there?

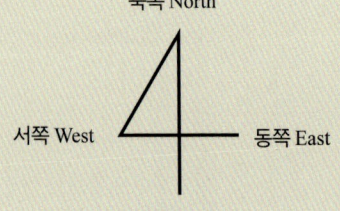

05 그늘
명 shade

나무 그늘 아래에서 도시락을 먹자.

Let's eat our lunch under the shade.

06 기온
명 temperature

낮의 기온이 30도를 넘었어요.

The daytime temperature is over 30 degree Celsius.

'기온'과 관련된 단어는 뭐가 있을까요?
What other words are related to the "기온(temperature)"?

영상(over zero), 영하(below zero), 온도(degree) 등이 있어요.

07 까닭
명 reason

연락을 하지 않은 까닭이 있을 것입니다.

There must be some reason for not contacting you.

08 껍질
명 skin

이 사과는 껍질을 먹어도 돼요.

You can eat skin off this apple.

 껍질째 skins on

09 끼다
동 cloud over

하늘에 구름이 잔뜩 끼었네요.

The sky is clouded over.

10 나름 　　　　　　　　　　　　　　　　　　　명 depend on

취직을 하고 못하고는 노력하기 나름이다.

Whether you get a job or not depends on your efforts.

관련어 나름대로 on one's own way

11 날마다 　　　　　　　　　　　　　　　　　　　부 everyday

날마다 조금씩 운동량을 늘려가야 합니다.

You should increase a bit of exercising every day.

12 내내 　　　　　　　　　　　　　　　　　　　부 throughout

여름 내내 비가 내렸어요.

It rained all throughout summer.

관련어 계속 continuous

13 녹다 　　　　　　　　　　　　　　　　　　　동 melt

더워서 아이스크림이 다 녹아버렸어요.

The ice cream melted away since it was so hot.

14 놀랍다 　　　　　　　　　　　　　　　　　　　형 amaze

그 사람이 그런 말을 하다니 정말 놀라운데요.

It is amazing that he had said such words.

15 놀이터 　　　　　　　　　　　　　　　　　　　명 play ground

놀이터에서 돌아오면 꼭 손을 씻도록 해.

When you come back from the play ground, you must wash off your hands.

16 곤란하다
형 it will be difficult to ~

더 이상 행사를 연기하는 것은 곤란합니다.

It will be difficult to delay the events any later than this.

17 굳이
부 obstinately

혼자 갈 수 있으니까 굳이 안 데려다 주셔도 돼요.

I can go by myself, so you don't have to take me home.

18 다
부 everything

다 끝내면 연락 드리겠습니다.

I'll let you know when everything is over.

19 다림질하다
동 iron

그 옷은 다림질해서 입으면 훨씬 단정해 보일 텐데….

If you iron the dress, it'll be much neater!

 다리다 iron   다리미 iron

20 석식
명 dinner

호텔비에는 보통 석식은 포함이 안 돼 있다.

Usually, dinners are not included in the room charges.

 또 어떤 종류의 식사가 있을까요?

What other kinds of meals are there?

조식(breakfast), 중식(lunch), 간식(snack), 야식(late-night snack) 등이 있어요.

21 다수 — 명 majority

다수의 국민들은 이번 선거에 참여하지 않을 것이다.
The majority of people will not be voting over this election.

관련어: 소수 minority   대다수 large majority

22 닫다 — 동 close

약국 문을 벌써 닫았네요.
The pharmacy has already closed.

23 달하다 — 동 reach

광장에 500명에 달하는 사람들이 모여들었습니다.
The number of people who gathered in the square reached up to 500.

24 당당하다 — 형 confident

큰 목소리로 당당하게 발표하면 좋겠습니다.
It would be nice to present confidently with a loud voice.

25 당분간 — 부 for a while

돈이 없어서 당분간 여행은 못 가겠다.
I can't go traveling for a while since I have no money.

26 당하다 — 동 be caught in~

갑자기 사고를 당해서 정신이 없었습니다.
I was out of my mind since I was caught in the accident so suddenly.

27 당황스럽다　　　　　　　　　　　　　　형 be embarrassed

그때 개인적인 질문을 해서 당황스러웠어요.

I was embarrassed to be asked personal questions.

당황하다 embarrass

28 대우　　　　　　　　　　　　　　명 treatments

김 대리는 대우가 더 좋은 회사로 옮기기로 결정했습니다.

Mr. Kim has decided to move to the company with better treatments.

29 더구나　　　　　　　　　　　　　　부 besides

이렇게 비가 심하게 오는데 집에 가겠다고요? 더구나 우산도 없잖아요.

Are you insisting on going home in this rain? Besides, you don't even have umbrella.

30 어버이날　　　　　　　　　　　　　　명 parent's day

어버이날이 되면 아이들이 부모님께 정성이 담긴 작은 선물을 드린다.

When the parent's day comes, children give a warm-hearted present with their hearts to their parents.

Tip

5월에는 어떤 기념일이 있을까요?

What days are there in May?

어린이날(children's day)(5.5.), 어버이날(parent's day)(5.8.), 스승의 날(teachers' day)(5.15)이 있어요.

31 데려다 주다　　　　　　　　　　　　　　동 take someone home

여자 친구를 집까지 데려다 주었다.

I took my girlfriend home.

모셔다 드리다 escort

32 도입하다 ⟨동⟩ introduce

이 차는 새로운 기술을 **도입해서** 만든 자동차입니다.

This car was made by applying the new technology.

 도입 introduction

33 도저히 ⟨부⟩ not..at all

속이 안 좋아서 지금은 **도저히** 못 먹겠어요.

I'm not feeling well; I can't eat at all now.

34 동참하다 ⟨동⟩ take part in

여러분, 불우 이웃 돕기에 **동참해** 주세요.

Everyone, please take part in the charity event.

TOPIK에서 혼동하기 쉬운 단어

다의어 Polysemy

짓다

❶ build
- 예: 은퇴하고 살 집을 **지으려고요**.
  I'm planning to build a house to live in after the retirement.

❷ have something made
- 예: 한방 병원에 가서 아이들에게 줄 한약을 **지었다**.
  I went to Oriental medicine clinic to have medicines made for my children.

❸ make
- 예: 새로운 음식을 맛 본 사람들이 이상한 표정을 **지었습니다**.
  People, who have tasted the new dish, made a weird face.

반의어 Antonym

선명하다 clear ↔ **희미하다** unclear

- 예: 결혼식을 한 지 10년이나 됐지만 아직도 그때가 **선명하게** 기억이 난다.
  It has been about 10 years since the wedding ceremony, but I still remember the time clearly.

  시간이 지날수록 추억들이 **희미해진다**.
  As the time passes, the memories become unclear.

유의어 Synonym

예정 schedule ≒ **계획** plan

- 예: 민호 씨는 내년에 결혼할 **예정**이라고 합니다.
  민호 씨는 내년에 결혼할 **계획**이라고 합니다.
  Minho is scheduled to get married next year.

DAY 29

복습해 보세요

 한국어는 영어로, 영어는 한국어로 써 보세요.
Write Korean in English, and English in Korean.

1. 굽다 _____   6. rights _____
2. 까닭 _____   7. amaze _____
3. 내내 _____   8. close _____
4. 다수 _____   9. be embarrassed _____
5. 도입하다 _____   10. treatments _____

 문장이 자연스럽도록 둘 중에서 알맞은 단어를 고르세요.
Choose the proper word that fits the sentence more naturally.

11. 더워서 아이스크림이 다 (a.녹아 / b.놓아) 버렸어요.
    The ice cream melted away since it was so hot.

12. 큰 목소리로 (a.얌전하게 / b.당당하게) 발표하면 좋겠습니다.
    It would be nice to present confidently with a loud voice.

13. 갑자기 사고를 (a.당해서 / b.생겨서) 정신이 없었습니다.
    I was out of my mind since I was caught in the accident so suddenly.

14. 광장에 500명에 (a.몰리는 / b.달하는) 사람들이 모여들었습니다.
    The number of people who gathered in the square reached up to 500.

15. 속이 안 좋아서 지금은 (a.도저히 / b.반드시) 못 먹겠어요.
    I'm not feeling well; I can't eat at all now.

정답

1.roast 2.reason 3.throughout 4.majority 5.introduce 6.권리 7.놀랍다 8.닫다 9.당황스럽다 10.대우 11.a 12.b 13.a 14.b 15.a

DAY 30

확인해 보세요

빨간 시트지로 가리고 단어의 뜻을 알면, ☐ 에 ✓ 해 보세요.
After covering up the words with red cover, please check(✓) the box (☐) when you know the meaning of the word.

☐ 01	동호회	club	☐ 13	먼지	dust	☐ 25	변환시키다	transform
☐ 02	뒤집다	turn something inside out	☐ 14	멋지다	lovely	☐ 26	부르다	call
☐ 03	따지다	calculate	☐ 15	발전소	power plant	☐ 27	분실하다	lost
☐ 04	딱딱하다	hard	☐ 16	몇몇	some	☐ 28	불리다	be called
☐ 05	뜻밖에	unexpectedly	☐ 17	무려	whopping	☐ 29	불만	dissatisfaction
☐ 06	마치다	finish	☐ 18	무리	beyond (one's ability)	☐ 30	비결	secret
☐ 07	입금	deposit	☐ 19	물다	bite	☐ 31	비다	vacant
☐ 08	막상	actually	☐ 20	문학	literature	☐ 32	기후	climate
☐ 09	망설이다	hesitate	☐ 21	물품	commodity	☐ 33	비평문	review
☐ 10	맞벌이	a couple of whom both has jobs	☐ 22	밑	under	☐ 34	빼앗다	take (something) from (somebody)
☐ 11	매력	attraction	☐ 23	바탕	based on			
☐ 12	매출	sales	☐ 24	범위	range			

DAY 30

 are the words that appeared in the former tests, and you may get a higher grade if you study them together.

01 동호회   명 club

인터넷 연극 **동호회**에 가입해서 활동하고 있다.

I am now a member of the drama club on the internet.

 how this word appears in the test

요즘 인터넷 동호회 활동이 활발해지면서 토픽에 동호회 모집 공고문 등이 자주 출제되고 있습니다.
Recently, as the people participate in the internet club activities, the recruiting notifications are frequently appearing in the TOPIK test.

동아리는 대학 안에서 학생들을 대상으로 하는 모임이라면 동호회는 나이나 성별에 크게 상관없이 같은 취미를 가진 사람들의 모임입니다.
The university circle is a group that targets the university students as a member, whereas the internet club is a group of a people gathered only based on common hobby regardless of their age or gender.

02 뒤집다   동 turn something inside out

알고 보니 셔츠를 **뒤집어** 입고 있었다.

I noticed that I was wearing my shirt inside out.

03 따지다   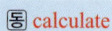 calculate

마트에서 물건을 살 때 가격을 잘 **따져** 보고 사는 편이에요.

When I buy a product in the market, I tend to calculate the cost of the product before I decide what to buy.

04 딱딱하다   형 hard

이가 아파서 **딱딱한** 음식을 먹기가 힘들어요.

I have a toothache and it is hard for me to eat hard food.

05 뜻밖에　　　　　　　　　　　　　　　　　　　　　　　　부 unexpectedly

시험을 못 본 것 같아서 걱정하고 있었는데 뜻밖에 성적이 좋았다.

I was worried I might fail the test but I unexpectedly got a very good score.

06 마치다　　　　　　　　　　　　　　　　　　　　　　　　동 finish

회사 일을 마치고 친구를 만나러 약속 장소로 향했다.

After finishing my work, I went to the place where I planned to meet my friend.

07 입금　　　　　　　　　　　　　　　　　　　　　　　　명 deposit

오늘 4시까지 이 계좌 번호로 입금 부탁드립니다.

Please make a deposit to this account number before 4 o'clock today.

> 은행에서 쓸 수 있는 단어는 뭐가 있을까요?
> What kinds of words can we use in the bank?
>
> 출금(withdraw), 송금(wire transfer), 예금(savings), 저금(savings), 적금(installment savings), 무통장입금(make a deposit without a bankbook) 등이 있어요.

08 막상　　　　　　　　　　　　　　　　　　　　　　　　부 actually

맛있어 보이길래 이 케이크를 샀는데 막상 먹어 보니 별로였어.

I bought a cake because it looked delicious, however, it was not that good when I actually tried it.

09 망설이다　　　　　　　　　　　　　　　　　　　　　　　　동 hesitate

회사를 그만둘까 말까 망설이고 있어요.

I am now hesitating whether to quit my job or not.

10 맞벌이 　　　　　　　　　　　　　　　　　　　몡 a couple of whom both has jobs

요즘은 맞벌이를 하는 부부가 많아지고 있습니다.

Lately the number of couples whom both have jobs is increasing.

 맞벌이 부부 a couple of whom both husband and wife working

 how this word appears in the test

최근 한국에서는 맞벌이 부부가 증가하고 있습니다. 육아 문제나 맞벌이 부부의 집안일 분담에 관한 주제들이 앞으로도 계속 출제될 가능성이 있습니다.

Lately the number of a couple of whom both has jobs is increasing. The topic related to childcare problem and dividing housework between husband and wife is possible to appear on the test.

11 매력 　　　　　　　　　　　　　　　　　　　　　　　　　몡 attraction

어떤 스타일의 남자에게 매력을 느껴요?

What kind of man are you attracted to?

 매력적 attractive

12 매출 　　　　　　　　　　　　　　　　　　　　　　　　　몡 sales

신상품 매출이 지난달에 비해 30% 정도 증가했다.

The number of the sales of the new product increased by 30% compared to the last month.

13 먼지 　　　　　　　　　　　　　　　　　　　　　　　　　　몡 dust

방에 먼지가 너무 많아서 청소를 하지 않을 수가 없었다.

I had no choice but to clean my room since there were too much dust.

14 멋지다 　　　　　　　　　　　　　　　　　　　　　　　　　　형 lovely

민호 씨 노래 부를 때 너무 멋지지 않아요?

Isn't Minho lovely when he sings?

 멋 style

15 발전소   명 power plant

풍력 발전소는 바람을 통해 에너지를 얻습니다.

A wind power plant generates energy from the wind.

> **Tip** '발전소'에는 어떤 것이 있을까요?
> What kind of "발전소(power plant)" is there?
>
> 풍력발전소(wind power plants),
> 수력 발전소(hydroelectric power generations),
> 화력 발전소(thermoelectric power plants),
> 원자력 발전소(nuclear power plants),
> 태양력 발전소(solar power plants) 등이 있어요.

16 몇몇   명 some

몇몇 학생들이 수업시간에 문자 메시지를 보냈다.

Some students were text messaging while they were in the class.

17 무려   부 whopping

대학교 학비가 작년에 비해서 무려 10%나 올랐다.

The university tuition grew by a whopping 10 percent.

18 무리   명 beyond (one's ability)

이틀이나 잠을 자지 않고 공부하는 건 무리라고 생각해.

I think studying for two days without sleeping is beyond one's ability.

 무리하게 by force   무리하다 V+ to hard

19 물다   동 bite

개가 내 다리를 물었어요.

A dog bit me on the leg.

20 문학　　　　　　　　　　　　　　　　　　　　　명 literature

고등학생 때는 문학 작품을 자주 읽었는데 요즘에는 거의 안 읽어요.

When I was a high school student I often read many literary works, however, now I rarely read them.

 소설 novel　　　　　시 poetry
수필 essay

21 물품　　　　　　　　　　　　　　　　　　　　　명 commodity

집을 청소하는 데 필요한 물품을 좀 사야겠다.

I should get some commodities that are needed when cleaning the house.

22 밑　　　　　　　　　　　　　　　　　　　　　　명 under

가방을 의자 밑에 두세요.

Please leave your bag under the chair.

23 바탕　　　　　　　　　　　　　　　　　　　　　명 based on

이 영화는 실제 있었던 이야기를 바탕으로 만든 거래요.

This movie was directed based on a true story.

24 범위　　　　　　　　　　　　　　　　　　　　　명 range

선생님께서 이번 시험 범위를 알려 주셨다.

Teacher told us the range of what the following test covers.

25 변환시키다　　　　　　　　　　　　　　　　　　동 transform

바람의 힘을 전기 에너지로 변환시키는 게 가능해졌다.

Now it has been possible for us to transform the wind power to electric energy.

변환하다 transform

26 부르다 — 동 call

친구를 불렀는데 듣지 못하고 가 버렸다.

I called my friend, but she did not hear my voice and just kept on going.

27 분실하다 — 동 lost

지하철에서 중요한 물건을 분실했다.

I lost my valuables while I was in the subway.

관련어 분실 lost   분실물 lost property

28 불리다 — 동 be called

그 사람은 어렸을 때부터 천재라고 불렸다.

He was called a genius from the time when he was young.

29 불만 — 명 dissatisfaction

회사의 정책에 대해 불만이 있는 사람들이 많다.

There are many people who have dissatisfaction with the company's policies.

관련어 불만 사항 dissatisfaction comments

30 비결 — 명 secret

그렇게 빠른 시간 안에 성공하게 된 비결을 알려 주세요.

Please tell me the secret that allowed you to succeed in such a short period of time.

31 비다 — 동 vacant

점심 시간이라 사무실이 텅 비었다.

The office was empty since it was lunch hours.

32 기후  climate

최근 기후 변화 때문에 힘들어하는 사람들이 많다.

Many people are going through a hard time because of the recent climate change.

'기후'의 종류는 뭐가 있을까요?

What different kinds of "기후(climate)" do we have?

열대 기후(tropical climate), 온대 기후(warm temperate climate), 건조 기후(an arid climate), 한대 기후(polar climate), 냉대 기후(cold temperate climate)가 있어요.

33 비평문  review

나는 영화 비평문을 써서 잡지에 실을 것이다.

I am planning to write a review and publish it in the magazine.

 비평가 critics

34 빼앗다   통 take (something) from (somebody)

동생한테서 장난감을 빼앗았더니 동생이 울고 말았다.

When I took the toy from my sister, she cried.

 뺏다 take away

TOPIK에서 혼동하기 쉬운 단어

다의어 Polysemy

빠지다

❶ fall (into a deep sleep)

예 동생을 깨웠지만 깊은 잠에 **빠져서** 일어나지 않았다.
I tried to wake my sister up, but she fell into a deep sleep and would not get up.

❷ go crooked

예 친구를 잘못 만나면 나쁜 길에 **빠질** 수 있어요.
You can go crooked if you get along with a wrong friend.

❸ be addicted to (computer game)

예 컴퓨터 게임에 **빠져서** 아무것도 하려고 하지 않아요.
He is addicted to computer games so he does not want to do anything else.

반의어 Antonym

흐릿하다 vague ↔ 뚜렷하다 clear

예 할머니는 나이가 들어 모든 것이 **흐릿하다고** 하셨다.
Grandmothers are old and have a vague sight.

아주 어릴 때 일이지만 그 일은 **뚜렷하게** 기억한다.
Even though it was something that happened when I was young I clearly remember it.

유의어 Synonym

의견 opinion ≒ 생각 thoughts

예 사람마다 **의견**이 다른 것은 당연합니다.
사람마다 **생각**이 다른 것은 당연합니다.
It is natural for each person to home a different opinion.

DAY 30 ★

복습해 보세요

한국어와 영어를 알맞게 연결해 보세요.
Connect the Korean words with the English words of same meaning.

1. 따지다 • • a. range
2. 막상 • • b. calculate
3. 맞벌이 • • c. bite
4. 무려 • • d. actually
5. 물다 • • e. vacant
6. 범위 • • f. whopping
7. 비다 • • g. have a dual income

다음 빈 칸에 알맞은 단어를 〈보기〉에서 골라 쓰세요.
Pick and write the suitable word among <the options> in the blank space.

〈보기〉
a. 비결을   b. 망설이고   c. 불렸다   d. 뜻밖에

8. 회사를 그만둘까 말까 (   ) 있어요.
   I am now hesitating whether to quit my job or not.

9. 시험을 못 본 것 같아서 걱정하고 있었는데 (   ) 성적이 좋았다.
   I was worried I might fail the test but I unexpectedly got a very good score.

10. 그 사람은 어렸을 때부터 천재라고 (   ).
    He was called a genius from the time when he was young.

11. 그렇게 빠른 시간 안에 성공하게 된 (   ) 알려 주세요.
    Please tell me the secret that allowed you to succeed in such a short period of time.

정답

1.b 2.d 3.g 4.f 5.c 6.a 7.e 8.b 9.d 10.c 11.a

주간 복습 day 26 – day 30

아래 단어를 보고 빈 칸에 뜻을 적어 보세요. 그리고 점선대로 접어서 적은 뜻이 맞는지 확인해 보세요. (만일 틀렸다면 뒷면의 단어 앞 □ 에 ✓ 하세요.)

Write down the meaning of the given word in the blank. Also, fold the page along a dotted line and check whether you got it right or wrong. (If you got it wrong check(✓) the box(□) in front of the word in next page.)

▼접는선

단어	뜻
소화	
시급하다	
여부	
욕심	
넘어지다	
늘	
접하다	
중요성	
차지하다	
택배	
아예	
까다롭다	
가리다	
관점	
괜히	
굽다	
까닭	
권리	
당황스럽다	
대우	
따지다	
막상	
맞벌이	
무려	
범위	

서울의 야경

주간 복습 day 26 – day 30

빈 칸에 한국어 단어를 3번 적고 다시 외워 봅시다.
Write down the Korean word 3 times in the blank and try to memorize it again.

◀ 접는선

뜻	단어		
☐ digest	소화		
☐ urgent	시급하다		
☐ whether	여부		
☐ greed	욕심		
☐ fall	넘어지다		
☐ always	늘		
☐ access	접하다		
☐ importance	중요성		
☐ occupy	차지하다		
☐ parcel service	택배		
☐ at all	아예		
☐ particular	까다롭다		
☐ choose over	가리다		
☐ perspective	관점		
☐ in vain	괜히		
☐ roast	굽다		
☐ reason	까닭		
☐ rights	권리		
☐ be embarrassed	당황스럽다		
☐ treatments	대우		
☐ calculate	따지다		
☐ actually	막상		
☐ have a dual income	맞벌이		
☐ whopping	무려		
☐ range	범위		

부록 Appendix

01 사동사
a causative verbs

02 피동사
a passive verbs

03 속담 및 관용 표현
proverbs, idomatic expressions

01 사동사 a causative verbs

끓이다 be boiled　`기본형` 끓다 boil
커피를 마시려고 물을 끓였어요.
I boiled water to drink coffee.

높이다 increase　`기본형` 높다 high
가격을 높이면 물건 판매량이 줄어들 거예요.
If you increase the price, the product will sell less.

먹이다 feed　`기본형` 먹다 eat
기침을 심하게 하면 아이에게 이 약을 먹이세요.
When your kid severely coughs, feed him this medicine.

보이다 show　`기본형` 보다 see
신분증을 보여야 이 건물로 들어갈 수 있습니다.
You should show your identification to enter the building.

붙이다 attach　`기본형` 붙다 stick
신청서에 꼭 사진을 붙여 주세요.
Please attach a photograph on the application form.

속이다 trick　`기본형` 속다 be fooled
다른 사람을 자주 속이는 사람과는 친구가 되고 싶지 않아요.
I do not want to be friends with the person who tricks others.

죽이다 kill　`기본형` 죽다 die
저는 벌레를 무서워해서 죽이지 못해요.
I cannot kill bugs because I get scared of them.

줄이다 shorten　`기본형` 줄다 decrease
바지가 너무 길어서 길이를 좀 줄여야겠어요.
The pants are too long so it should be shortened.

끝내다 finish　`기본형` 끝나다 be finished
이 일을 끝내면 좀 쉬고 싶어요.
I want to take a break after this is finished.

넓히다 widen　`기본형` 넓다 broad
우리 집이 좁아서 집을 넓히는 공사를 했어요.
Our house was small, so we built an extention to it.

눕히다 lay　`기본형` 눕다 lie
잠이 든 아이를 침대에 눕혔어요.
I laid the sleeping baby on the bed.

맞히다 hit　`기본형` 맞다 be hit
아이에게 주사를 맞히기는 쉽지가 않네요.
It is not easy to make the children get a shot.

앉히다 have one seated　`기본형` 앉다 sit
버스가 곧 출발하니까 아이를 자리에 앉혀 주세요.
The bus will depart soon, so please have your child seated.

읽히다 have one read	기본형	읽다 read	선생님이 상희 씨에게 책을 읽혔어요. Teacher has Sang-hee read his book.
입히다 have one wear	기본형	입다 wear	이 옷이 잘 어울릴 것 같은데 아이에게 한번 입혀 보세요. This outfit seems to look good on your child, have him try this.
날리다 fly	기본형	날다 fly	종이 비행기를 만들어서 창 밖으로 날렸어요. I made an airplane out of paper and had it fly outside the window.
돌리다 operate	기본형	돌다 operate	저는 세탁기를 돌릴 테니까 혜경 씨는 청소를 해 주세요. I will do the laundry, Hea-Kyung please clean the apartment.
살리다 save	기본형	살다 live	의사가 물에 빠진 아이를 살렸어요. The doctor saved the drowning child.
알리다 notice	기본형	알다 know	새로운 소식이 있으면 꼭 저에게 알려 주세요. If you have any new information, please tell me what it is.
울리다 make one cry	기본형	울다 cry	저는 어렸을 때 동생을 자주 울렸어요. When I was young, I often made my younger brother cry.
감기다 wash	기본형	감다 wash	미용실에 가면 미용사가 제 머리를 감겨 줘서 참 편해요. When I visit hair salon, it is really comfortable since the hair dresser washes my hair.
남기다 leave (to remain)	기본형	남다 leave	밥을 남기지 말고 다 드세요. Do not leave any food on your plate and eat all of them.
맡기다 leave (to go)	기본형	맡다 take	그 옷은 세탁기에 빨지 말고 세탁소에 맡겨야 해요. You should take those clothes to the laundry instead of washing them yourself.
벗기다 take one's clothes off	기본형	벗다 take off	아이가 비를 맞고 집에 와서 젖은 옷을 벗겨 줬어요. My kid came back home soaked in rain, so I took his clothes off.
숨기다 hide	기본형	숨다 hide	그 사람 표정을 보니까 뭔가 숨기는 것이 있는 것 같아요. The look on his face says that he is hiding something.
신기다 have one wear	기본형	신다 wear	지금 나가야 하니까 얼른 아이에게 신발을 신겨 주세요. We have to go out now, so please have the child wear his shoes.

부록

단어	뜻	기본형	기본형 뜻	예문
씻기다	wash	기본형	씻다 wash	강아지가 더러워서 좀 씻겨야겠어요. You should wash your dog.
웃기다	make one laugh	기본형	웃다 laugh	전 재미있는 말로 다른 사람들을 웃기는 것을 좋아해요. I like to make other people laugh with funny stories.
깨우다	wake one up	기본형	깨다 wake up	시간이 없으니까 빨리 상희 씨를 깨우세요. There's no time, so wake Sang-hee up.
비우다	be emptied	기본형	비다 empty	사무실 쓰레기통을 누가 비웠지요? Who emptied the trashcan in the office?
세우다	be stopped	기본형	서다 stop	친구 집 앞에 차를 세우고 기다렸어요. I stopped the car in front of my friend's house and waited.
씌우다	have one wear	기본형	쓰다 wear	밖이 추우니까 아이에게 모자를 씌워 주세요. It is cold outside so have your kid wear a cap.
재우다	have one sleep	기본형	자다 sleep	아기를 재워야하니 잠시만 조용히 해 주세요. Please be silent since I need to have the baby asleep.
태우다	have one ride	기본형	타다 ride	승준 씨는 여자 친구를 자전거에 태우고 소풍을 갔어요. Seung-Jun went on a picnic with his girlfriend, riding on the back of his bike.

02 피동사 a passive verbs

놓이다 be placed	기본형	놓다 place	저기 테이블 위에 놓여 있는 물건이 뭐예요? What is that placed on the table?
바뀌다 be changed	기본형	바꾸다 change	혜경 씨가 이사를 가서 주소가 바뀌었어요. Hea-Kyung moved and her address changed.
보이다 be seen	기본형	보다 see	창문을 열면 바다가 보이는 집에 살고 싶어요. I want to live in the house where I can see the ocean.
쌓이다 be piled	기본형	쌓다 pile	한동안 청소를 안 했더니 집에 먼지가 쌓여 있네요. There is a pile of dust in the house since I have not cleaned the place for a while.
쓰이다 be written	기본형	쓰다 write	책에 이름이 쓰여 있으니까 주인을 찾을 수 있을 거예요. You may find the owner of the book since the name is written on it.
잠기다 be locked	기본형	잠그다 lock	가게 문이 잠겨 있는 것을 보니 아무도 없나 봐요. There must be no one in the store since the door is locked.
닫히다 be closed	기본형	닫다 close	바람 때문에 문이 저절로 닫혔어요. The door closed by itself because of the wind.
막히다 be blocked	기본형	막다 block	출퇴근 시간에는 길이 많이 막혀요. The traffic jam is serious every morning and evening when people are going and coming back from work.
먹히다 be eaten	기본형	먹다 eat	쥐가 고양이에게 먹혔어요. The rat was eaten by the cat.
밟히다 be stepped	기본형	밟다 step	지하철에 사람이 많아서 계속 발을 밟혔어요. Too many people were in the subway and my foot was constantly stepped on.
업히다 carry somebody or something on one's back	기본형	업다 ride on somebody's back	어젯밤에 혜경 씨는 취해서 친구에게 업혀서 집에 왔어요. Last night Hea-Kyung was so drunk that she was carried here on her friend's back.
읽히다 be read	기본형	읽다 read	책 내용이 어려워서 잘 읽히지 않네요. The book's content is too challenging, so it is hard to read.
잡히다 be caught	기본형	잡다 catch	지난주에 일어난 살인사건의 용의자가 잡혔대요. The suspect of the homicide was caught last week.

부록

걸리다	be hanged	기본형	걸다 hang	우리 집에는 가족 사진이 걸려 있어요. There is a family picture hanging on our house wall.
날리다	fly	기본형	날다 fly	봄에는 바람이 불면 꽃잎이 날려서 참 예뻐요. It is beautiful in the spring to see the petals fly in the wind.
들리다	hear	기본형	듣다 hear	소리가 잘 안 들리는데 소리를 좀 크게 해 주세요. I cannot hear the sound, so can you please turn up the volume?
물리다	be bitten	기본형	물다 bite	여름철에 창문을 열고 자면 모기에게 많이 물려요. If you let your window open in the summer while you are sleeping, you will get many bites from mosquitoes.
열리다	be opened	기본형	열다 open	집에 와 보니 문이 열려 있어서 깜짝 놀랐어요. I was shocked to see my window being opened when I came back from work.
팔리다	be sold	기본형	팔다 sell	이 옷이 요즘 잘 팔리는 옷이에요. These clothes are the ones that are being sold well these days.
풀리다	be solved	기본형	풀다 solve	이 수학 문제는 너무 어려워서 잘 풀리지 않네요. This math problem is too challenging to be solved.
끊기다	stopped operating	기본형	끊다 disconnect	너무 늦어서 마지막 지하철마저 끊겼어요. I was too late that the last subway already left.
담기다	be filled with	기본형	담다 put something in	식탁 위에 있는 소금이 담긴 통을 갖다 주세요. Can you please take the jar filled with salt on the kitchen table and bring it to me?
빼앗기다	be robbed	기본형	빼앗다 rob	집에 오는 길에 나쁜 사람에게 돈을 빼앗겼어요. While I was coming back home, I had a bad man rob me.
안기다	be in one's arm	기본형	안다 hug	아이가 엄마에게 안겨서 자고 있는 모습이 참 귀엽네요. The child sleeping in his mother's arms is just too cute.
쫓기다	be chased	기본형	쫓다 chase	그 도둑은 경찰에게 쫓기다가 넘어졌다. The thief tripped while he was chased by the police.

03 속담 및 관용표현 proverbs, idomatic expressions

- **가는 날이 장날**

  As luck would have it

  This expression is used when you end up with something unexpected while you were doing something.

- **가는 말이 고와야 오는 말이 곱다**

  What goes around comes around

  It means that in order to hear good things from the counterpart, you should tell him good things first.

- **갈수록 태산이다**

  Out of the frying pan into the fire

  You use this expression when you face work that becomes harder and harder as it proceeds.

- **겉 다르고 속 다르다**

  Appearances are deceptive

  It means that the expression that is revealed outside is totally different from what is in one's mind.

- **계란으로 바위 치기**

  Beat one's head against the wall

  This expression is used when you are too weak so that you will never win no matter how hard you try.

- **공든 탑이 무너지랴**

  A man's labors will be crowned with success

  It means that the work with paintaking care will always create positive results.

- **그림의 떡**

  Pie in the sky

  It describes an object that one will never get and almost impossible to reach.

- **긁어 부스럼 만들기**

  Let sleeping dog lie

  This expression is used when someone is unecessarily involed with the work and even make it worse than before.

- **꿩 대신 닭**

  Something is better than nothing

  This is used when something is needed but you don't have it, you use different but similar thing instead that is usually not good enough than the original thing that you needed in the first place.

- **남의 떡이 더 커 보인다**

  The grass is greener on the other side of the fence

  You use this expression when the thing that other people have looks better than your's.

- **도토리 키 재기**

  A miss is as good as a mile

  This exepression is used when two people argue that he is better than the other, but actually both of them has no big of a difference.

- **돌다리도 두둘겨 보고 건너라**

  Look before you leap

  It means that you should be careful of doing whatever you do.

■ 등잔 밑이 어둡다

A beacon does not shine on its own base

It means that it is rather hard for you to know what happens close to you than what happens far from you.

■ 땅 짚고 헤엄치기

Swimming while touching the ground.
= it's a piece of cake

It means that the thing that you are trying to do is easy.

■ 말 속에 뼈가 있다

Many a true word is spoken in jest

You use this expression when you hear a normal expression but it has a sarcasm behind the apparent meaning.

■ 모르는 게 약

Nothing hurts like the truth

It means that it may be better for you to not know about it since knowing will only make you worse.

■ 믿는 도끼에 발등 찍힌다

(get) Stabbed in the back

You use this expression when the work that you believed will turn out fine but not or you were betrayed by the person you believed in.

■ 밑 빠진 독에 물 붓기

All that is put in a riven dish is lost

This expression is used when there is no positive outcome of what you are doing or you cannot do anything about it.

■ 배보다 배꼽이 크다

It is the tail wagging the dog

This is used when the basic thing needs more attention or cost that is spent while doing the main task.

■ 보기 좋은 떡이 먹기에도 좋다

Names and natures do often agree

It means that there is a moment when a good appearance is also important.

■ 산 넘어 산

Out of the frying pan into the fire

It is an expression that used when after getting out of a bad situation you end up in the worse one.

■ 쇠귀(소귀)에 경 읽기

Talking to the wall.

This expression is used when the person that you are teaching does not understand what you are saying no matter how many times you repeat what you tell him.

- **수박 겉 핥기**

  Scratching the surface

  This expression is used when someone does a lazy work and does not do the important thing that he should do.

- **시간은 금**

  Time is gold

  It means that the time is invaluable as gold is.

- **시간이 약**

  Time heals all wounds

  It means that even though you have gone through a devastating thing or heart breaking thing, time will always make the pain heal.

- **식은 죽 먹기**

  Something is a breeze = it's a piece of cake

  It means that the thing that you are trying to do is easy.

- **실패는 성공의 어머니**

  Failure is but a stepping stone to success

  This means that in order to succeed in the longrun, it is necessary for you to fail first, and you should not be afraid of failing.

- **싼 게 비지떡**

  You get what you pay for

  It means that the cheap product is bad.

- **아는 길도 물어서 가라**

  Look before you leap

  It means that you should be cautious even while you are doing the thing that you are familiar with.

- **아니 땐 굴뚝에 연기 날까**

  Where there's smoke, there's fire

  It means that when there is a result, there must be a cause that made that result.

- **앓던 이가 빠진 것 같다**

  Feel sudden relief

  This expression is used when someone finally solved a big problem that had been bothering him greatly

- **어깨가 무겁다**

  Feeling a big burden on my shoulders

  This is an expression that describes the status that is highly stressed with heavy responsibility.

- **열번 찍어 안 넘어가는 나무 없다**

  Little strokes fell great oaks

  This means that even the hardest work can be done when you constantly try to do it.

- **오르지 못할 나무는 쳐다 보지 마라**

  Don't bite off more than you can chew

  It means that you should never try to do the thing that is hard for you to do with your ability.

- **윗물이 맑아야 아랫물이 맑다**

  The fish always stinks from the head downwards

  This means that the elder should act well, so that the young can learn from that and do well in the future.

- **입에 쓴 약이 병에는 좋다**

  A good medicine tastes bitter

  This means that even though the course of doing a certain work can be hard, the result will pay off after you endure the pain and accomplish it.

- **자식 이기는 부모 없다**

  There's no parent who win their children.
  = No parent win their children

  This means that when the child seriously decides to do certain thing, no parents can prevent them from doing that.

- **천 리 길도 한 걸음부터**

  Step by step one goes a long way

  It means that no matter how fast you want to finish a certain job, you should never be hasty but be patient by slowly doing the proper things step by step starting from the beginning.

- **티끌 모아 태산**

  Many a little makes a miracle

  This means that you can get a big thing in the long run after gathering the smallest things.

- **하늘의 별 따기**

  Catching a star in the sky

  It is an expression that shows that the goal that you are trying to achieve is beyond your ability so that the possibility that you will succeed is low.

- **원숭이도 나무에서 떨어진다**

  Even homer sometimes nods

  It means that even an expert can sometimes make a mistake in the field where he specialize.

단어장

self-vocabulary booklet
day 01 - day 30

Now, cheer up until you reach the mid-level of TOPIK!

DAY 01 | 일일 단어 리스트

- [ ] 01 필요하다 — need
- [ ] 02 방법 — method
- [ ] 03 이용하다 — use, take
- [ ] 04 생각하다 — think
- [ ] 05 관심 — attention
- [ ] 06 가능하다 — be possible
- [ ] 07 결과 — result
- [ ] 08 늘다 — increase
- [ ] 09 바꾸다 — exchange
- [ ] 10 노력하다 — make an effort
- [ ] 11 느끼다 — feel
- [ ] 12 경우 — case
- [ ] 13 상품 — goods
- [ ] 14 생기다 — come up
- [ ] 15 도움 — help
- [ ] 16 환경 — environment
- [ ] 17 내용 — content
- [ ] 18 상황 — situation
- [ ] 19 바로잡다 — correct
- [ ] 20 사회 — society
- [ ] 21 생활 — living
- [ ] 22 이상하다 — strange
- [ ] 23 경험 — experience
- [ ] 24 다양하다 — various, different kinds of
- [ ] 25 최근 — recently
- [ ] 26 선택하다 — choose, select, decide
- [ ] 27 효과 — effect
- [ ] 28 문제 — problem
- [ ] 29 자신 — oneself
- [ ] 30 찾다 — find
- [ ] 31 관계 — relationship
- [ ] 32 기간 — period
- [ ] 33 전문가 — expert

DAY 02 | 일일 단어 리스트

- [ ] 01 행사 — event
- [ ] 02 대상 — target
- [ ] 03 설명하다 — explain
- [ ] 04 연구 — research
- [ ] 05 직접 — in person, directly
- [ ] 06 대부분 — most (of)
- [ ] 07 물건 — thing, object
- [ ] 08 안내하다 — show
- [ ] 09 직장 — job
- [ ] 10 참여하다 — participate
- [ ] 11 시작하다 — start
- [ ] 12 변화 — change
- [ ] 13 편하다 — comfortable
- [ ] 14 성공하다 — succeed
- [ ] 15 영향 — influence
- [ ] 16 걱정하다 — worry about
- [ ] 17 교통 — traffic
- [ ] 18 모으다 — save
- [ ] 19 세계 — world
- [ ] 20 신청 — apply
- [ ] 21 오히려 — rather
- [ ] 22 지역 — area
- [ ] 23 판매하다 — sell
- [ ] 24 계속 — continue
- [ ] 25 버리다 — throw away
- [ ] 26 경력 — experience
- [ ] 27 계획 — plan
- [ ] 28 끝나다 — finish
- [ ] 29 어리다 — young
- [ ] 30 직원 — employee
- [ ] 31 관리 — management
- [ ] 32 사실 — truth
- [ ] 33 불편하다 — inconvenient

DAY 03 | 일일 단어 리스트

- ☐ 01 소비 — consumption
- ☐ 02 실제로 — actually
- ☐ 03 충분하다 — plenty of, be enough
- ☐ 04 표현하다 — express
- ☐ 05 해결하다 — solve
- ☐ 06 개인 — individual, personal
- ☐ 07 경제 — economy
- ☐ 08 늦다 — be late
- ☐ 09 따라하다 — follow
- ☐ 10 인기 — popularity
- ☐ 11 장단점 — strong and weak points
- ☐ 12 지키다 — keep
- ☐ 13 통하다 — through
- ☐ 14 참가하다 — participate in
- ☐ 15 문화 — culture
- ☐ 16 받다 — receive
- ☐ 17 발생 — occurrence
- ☐ 18 심하다 — severe
- ☐ 19 장소 — place
- ☐ 20 제대로 — properly
- ☐ 21 개발하다 — develop
- ☐ 22 구입하다 — purchase
- ☐ 23 기분 — mood
- ☐ 24 기억 — memory
- ☐ 25 기회 — chance
- ☐ 26 무료 — free of charge
- ☐ 27 상대방 — counterpart
- ☐ 28 색 — color
- ☐ 29 알려주다 — notice
- ☐ 30 포함되다 — be included
- ☐ 31 힘 — power
- ☐ 32 대회 — competition
- ☐ 33 발표 — presentation

DAY 04 | 일일 단어 리스트

- ☐ 01 소개하다 — introduce
- ☐ 02 역할 — role, part
- ☐ 03 일반적 — in general
- ☐ 04 입장 — entrance
- ☐ 05 자료 — data
- ☐ 06 제품 — product
- ☐ 07 주변 — surroundings
- ☐ 08 주의 사항 — matters that require attention
- ☐ 09 피해 — be harmed
- ☐ 10 부탁 — request
- ☐ 11 고르다 — pick
- ☐ 12 돌아가다 — go back (to)
- ☐ 13 들어오다 — come
- ☐ 14 사고 — accident
- ☐ 15 소리 — sound
- ☐ 16 연락하다 — contact
- ☐ 17 모습 — appearance
- ☐ 18 오래되다 — old
- ☐ 19 원인 — reason
- ☐ 20 인간 — man, human
- ☐ 21 잃다 — lose
- ☐ 22 자리 — seat
- ☐ 23 조사하다 — investigate
- ☐ 24 주민 — (local) resident
- ☐ 25 차이 — difference
- ☐ 26 책임 — responsibility
- ☐ 27 행동하다 — act
- ☐ 28 확인하다 — check
- ☐ 29 광고 — advertisement
- ☐ 30 급하다 — urgent
- ☐ 31 실시하다 — practice
- ☐ 32 작품 — work
- ☐ 33 적극적 — active

DAY 05 | 일일 단어 리스트

- [ ] 01 정보 — information
- [ ] 02 할인되다 — discount
- [ ] 03 활용하다 — apply, use
- [ ] 04 꿈 — dream
- [ ] 05 노인 — older people
- [ ] 06 반면 — on the other hand
- [ ] 07 자기 — self
- [ ] 08 키우다 — raise
- [ ] 09 해외 — abroad
- [ ] 10 각종 — of every kind
- [ ] 11 고민 — worry
- [ ] 12 글 — (a piece of) writing
- [ ] 13 따르다 — follow
- [ ] 14 모집 — recruitment
- [ ] 15 믿다 — trust
- [ ] 16 부족하다 — be short of
- [ ] 17 상태 — status, condition
- [ ] 18 시민 — citizen
- [ ] 19 공연 — performance
- [ ] 20 여성 — female
- [ ] 21 역사 — history
- [ ] 22 예전 — back in the days
- [ ] 23 원하다 — desire
- [ ] 24 유지하다 — maintain
- [ ] 25 이해하다 — understand
- [ ] 26 정리하다 — organize
- [ ] 27 방식 — method
- [ ] 28 감정 — emotion
- [ ] 29 과학 — science
- [ ] 30 나타나다 — appear
- [ ] 31 따로 — apart
- [ ] 32 밝히다 — disclose
- [ ] 33 벌써 — already

DAY 06 | 일일 단어 리스트

- [ ] 01 삶 — life
- [ ] 02 성격 — characteristic
- [ ] 03 습관 — habit
- [ ] 04 업무 — work
- [ ] 05 위험하다 — dangerous
- [ ] 06 자녀 — children
- [ ] 07 자연스럽다 — it is natural to
- [ ] 08 치료하다 — cure
- [ ] 09 함께 — together
- [ ] 10 혼자 — alone
- [ ] 11 등등 — etc. (et cetera), ~and so on
- [ ] 12 국내 — domestic
- [ ] 13 기능 — function
- [ ] 14 꾸준히 — constantly
- [ ] 15 맛 — taste
- [ ] 16 신경 — nerve
- [ ] 17 심각하다 — serious
- [ ] 18 인정하다 — appreciate (one's ability)
- [ ] 19 진행되다 — in progress
- [ ] 20 하루 — a day
- [ ] 21 행복하다 — be happy
- [ ] 22 적당하다 — proper
- [ ] 23 정부 — administration, government
- [ ] 24 내리다 — decrease
- [ ] 25 동료 — coworker
- [ ] 26 떠나다 — leave
- [ ] 27 그만두다 — quit
- [ ] 28 무조건 — unconditionally
- [ ] 29 물론 — as well as
- [ ] 30 바라다 — wish
- [ ] 31 발명되다 — be invented
- [ ] 32 방문 — visit
- [ ] 33 방송 — broadcasting

DAY 07 | 일일 단어 리스트

- 01 붙다 — stick
- 02 비슷하다 — be similar to
- 03 상담하다 — consult
- 04 시설 — facility
- 05 실수 — mistake
- 06 안전하다 — be safe
- 07 없애다 — get rid of
- 08 자격 — qualification
- 09 작가 — writer
- 10 전하다 — send
- 11 제공하다 — provide
- 12 제시하다 — suggest
- 13 조건 — condition
- 14 조심하다 — be careful
- 15 즐기다 — enjoy
- 16 증가하다 — increase
- 17 취업하다 — get a job
- 18 팔다 — sell
- 19 프로그램 — program
- 20 피하다 — avoid
- 21 넘다 — after
- 22 발길 — coming and going
- 23 가득하다 — be filled with
- 24 가지다(=갖다) — have
- 25 거의 — almost
- 26 결국 — finally
- 27 공공장소 — public place
- 28 관광객 — tourist
- 29 기대하다 — expect
- 30 대신하다 — replace, instead (of)
- 31 대중교통 — public transportation
- 32 미리 — in advance
- 33 반응 — reaction

DAY 08 | 일일 단어 리스트

- 01 봉사하다 — volunteer
- 02 서비스 — service
- 03 스트레스 — stress
- 04 시청 — watch
- 05 신문 — newspaper
- 06 움직이다 — move
- 07 가격 — price
- 08 전통 — tradition
- 09 젊다 — young
- 10 점 — point
- 11 정확하다 — precise
- 12 주문하다 — order
- 13 지나치다 — excessively
- 14 지원하다 — apply for
- 15 청소년 — teenager
- 16 추억 — memory
- 17 현재 — present, now
- 18 활동하다 — be active
- 19 희망하다 — look forward to
- 20 관람하다 — watch
- 21 기준 — standard
- 22 감상하다 — appreciate
- 23 경쟁 — competition
- 24 공기 — air
- 25 담다 — contain
- 26 도시 — city
- 27 뛰다 — run
- 28 분위기 — atmosphere
- 29 빛 — light
- 30 생명 — life
- 31 세탁하다 — wash
- 32 안정 — stability
- 33 어울리다 — go with

DAY 09 | 일일 단어 리스트

- 01 연장하다 — extend
- 02 옮기다 — move
- 03 유행하다 — be in fashion
- 04 일부 — part, portion, section
- 05 전시회 — exhibition
- 06 처리하다 — handle
- 07 처음 — for the first time
- 08 선배 — senior alumnus
- 09 고생 — (have) a hard time + ~ing
- 10 구매하다 — purchase
- 11 기업 — firm
- 12 남 — other people
- 13 다치다 — injured
- 14 마침 — just (about to)
- 15 물질 — material
- 16 미래 — future
- 17 미술 — art
- 18 별로 — particularly
- 19 분석하다 — analyze
- 20 비교하다 — compare
- 21 사무실 — office
- 22 살펴보다 — look around
- 23 어른 — an adult
- 24 예방하다 — prevent
- 25 음식 — food
- 26 의미 — (the) meaning
- 27 일시적 — temporary
- 28 일으키다 — raise
- 29 자신감 — self-esteem
- 30 재산 — asset, property
- 31 정신 — mind
- 32 얻다 — get, gain
- 33 제도 — policy

DAY 10 | 일일 단어 리스트

- 01 제출하다 — submit
- 02 지속되다 — continue
- 03 집중하다 — concentrate (on)
- 04 체험하다 — experience
- 05 최선 — do one's best
- 06 평소 — usual
- 07 학습하다 — learn
- 08 고객 — customer
- 09 고려하다 — consider
- 10 고장나다 — break
- 11 교환 — exchange
- 12 그냥 — just
- 13 기술 — technology
- 14 나중에 — afterward
- 15 드러내다 — reveal
- 16 디자인 — design
- 17 마찬가지 — as ~ as
- 18 초대하다 — invite
- 19 목표 — goal
- 20 방해하다 — bother
- 21 보내다 — send
- 22 빌리다 — borrow
- 23 설문조사 — survey
- 24 사건 — incident, case
- 25 실패하다 — fail
- 26 실험 — experiment
- 27 아무리 — no matter
- 28 아이디어 — idea
- 29 안타깝다 — feel sorry for
- 30 알아보다 — recognize
- 31 연결되다 — be connected
- 32 예 — example
- 33 변하다 — change

DAY 11 | 일일 단어 리스트

- 01 운전 — drive
- 02 이미 — already
- 03 조용하다 — be quite
- 04 주로 — mainly
- 05 주차장 — parking lot
- 06 직업 — occupation
- 07 특징 — (special) feature
- 08 평균 — average
- 09 끌다 — draw (attention)
- 10 포기하다 — give up
- 11 현상 — phenomenon
- 12 현실 — reality
- 13 현장 — scene
- 14 홈페이지 — homepage
- 15 환영하다 — welcome
- 16 양 — quantity
- 17 걸리다 — catch
- 18 경기 — game
- 19 기타 — other, further
- 20 긴장 — tension
- 21 깊다 — deep
- 22 낭비하다 — waste
- 23 낮잠 — nap
- 24 농사 — farming
- 25 능력 — ability
- 26 단 — only
- 27 안심하다 — calm down
- 28 대형 — big
- 29 대화 — conversation
- 30 도로 — (take it) back
- 31 떠오르다 — come up
- 32 만족하다 — satisfy
- 33 멀리하다 — keep away from

DAY 12 | 일일 단어 리스트

- 01 목적 — goal
- 02 문의 — inquire
- 03 및 — and
- 04 바라보다 — look
- 05 발견하다 — find out
- 06 보고서 — report
- 07 부담 — pressure
- 08 부분 — part
- 09 분야 — area
- 10 상상력 — imagination
- 11 서두르다 — hurry
- 12 서류 — document
- 13 설득하다 — persuade
- 14 본 — this
- 15 성장하다 — grow
- 16 소중하다 — be precious
- 17 숲 — forest
- 18 시각 — vision
- 19 영양 — ingredient
- 20 옛 — old
- 21 운동 — movement, campaign
- 22 일정하다 — steady
- 23 자원봉사 — volunteer
- 24 재료 — ingredient
- 25 전달하다 — give
- 26 점점 — more and more
- 27 정기적 — regular
- 28 정작 — actually
- 29 정치 — politics
- 30 즐겁다 — enjoy
- 31 진정하다 — calm down
- 32 집안일 — housework
- 33 축제 — festival

DAY 13 | 일일 단어 리스트

- [ ] 01 편 — piece
- [ ] 02 포장하다 — wrap (up)
- [ ] 03 품질 — quality
- [ ] 04 화 — angry
- [ ] 05 훌륭하다 — excellent
- [ ] 06 이웃 — neighbor
- [ ] 07 고등학교 — high school
- [ ] 08 가장 — head of the household
- [ ] 09 가져오다 — bring (about)
- [ ] 10 간단하다 — simple
- [ ] 11 거리 — distance
- [ ] 12 구체적 — in detail
- [ ] 13 극복하다 — overcome
- [ ] 14 기름 — oil
- [ ] 15 먹이 — food
- [ ] 16 기본 — basic
- [ ] 17 기사 — article
- [ ] 18 냄새 — smell
- [ ] 19 다가가다 — approach
- [ ] 20 담당하다 — be in charge of
- [ ] 21 도전하다 — challenge
- [ ] 22 뛰어나다 — fluent
- [ ] 23 면접 — interview
- [ ] 24 목소리 — voice
- [ ] 25 무시하다 — look down on
- [ ] 26 바닷가 — the seaside
- [ ] 27 밤새우다 — stay up all night
- [ ] 28 배달 — delivery
- [ ] 29 벌다 — earn
- [ ] 30 보관하다 — store
- [ ] 31 부드럽다 — soften
- [ ] 32 불러일으키다 — cause
- [ ] 33 비율 — rate

DAY 14 | 일일 단어 리스트

- [ ] 01 비판하다 — criticize
- [ ] 02 소설 — novel
- [ ] 03 소재 — material
- [ ] 04 속 — inside
- [ ] 05 승객 — passenger
- [ ] 06 시 — poem
- [ ] 07 시절 — time
- [ ] 08 싸다 — pack
- [ ] 09 쓰레기 — waste
- [ ] 10 아까 — a while ago
- [ ] 11 앞장서다 — lead
- [ ] 12 약하다 — weak
- [ ] 13 에너지 — energy
- [ ] 14 언기하다 — act
- [ ] 15 예상되다 — be expected
- [ ] 16 온도 — temperature
- [ ] 17 원고 — manuscript
- [ ] 18 N위 — rank
- [ ] 19 의심하다 — suspect
- [ ] 20 이어지다 — lead
- [ ] 21 인물 — person
- [ ] 22 인생 — life
- [ ] 23 인식하다 — recognize
- [ ] 24 자유롭다 — free
- [ ] 25 절약하다 — save
- [ ] 26 정책 — policy
- [ ] 27 종류 — kinds
- [ ] 28 종종 — often
- [ ] 29 주장하다 — argue
- [ ] 30 주제 — theme
- [ ] 31 소식 — news
- [ ] 32 중심 — main
- [ ] 33 지나다 — pass

DAY 15 | 일일 단어 리스트

- [ ] 01 채소 vegetable
- [ ] 02 특성 characteristics
- [ ] 03 특히 especially
- [ ] 04 평가하다 evaluate
- [ ] 05 향상시키다 improve
- [ ] 06 혹시 perhaps
- [ ] 07 홍보하다 advertise
- [ ] 08 회원 member
- [ ] 09 머릿결 hair
- [ ] 10 감독 director
- [ ] 11 계단 stairs
- [ ] 12 골고루 balanced
- [ ] 13 공동 commune
- [ ] 14 과연 truly
- [ ] 15 관객 audience
- [ ] 16 규모 size
- [ ] 17 규칙 rule
- [ ] 18 스스로 by oneself
- [ ] 19 기부하다 donate
- [ ] 20 깨다 wake up
- [ ] 21 나누다 divide
- [ ] 22 뇌 brain
- [ ] 23 눕다 lie
- [ ] 24 다행이다 fortunate
- [ ] 25 당연하다 natural
- [ ] 26 대책 measures
- [ ] 27 훨씬 way
- [ ] 28 두렵다 fear
- [ ] 29 등장 appear
- [ ] 30 또한 also
- [ ] 31 말리다 dry
- [ ] 32 맑다 clear
- [ ] 33 무대 stage

DAY 16 | 일일 단어 리스트

- [ ] 01 묻다 ask
- [ ] 02 반영하다 reflect
- [ ] 03 밝다 bright
- [ ] 04 발달 development
- [ ] 05 발전 progress
- [ ] 06 병 disease
- [ ] 07 보호 protection
- [ ] 08 부딪치다 hit
- [ ] 09 비상구 emergency exit
- [ ] 10 사귀다 get along
- [ ] 11 사례 case
- [ ] 12 상관없이 regardless of
- [ ] 13 선호하다 prefer
- [ ] 14 소득 income
- [ ] 15 손님 guest
- [ ] 16 수면 sleep
- [ ] 17 순간 at the moment
- [ ] 18 시끄럽다 noise
- [ ] 19 실력 ability
- [ ] 20 직급 position
- [ ] 21 실천하다 practice
- [ ] 22 심리 psychology
- [ ] 23 약속 promise
- [ ] 24 업체 enterprise
- [ ] 25 여기다 consider
- [ ] 26 영업 business
- [ ] 27 오염되다 be polluted
- [ ] 28 요구되다 be required
- [ ] 29 원래 originally
- [ ] 30 위하다 care for
- [ ] 31 음악 music
- [ ] 32 응답자 respondent
- [ ] 33 작성하다 write

DAY 17 | 일일 단어 리스트

- [ ] 01 접수하다 — sign up
- [ ] 02 정서 발달 — emotional development
- [ ] 03 정성 — one's heart
- [ ] 04 정하다 — settle
- [ ] 05 제한하다 — limit
- [ ] 06 짐 — baggage
- [ ] 07 창업하다 — establish a business
- [ ] 08 창의력 — creativity
- [ ] 09 출퇴근하다 — commute
- [ ] 10 토론하다 — discuss
- [ ] 11 파악하다 — figure out
- [ ] 12 평범하다 — normal
- [ ] 13 함부로 — indiscreetly
- [ ] 14 화재 — fire
- [ ] 15 화제 — issue
- [ ] 16 활발하다 — active
- [ ] 17 후회하다 — regret
- [ ] 18 흔히 — usually
- [ ] 19 부정적 — negative
- [ ] 20 연습하다 — practice
- [ ] 21 상 — award
- [ ] 22 가만히 — stay still
- [ ] 23 개성 — individuality
- [ ] 24 개최하다 — host
- [ ] 25 공포감 — fear
- [ ] 26 관련되다 — be related to
- [ ] 27 그립다 — miss
- [ ] 28 그만 — stop
- [ ] 29 근거 — reason
- [ ] 30 기념 — commemoration
- [ ] 31 금방 — soon
- [ ] 32 기뻐하다 — be happy
- [ ] 33 날개 — wings

DAY 18 | 일일 단어 리스트

- [ ] 01 날다 — fly
- [ ] 02 낮추다 — turn down
- [ ] 03 넘치다 — flood
- [ ] 04 놀라다 — be surprised
- [ ] 05 승진 — promotion
- [ ] 06 대표 — representative
- [ ] 07 독자 — readers
- [ ] 08 돌보다 — take care of
- [ ] 09 동아리 — club
- [ ] 10 등산객 — mountain climber
- [ ] 11 땀 — sweat
- [ ] 12 로봇 — robot
- [ ] 13 마라톤 — marathon
- [ ] 14 아무 — anyone
- [ ] 15 막 — just
- [ ] 16 면 — (many) ways
- [ ] 17 모 — anonymous
- [ ] 18 모기 — mosquito
- [ ] 19 미끄럽다 — slippery
- [ ] 20 반복 — repeat
- [ ] 21 법 — law
- [ ] 22 벽 — wall
- [ ] 23 불가 — not allowed to
- [ ] 24 비밀 — secret
- [ ] 25 사물 — object
- [ ] 26 사업 — business
- [ ] 27 사정 — excuse
- [ ] 28 속도 — speed
- [ ] 29 시기 — timing
- [ ] 30 신설하다 — create
- [ ] 31 시대 — age
- [ ] 32 심다 — plant
- [ ] 33 쌀 — rice

DAY 19 | 일일 단어 리스트

- [ ] 01 아무래도 somehow
- [ ] 02 양심 conscience
- [ ] 03 연주하다 performance
- [ ] 04 과소비 overconsumption
- [ ] 05 예술가 artist
- [ ] 06 예의 manner
- [ ] 07 외 but also
- [ ] 08 외모 appearance
- [ ] 09 외출하다 go out
- [ ] 10 우수하다 superb
- [ ] 11 위기 crisis
- [ ] 12 이내 in
- [ ] 13 이사하다 move
- [ ] 14 예매하다 get a ticket
- [ ] 15 이익 profit
- [ ] 16 이제 now
- [ ] 17 자랑하다 brag
- [ ] 18 저렴하다 cheap
- [ ] 19 전공하다 major
- [ ] 20 전국 all over the country
- [ ] 21 전기 electricity
- [ ] 22 전자 electronic
- [ ] 23 전체 whole
- [ ] 24 전혀 not at all
- [ ] 25 절대로 never
- [ ] 26 조정하다 rearrange
- [ ] 27 졸업 graduation
- [ ] 28 졸음 sleepy
- [ ] 29 주고받다 exchange
- [ ] 30 증정하다 give out
- [ ] 31 최고 the best
- [ ] 32 출연하다 appear
- [ ] 33 취소되다 be canceled
- [ ] 34 가꾸다 grow

DAY 20 | 일일 단어 리스트

- [ ] 01 친하다 close
- [ ] 02 파괴하다 destroy
- [ ] 03 피로 fatigue
- [ ] 04 한꺼번에 at once
- [ ] 05 화려하다 fancy
- [ ] 06 화면 screen
- [ ] 07 화장품 cosmetics
- [ ] 08 횡단보도 crosswalk
- [ ] 09 효율성 efficiency
- [ ] 10 휴식 rest, break time
- [ ] 11 흔하다 common
- [ ] 12 켜다 turn on
- [ ] 13 가정 family
- [ ] 14 감각 sense
- [ ] 15 강화하다 improve
- [ ] 16 갖추다 possess
- [ ] 17 거짓말 lie
- [ ] 18 검사 examination
- [ ] 19 겨우 barely
- [ ] 20 계산 calculation
- [ ] 21 고속도로 expressway
- [ ] 22 공지 announcement
- [ ] 23 공통되다 overlap
- [ ] 24 구조하다 rescue
- [ ] 25 국가 nation
- [ ] 26 궁금하다 be curious
- [ ] 27 귀찮다 tiresome
- [ ] 28 그치다 stop
- [ ] 29 깜빡 slip out
- [ ] 30 깜짝 be startled
- [ ] 31 깨닫다 realize
- [ ] 32 꺼내다 bring up
- [ ] 33 이혼 divorce

DAY 21 | 일일 단어 리스트

- 01 꽤 — quite
- 02 끊임없이 — endlessly
- 03 노동 — labor
- 04 강조되다 — be emphasized
- 05 길이 — length
- 06 논리적 — logical
- 07 누르다 — push
- 08 닦다 — brush
- 09 단위 — unit
- 10 대기하다 — stand by
- 11 대하다 — treat
- 12 남기다 — leave
- 13 독창성 — creativity
- 14 돌 — first birthday
- 15 동화책 — fairy tale book
- 16 마치 — as if
- 17 못지않다 — as (adjective) as
- 18 무척 — really
- 19 미치다 — affect
- 20 별 — not much
- 21 배 — be doubled
- 22 벗어나다 — get out of
- 23 보험 — insurance
- 24 복사 — copy
- 25 부럽다 — envy
- 26 부부 — couple
- 27 불쾌하다 — (be) unpleasant
- 28 비치다 — be reflected (in)
- 29 사연 — story
- 30 성과 — accomplishment
- 31 상하다 — go bad
- 32 성분 — ingredient
- 33 세상 — world
- 34 세제 — detergent

DAY 22 | 일일 단어 리스트

- 01 소극장 — small theater
- 02 수상하다 — be awarded
- 03 숨 — breath
- 04 시장 — mayor
- 05 식품 — food
- 06 신제품 — new product
- 07 신체 — body
- 08 주인공 — main character
- 09 신호 — signal
- 10 실외 — outdoor
- 11 심장 — heart
- 12 교사 — teacher
- 13 씹다 — chew
- 14 아쉽다 — feel sorry for~
- 15 악화되다 — get worse
- 16 애쓰다 — make (put) an effort
- 17 애완동물 — pet
- 18 양보하다 — yield
- 19 얼른 — hurry
- 20 연말 — the end of the year
- 21 완성되다 — be completed
- 22 외면 — ignore
- 23 운영하다 — operate, run
- 24 위협하다 — threaten
- 25 유리창 — window
- 26 유익하다 — beneficial
- 27 이 — teeth
- 28 입다 — get (damaged)
- 29 잊다 — forget
- 30 자꾸 — often
- 31 자라다 — grow up
- 32 자세하다 — in detail
- 33 저축하다 — save
- 34 N별 — distinction

DAY 23 | 일일 단어 리스트

- [ ] 01 적성 — aptitude
- [ ] 02 적절하다 — proper
- [ ] 03 조언 — advice
- [ ] 04 좌석 — seat
- [ ] 05 중소기업 — smaller firms
- [ ] 06 지구 — the earth
- [ ] 07 슬프다 — sad
- [ ] 08 지적하다 — point out
- [ ] 09 첫인상 — the first impression
- [ ] 10 초 — candle
- [ ] 11 최대한 — at most
- [ ] 12 추천하다 — recommend
- [ ] 13 치우다 — clean
- [ ] 14 내 — in
- [ ] 15 통행 — pass by
- [ ] 16 튼튼하다 — olid
- [ ] 17 퍼센트 — percent
- [ ] 18 한자 — chinese character
- [ ] 19 한참 — (for) a while
- [ ] 20 허락하다 — give one a permission
- [ ] 21 혜택 — benefit
- [ ] 22 호기심 — curiosity
- [ ] 23 흘러가다 — pass
- [ ] 24 늙다 — get older
- [ ] 25 흥미 — interest
- [ ] 26 일상생활 — daily life
- [ ] 27 특정 — certain
- [ ] 28 두통 — headache
- [ ] 29 이상 — more than
- [ ] 30 간식 — snack
- [ ] 31 감동적 — emotional
- [ ] 32 거칠다 — rough
- [ ] 33 건설 — construction
- [ ] 34 경향 — tendency

DAY 24 | 일일 단어 리스트

- [ ] 01 곧 — soon
- [ ] 02 골목 — street
- [ ] 03 곱다 — pretty
- [ ] 04 공격적 — offensive
- [ ] 05 공급하다 — supply
- [ ] 06 명절 — holiday
- [ ] 07 공모하다 — invite public participation
- [ ] 08 공사 — construction
- [ ] 09 과정 — process
- [ ] 10 구독 — subscription
- [ ] 11 금지되다 — be prohibited
- [ ] 12 기관 — organization
- [ ] 13 기운 — energy
- [ ] 14 기존 — existing
- [ ] 15 깎다 — cut
- [ ] 16 깨지다 — be broken
- [ ] 17 미루다 — delay
- [ ] 18 껌 — gum
- [ ] 19 꼽다 — pick
- [ ] 20 남녀노소 — men and women of all ages
- [ ] 21 널리 — widely
- [ ] 22 단체 — group
- [ ] 23 달리다 — run
- [ ] 24 답답하다 — stuffy
- [ ] 25 당일 — on that day
- [ ] 26 대비 — prepare
- [ ] 27 덜다 — take (out)
- [ ] 28 동네 — neighborhood
- [ ] 29 순서 — turn
- [ ] 30 동시 — at the same time
- [ ] 31 동의하다 — agree with
- [ ] 32 둘러보다 — look around
- [ ] 33 뚜렷하다 — clear
- [ ] 34 마감 — deadline

DAY 25 | 일일 단어 리스트

- ☐ 01 마땅하다 — suitable
- ☐ 02 마지막 — last
- ☐ 03 만 — american age
- ☐ 04 약 — approximately
- ☐ 05 멈추다 — stop
- ☐ 06 명함 — business card
- ☐ 07 몰리다 — be accused of
- ☐ 08 무늬 — pattern
- ☐ 09 무역 — trade
- ☐ 10 민속 — folk
- ☐ 11 바닥 — floor
- ☐ 12 바람직하다 — desirable
- ☐ 13 반사되다 — be reflected
- ☐ 14 발송 — send
- ☐ 15 방안 — option
- ☐ 16 버릇 — habit
- ☐ 17 벌이다 — start
- ☐ 18 범죄 — crime
- ☐ 19 변경하다 — change
- ☐ 20 보람 — worthwhile
- ☐ 21 보수 — pay
- ☐ 22 보상 — compensate
- ☐ 23 입원 — enter a hospital
- ☐ 24 부상 — injury
- ☐ 25 부작용 — side effects
- ☐ 26 부지런하다 — diligent
- ☐ 27 불가능하다 — impossible
- ☐ 28 빨다 — wash
- ☐ 29 빼다 — without
- ☐ 30 상승하다 — increase
- ☐ 31 서투르다 — unskilled
- ☐ 32 선거 — election
- ☐ 33 선발하다 — select
- ☐ 34 재학생 — registered student

DAY 26 | 일일 단어 리스트

- ☐ 01 세기 — century
- ☐ 02 소화 — digest
- ☐ 03 손쉽다 — easy (to do)
- ☐ 04 근무 — work
- ☐ 05 수분 — water
- ☐ 06 수출 — export
- ☐ 07 시급하다 — urgent
- ☐ 08 시키다 — make (someone to do)
- ☐ 09 신고하다 — report
- ☐ 10 신분증 — identification
- ☐ 11 심사 — screening
- ☐ 12 언어 — language
- ☐ 13 여부 — whether
- ☐ 14 열람 — reading
- ☐ 15 열쇠 — key
- ☐ 16 열차 — train
- ☐ 17 영수증 — receipt
- ☐ 18 내놓다 — release
- ☐ 19 예 — old times
- ☐ 20 올라가다 — rise
- ☐ 21 올바르다 — right
- ☐ 22 욕심 — greed
- ☐ 23 용도 — use
- ☐ 24 음료수 — beverage
- ☐ 25 의무 — duty
- ☐ 26 의사소통 — communicate
- ☐ 27 이성 — opposite sex
- ☐ 28 넘어지다 — fall
- ☐ 29 자극하다 — stimulate
- ☐ 30 자동 — automaticallly
- ☐ 31 잠시 — for a moment
- ☐ 32 자율 — autonomy
- ☐ 33 장난 — joke

DAY 27 | 일일 단어 리스트

- [ ] 01 장사 — business
- [ ] 02 재능 — talent
- [ ] 03 적용하다 — apply
- [ ] 04 전 N — all
- [ ] 05 적응하다 — adapt
- [ ] 06 절반 — half
- [ ] 07 늘 — always
- [ ] 08 접종 — vaccination
- [ ] 09 접하다 — access
- [ ] 10 제거하다 — remove
- [ ] 11 제안하다 — suggest
- [ ] 12 제작하다 — produce
- [ ] 13 조절하다 — control
- [ ] 14 존경하다 — respect
- [ ] 15 주택 — house
- [ ] 16 중요성 — importance
- [ ] 17 지르다 — shout out
- [ ] 18 진심 — sincerity
- [ ] 19 차지하다 — occupy
- [ ] 20 비롯하다 — including
- [ ] 21 챙기다 — take
- [ ] 22 최신 — latest
- [ ] 23 추가하다 — add
- [ ] 24 출입 — enter
- [ ] 25 가전제품 — home appliances
- [ ] 26 취하다 — get
- [ ] 27 친밀하다 — friendly
- [ ] 28 택배 — parcel service
- [ ] 29 통화하다 — talk on the phone
- [ ] 30 표시하다 — mark
- [ ] 31 풍부하다 — abundant
- [ ] 32 프린터 — printer
- [ ] 33 피부 — skin
- [ ] 34 협조하다 — cooperate

DAY 28 | 일일 단어 리스트

- [ ] 01 형식 — format
- [ ] 02 대여하다 — lend
- [ ] 03 아예 — at all
- [ ] 04 오해 — misunderstanding
- [ ] 05 원망스럽다 — blame
- [ ] 06 응모 — enter
- [ ] 07 이동하다 — move
- [ ] 08 인류 — human
- [ ] 09 현금 — cash
- [ ] 10 저장하다 — store
- [ ] 11 정체 — congestion
- [ ] 12 체조 — stretching
- [ ] 13 해당되다 — apply to
- [ ] 14 해소하다 — alleviate
- [ ] 15 까다롭다 — particular
- [ ] 16 곁 — on someone's side
- [ ] 17 가리다 — choose over
- [ ] 18 간편하다 — easy
- [ ] 19 강요하다 — force
- [ ] 20 객관적 — objective
- [ ] 21 건조하다 — dry
- [ ] 22 겉 — out[side]
- [ ] 23 경조사비 — gratuity (for family events)
- [ ] 24 고유하다 — original
- [ ] 25 고집 — stubborn
- [ ] 26 도구 — tool
- [ ] 27 고통 — pain
- [ ] 28 공개 — open
- [ ] 29 공고 — notice
- [ ] 30 과장되다 — exaggerate
- [ ] 31 관점 — perspective
- [ ] 32 괜히 — in vain
- [ ] 33 괴롭다 — painful
- [ ] 34 교과서 — textbook

DAY 29 | 일일 단어 리스트

- [ ] 01 굽다 — roast
- [ ] 02 권리 — rights
- [ ] 03 귀가 — returning home
- [ ] 04 동쪽 — east
- [ ] 05 그늘 — shade
- [ ] 06 기온 — temperature
- [ ] 07 까닭 — reason
- [ ] 08 껍질 — skin
- [ ] 09 끼다 — cloud over
- [ ] 10 나름 — depend on
- [ ] 11 날마다 — everyday
- [ ] 12 내내 — throughout
- [ ] 13 녹다 — melt
- [ ] 14 놀랍다 — amaze
- [ ] 15 놀이터 — play ground
- [ ] 16 곤란하다 — it will be difficult to ~
- [ ] 17 굳이 — obstinately
- [ ] 18 다 — everything
- [ ] 19 다림질하다 — iron
- [ ] 20 석식 — dinner
- [ ] 21 다수 — majority
- [ ] 22 닫다 — close
- [ ] 23 달하다 — reach
- [ ] 24 당당하다 — confident
- [ ] 25 당분간 — for a while
- [ ] 26 당하다 — be caught in~
- [ ] 27 당황스럽다 — be embarrassed
- [ ] 28 대우 — treatments
- [ ] 29 더구나 — besides
- [ ] 30 어버이날 — parent's day
- [ ] 31 데려다 주다 — take someone home
- [ ] 32 도입하다 — introduce
- [ ] 33 도저히 — not..at all
- [ ] 34 동참하다 — take part in

DAY 30 | 일일 단어 리스트

- [ ] 01 동호회 — club
- [ ] 02 뒤집다 — turn something inside out
- [ ] 03 따지다 — calculate
- [ ] 04 딱딱하다 — hard
- [ ] 05 뜻밖에 — unexpectedly
- [ ] 06 마치다 — finish
- [ ] 07 입금 — deposit
- [ ] 08 막상 — actually
- [ ] 09 망설이다 — hesitate
- [ ] 10 맞벌이 — a couple of whom both has jobs
- [ ] 11 매력 — attraction
- [ ] 12 매출 — sales
- [ ] 13 먼지 — dust
- [ ] 14 멋지다 — lovely
- [ ] 15 발전소 — power plant
- [ ] 16 몇몇 — some
- [ ] 17 무려 — whopping
- [ ] 18 무리 — beyond (one's ability)
- [ ] 19 물다 — bite
- [ ] 20 문학 — literature
- [ ] 21 물품 — commodity
- [ ] 22 밑 — under
- [ ] 23 바탕 — based on
- [ ] 24 범위 — range
- [ ] 25 변환시키다 — transform
- [ ] 26 부르다 — call
- [ ] 27 분실하다 — lost
- [ ] 28 불리다 — be called
- [ ] 29 불만 — dissatisfaction
- [ ] 30 비결 — secret
- [ ] 31 비다 — vacant
- [ ] 32 기후 — climate
- [ ] 33 비평문 — review
- [ ] 34 빼앗다 — take (something) from (somebody)

INDEX

ㄱ

가격	91	강조되다	226	경기	125
가꾸다	210	강화하다	216	경력	33
가능하다	19	갖추다	217	경우	20
가득하다	84	개발하다	42	경쟁	94
가리다	301	개성	188	경제	39
가만히	188	개인	39	경조사비	302
가입	25	개최하다	188	경향	252
가장	143	객관적	302	경험	22
가전제품	292	거리	144	곁	301
가정	216	거의	85	계단	164
가져오다	144	거절하다	55	계산	217
가지다(=갖다)	84	거짓말	217	계속	33
각종	60	거칠다	252	계획	33, 315
간단하다	144	걱정하다	31, 191	고객	111
간식	251	건설	252	고등학교	143
간편하다	301	건조하다	302	고려하다	111
감각	216	걸다	35	고르다	50
감다	25	걸리다	125	고민	60
감독	164	검사	217	고생	101
감동적	252	겉	302	고속도로	218
감상하다	94	게다가	35	고유하다	302
감소하다	35, 211	게으르다	65	고장나다	111
감정	63	겨우	217	고집	303
감추다	45	견디다	149	고치다	253
갑자기	106	결과	19	고통	303
강요하다	301	결국	85	곤란하다	311
		결심하다	87	곧	256

INDEX | 355

골고루	164	관점	304	그만	189
골목	256	광고	54	그만두다	75
곱다	256	괜히	304	그치다	219
공개	303	괴롭다	304	극복하다	144
공격적	256	교과서	304	근거	189
공고	303	교사	238	근무	278
공공장소	85	교통	31	글	60
공급하다	256	교환	112	금방	190
공기	94	구독	257	금지되다	258
공동	164	구매하다	101	급하다	54
공모하다	257	구입하다	42	긍정적	87
공사	257	구조하다	219	기간	24
공연	61	구체적	144	기관	258
공지	218	구하다	45	기념	189
공통되다	218	국가	219	기능	72
공포감	189	국내	72	기대하다	85
과소비	204	굳이	311	기르다	117
과연	164	굽다	308	기름	144
과장되다	303	궁금하다	219	기본	145
과정	257	권리	308	기부하다	166
과학	63	귀가	308	기분	42
관객	165	귀찮다	219	기뻐하다	190
관계	24	귀하다	77	기사	145
관광객	85	규모	165	기술	112
관람하다	94	규칙	165	기억	42
관련되다	189	그냥	112	기업	101
관리	34	그늘	309	기온	309
관심	19	그립다	189	기운	258

기존	258	**ㄴ**		넘어지다	283
기준	94	나가다	55	넘치다	194
기타	125	나누다	166	노동	226
기회	42	나다	65	노력하다	20
기후	324	나름	310	노인	59
긴장	125	나오다	77	녹다	310
길이	227	나중에	112	논리적	227
깊다	125	나타나다	64, 149	놀라다	194
까다롭다	301	날개	190	놀랍다	310
까닭	309	날다	194	놀이터	310
깎다	258	날마다	310	농사	126
깜빡	219	남	102	뇌	166
깜짝	220	남기다	228	누르다	227
깨다	166	남녀노소	259	눕다	166
깨닫다	220	낫다	87	느끼다	20
깨지다	258	낭비하다	126	늘	289
꺼내다	220	낮잠	126	늘다	19
껌	259	낮추다	194	늘리다	169
껍질	309	낯설다	97	늘어나다	233
꼽다	259	내	248	늙다	250
꽤	226	내내	310	능력	127
꾸준히	72	내놓다	281	늦다	39
꿈	58	내다	285	늦추다	181
끊임없이	226	내리다	74		
끌다	123	내용	21	**ㄷ**	
끝나다	33	냄새	145	다	311
끼다	309	널리	260	다가가다	145
		넘다	84	다림질하다	311

다수	312	대여하다	298	동아리	195
다양하다	23	대우	313	동의하다	262
다치다	102	대중교통	86	동쪽	308
다투다	243	대책	167	동참하다	314
다행이다	166	대표	195	동호회	318
닦다	227	대하다	228	동화책	228
단	127	대형	127	두다	97
단순하다	273	대화	127	두렵다	167
단위	227	대회	44	두통	251
단체	260	더구나	35, 313	둘러보다	262
닫다	312	덜다	261	뒤집다	318
달리	285	데려다 주다	313	드디어	77
달리다	260	데우다	295	드러내다	45, 112
달하다	312	도구	303	드물다	106
담다	95	도로	127	들다	295
담당하다	146	도시	95	들어오다	50
답답하다	260	도움	21	등등	72
당당하다	312	도입하다	314	등산객	195
당분간	312	도저히	314	등장	167
당연하다	167	도전하다	146	디자인	112
당일	260	독자	195	따라하다	39
당하다	312	독창성	228	따로	64
당황스럽다	313	돌	228	따르다	60
대기하다	227	돌보다	195	따지다	318
대부분	29	돌아가다	50	딱딱하다	318
대비	261	동네	261	땀	196
대상	28	동료	74	떠나다	74
대신하다	86	동시	262	떠오르다	128

떨어지다	305	만족하다	128	모자라다	97
또한	168	말리다	168	모집	60
뚜렷하다	262, 325	맑다	168	목소리	146
뛰다	95	맛	72	목적	132
뛰어나다	146	망설이다	319	목표	113
뜨다	106	맞다	117	몰리다	267
뜻밖에	319	맞벌이	320	못지않다	229
		맞추다	129	무늬	267
ㄹ		맡기다	129	무대	168
로봇	196	맡다	139	무려	321
		매력	320	무료	43
ㅁ		매출	320	무리	321
마감	262	머릿결	163	무시하다	146
마땅하다	266	먹이	145	무역	267
마라톤	196	먼저	295	무조건	75
마련하다	45	먼지	320	무척	229
마음껏	169	멀리하다	128	문득	106
마음먹다	87	멈추다	263, 267	문의	132
마중하다	117	멋지다	320	문제	23
마지막	266	면	197	문학	322
마찬가지	113, 285	면접	146	문화	41
마치	229	명절	257	묻다	174
마치다	319	명함	267	물건	29
마침	102	몇몇	321	물다	321
마침내	77	모	197	물론	75
막	197	모기	197	물질	102
막상	319	모습	51	물품	322
만	266	모으다	31	미끄럽다	197

미래	102	발견하다	133	범위	322
미루다	221, 259	발길	84	범죄	269
미리	86	발달	175	법	198
미술	102	발명되다	75	벗어나다	230
미치다	229	발생	41	벽	198
민속	267	발송	268	변경하다	269
믿다	61	발전	175	변하다	116
및	132	발전소	321	변화	30
밑	322	발표	44	변환시키다	322
		밝다	174	별	229
ㅂ		밝히다	64	별로	103
바꾸다	19	밤새우다	147	병	175
바닥	268	방문	76	보고서	133
바닷가	147	방법	18	보관하다	148
바라다	75	방송	76	보내다	113
바라보다	132	방식	63	보람	269
바람직하다	268	방안	268	보상	270
바로잡다	21	방해하다	113	보수	269
바르다	149	배	230	보험	230
바탕	322	배달	147	보호	175
반대하다	139	배웅하다	117	복사	230
반드시	129	뱉다	305	복잡하다	273
반면	59	버릇	268	본	134
반복	198	버리다	33	봉사하다	90
반사되다	268	번지다	159	부끄럽다	273
반영하다	174	벌다	147	부담	133
반응	86	벌써	64	부드럽다	148
받다	41	벌이다	269	부딪치다	175

부럽다	230	비밀	198	사회	22
부르다	323	비상구	175	살펴보다	103
부부	230	비슷하다	80	삶	70
부분	133	비율	148	삼키다	305
부상	270	비치다	231	상	188
부작용	270	비판하다	152	상관없이	176
부정적	87, 187	비평문	324	상담하다	80
부족하다	61, 97	빌리다	113	상대방	43
부지런하다	65, 270	빛	95	상상력	133
부탁	50	빠지다	233, 325	상승하다	271
분명하다	285	빨다	271	상의하다	65
분석하다	103	빼다	271	상태	61
분실하다	323	빼앗다	324	상품	20
분야	133	뽑다	169	상하다	231
분위기	95			상황	21
불가	198	**ㅅ**		색	43
불가능하다	271	사건	114	생각하다	18, 325
불러일으키다	148	사고	50	생기다	20
불리다	323	사귀다	176	생명	95
불만	323	사라지다	149	생산하다	159
불쾌하다	231	사례	176	생활	22
불편하다	34	사무실	103	서두르다	134
붓다	273	사물	199	서류	134
붙다	80	사실	34	서비스	90
비결	323	사업	199	서운하다	181
비교하다	103	사연	231	서투르다	271
비다	323	사용하다	55	석식	311
비롯하다	291	사정	199	선거	271

선명하다	315	소중하다	135	시대	200
선발하다	272	소화	278	시민	61
선배	101	속	152	시설	80
선택하다	23	속도	199	시작하다	30
선호하다	176	손님	176	시장	236
설득하다	134	손쉽다	278	시절	153
설명하다	28	수리하다	253	시청	90
설문조사	114	수면	177	시키다	279
섭섭하다	181	수분	279	식품	236
성격	70	수상하다	236	식히다	295
성공하다	31	수출	279	신경	73
성과	231	순간	177	신고하다	279
성분	232	순서	261	신문	91
성장하다	135	숨	236	신분증	279
세계	32	숲	135	신설하다	199
세기	278	스스로	165	신제품	237
세상	232	스트레스	90	신청	32
세우다	181	슬프다	247	신체	237
세제	232	습관	70	신호	237
세탁하다	96	승객	152	실력	177
소개하다	48	승낙하다	55	실수	80
소극장	236	승진	194	실시하다	54
소득	176	승차하다	263	실외	238
소리	51	시	153	실제로	38
소비	38, 159	시각	135	실천하다	178
소설	152	시급하다	279	실컷	169
소식	158	시기	199	실패하다	114
소재	152	시끄럽다	177	실험	114

심각하다	73	알려주다	43	역사	62
심다	200	알아보다	115	역할	48
심리	178	앞당기다	181	연결되다	115
심사	280	앞장서다	154	연구	28
심장	238	애쓰다	239	연기하다	155, 221
심하다	41	애완동물	239	연락하다	51
싸다	153	약	266	연말	240
싸우다	243	약속	178	연습하다	188
쌀	200	약하다	154	연장하다	100
쏟다	191	양	125	연주하다	204
쓰다	201	양보하다	239	연하다	221
쓰레기	153	양심	204	열람	280
씹다	238	어둡다	191	열쇠	280
		어른	103	열차	280
		어리다	34	염려하다	191
ㅇ		어버이날	313	영수증	281
아까	154	어울리다	96	영양	135
아무	196	언어	280	영업	179
아무래도	204	얻다	105	영향	31
아무리	115	얼굴빛	159	예	115, 281
아쉽다	238	얼른	240	예매하다	206
아예	298	업무	70	예방하다	104
아이디어	115	업체	178	예상되다	155
악화되다	239	없애다	81	예술가	205
안내하다	29	에너지	154	예의	205
안심하다	127	여기다	178	예전	62
안전하다	81	여부	280	예정	315
안정	96	여성	62	예측	305
안타깝다	115				

옛	136	위기	206	이성	282
오래되다	52	위하다	180	이어지다	156
오염되다	179	위험하다	70	이용하다	18, 55
오해	298	위협하다	240	이웃	143
오히려	32	유리창	241	이익	207
온도	155	유익하다	241	이제	207
올라가다	281	유지하다	62	이해하다	63
올바르다	281	유행하다	100	이혼	220
옮기다	100	음료수	282	익숙하다	97
완성되다	240	음식	104	인간	52
외	205	음악	180	인기	40
외면	240	응답자	180	인내심	139
외모	205	응모	299	인류	299
외출하다	205	의견	325	인물	156
요구되다	179	의논하다	65	인생	156
욕심	282	의무	282	인식하다	156
용도	282	의미	104	인정하다	73
우선	295	의사소통	282	일반적	48
우수하다	205	의심하다	155	일부	100
운동	136	이	241	일상생활	251
운영하다	240	이기다	201	일시적	104
운전	122	이내	206	일으키다	104
움직이다	91	이동하다	299	일정하다	136
원고	155	이륙하다	211	잃다	52
원래	179	이미	122	입금	319
원망스럽다	298	이사하다	206	입다	241
원인	52	이상	251	입원	270
원하다	62	이상하다	22	입장	48

잊다	241	장사	288	전혀	208
		장소	41	절대로	208
ㅈ		재능	288	절반	289
자격	81	재료	136	절약하다	156
자극하다	283	재산	105	젊다	92
자기	59	재학생	272	점	92
자꾸	242	저렴하다	207	점점	137
자녀	71	저장하다	300	접수하다	184
자동	283	저축하다	242	접종	289
자라다	242	적극적	54	접하다	289
자랑하다	207	적다	201	정기적	137
자료	48	적당하다	74	정리하다	63
자리	52	적성	246	정보	58
자세하다	242	적용하다	288	정부	74
자신	24	적응하다	289	정서 발달	184
자신감	104	적절하다	246	정성	184
자연스럽다	71	전 N	288	정신	105
자원봉사	136	전공하다	207	정작	137
자유롭다	156	전국	208	정책	157
자율	284	전기	208	정체	300
작가	81	전달하다	137	정치	137
작성하다	180	전망	305	정하다	184
작품	54	전문가	24	정확하다	92
잠그다	253	전시회	100	제거하다	290
잠시	283	전자	208	제공하다	82
잡다	201	전체	208	제대로	41
장난	284	전통	92	제도	105
장단점	40	전하다	82	제시하다	82

제안하다	290	주택	290	진정하다	138
제작하다	290	준비하다	45	진하다	25, 221
제출하다	110	줄이다	169	진행되다	73
제품	49	중단하다	263	짐	185
제한하다	185	중소기업	246	집안일	138
조건	82	중심	158	집중하다	110
조사하다	53	중요성	291	짓다	315
조심하다	82	즐겁다	138	짙다	25
조언	246	즐기다	82	찌다	233
조용하다	122	증가하다	35, 83, 233		
조절하다	290	증정하다	209	**ㅊ**	
조정하다	209	지구	247	차다	243
존경하다	290	지나다	158	차이	53
졸업	209	지나치다	92	차지하다	291
졸음	209	지내다	211	착륙하다	211
종류	157	지다	201, 221	찬성하다	139
종종	157	지르다	291	참가하다	40
좌석	246	지속되다	110	참다	149
주고받다	209	지역	32	참석하다	233
주로	122	지원하다	93	참여하다	30
주문하다	92	지적하다	247	참을성	139
주민	53	지키다	40	창업하다	185
주변	49	직급	177	창의력	185
주의 사항	49	직업	123	창피하다	273
주인공	237	직원	34	찾다	24, 129
주장하다	157	직장	30	채소	162
주제	157	직접	29	책임	53
주차장	122	진심	291	챙기다	292

처리하다	101
처음	101
첫인상	247
청소년	93
체조	300
체험하다	110
초	248
초대하다	113
최고	210
최근	23
최대한	248
최선	111
최신	292
추가하다	292
추억	93
추천하다	248
축제	138
출연하다	210
출입	292
출퇴근하다	185
충분하다	38
취소되다	210
취업하다	83
취하다	293
치료하다	71
치우다	248
친밀하다	293
친하다	214

ㅋ

켜다	216
키우다	59, 117

ㅌ

타다	253
탈퇴	25
택배	293
토론하다	186
통하다	40
통행	249
통화하다	293
특별하다	243
특성	162
특정	251
특징	123
특히	162
튼튼하다	249
틀다	253
틀림없이	129

ㅍ

파괴하다	214
파악하다	186
판매하다	32
팔다	83
퍼센트	249
편	142

편하다	30
평가하다	162
평균	123
평범하다	186, 243
평소	111
포기하다	123
포장하다	142
포함되다	43
표시하다	293
표정	159
표현하다	38
풀다	263
품질	142
풍부하다	293
프로그램	83
프린터	294
피로	214
피부	294
피하다	84
피해	49
필요하다	18

ㅎ

하락하다	211
하루	73
하차하다	263
학습하다	111
한꺼번에	214

한자	249	화려하다	214	힘	44
한참	249	화면	215		
할인되다	58	화장품	215	**N**	
함께	71	화재	186	N별	242
함부로	186	화제	187	N위	155
해결하다	39	확실하다	285		
해당되다	300	확인하다	54		
해소하다	300	환경	21		
해외	59	환영하다	124		
행동하다	53	환하다	191		
행복하다	74	활동하다	93		
행사	28	활발하다	187		
향상시키다	162	활용하다	58		
허락하다	250	회원	163		
현금	299	횡단보도	215		
현상	124	효과	23		
현실	124	효율성	215		
현장	124	후회하다	187		
현재	93	훌륭하다	143		
협조하다	294	훨씬	167		
형식	298	휴식	215		
혜택	250	흐릿하다	325		
호기심	250	흔하다	77, 106, 215		
혹시	163	흔히	187		
혼자	71	흘러가다	250		
홈페이지	124	흥미	251		
홍보하다	163	희망하다	94		
화	142	희미하다	315